Tuesday 25th Octr 1825

Ordered by the Court that Job Bennett 14 Years old the 24th day of March next be bound as an apprentice to George Boyle until he shall attain the age of Twenty one Years the said Boyle to teach him to read the old and new Testaments intelligibly, to write a legible hand, to cypher through the single rule of three to teach him the art and mystery of a Tailor and at his freedom to give him two suits of Clothes one home spun and the other a second rate Store suit, and a set of tools to carry on the tailors Trade —

Ordered by the Court that Betsy Cross a female child supposed to be 7 Years old be bound as an Apprentice to George W. Kennedy until she shall attain the age of 18 Years — the said Kennedy to teach her to read the old and new testaments intelligibly, to do the duties of a good house wife and at her freedom to give her two Suits of Clothes one home spun and the other a second rate Store suit a good feather bed and furniture, a second rate Cow and Calf and a spinning Wheel —

Minutes of the Court of Pleas and Quarter Sessions, Greene County, Tennessee, October 25, 1825

EAST TENNESSEE'S FORGOTTEN CHILDREN

Apprentices from 1778 to 1911

by

Alan N. Miller

CLEARFIELD

Printed for
Clearfield Company, Inc. by
Genealogical Publishing Co., Inc.
Baltimore, Maryland
2000

Reprinted for
Clearfield Company, Inc. by
Genealogical Publishing Co., Inc.
Baltimore, Maryland
2001

International Standard Book Number: 0-8063-4966-2

Made in the United States of America

Table of Contents

List of Abbreviations

bnd	bound	mos	months
canc	cancelled	prev	previous(ly)
d	days	prob	probated
dau	daughter	req	request
dcd	deceased	resc	rescinded
GF	grandfather	ret	returned
GM	grandmother	sib(s)	sibling(s)
illeg	illegtimate	sur	surety
ind	indenture	yrs	years

Introduction

Apprenticeships have been known since ancient times, but the system which evolved in America had its roots in the England of the 16th century. The practice spread to the colonies along with other English customs but gradually became less of a method of training in the professions and crafts, developing instead into a system whereby children who were or were likely to become indigent could be supported without cost to the local government.

When Tennessee became a state in 1796, she inherited the legal code of her mother state, North Carolina. Their laws of 1762 applicable to orphans specified the following:

1. Annually the names of all orphans who had no guardian or who were not previously bound were to be reported to the Orphan Court.
2. Where their estate was too small to support them, orphans or base-born children were to be bound as apprentices: the males until age 21, the females until age 18, and mulatto or mustee females until age 21.
3. The master was to provide "diet, clothes, lodging and accommodations, fit and necessary, and to teach or cause him or her to be taught to read and write."
4. At the expiration of the apprenticeship, the master was to pay the apprentice an amount specified by law [or in the indenture].
5. If the child were ill used or not taught as required, the court could cancel the indenture and rebind him or her.
6. The bond was to be by indenture, made between the presiding officer of the court (and his successor) and the master or mistress, recorded, and a copy kept in the clerk's office for the benefit of the apprentice.
7. Any illy-treated apprentice could prosecute in the name of the Justices of the Court and recover damages.

Originally, an orphan was considered to be any fatherless child. In 1825 Tennessee law was amended to include any child as bindable whose father had abandoned him or utterly failed and refused to support him, provided that the mother gave assent in open court. In the minutes these children also are sometimes referred to as orphans. In 1854 the courts were given the discretion to bind apprentices for shorter periods if desired. By 1858 the Code of Tennessee specified other changes, as follows:

1. No apprentice could be removed from the county without his consent and the consent of the court.
2. No householder could harbor or conceal any orphan child, or hire him, without first obtaining leave from some Justice of the Peace.
3. The apprentice was to be taught to read, write, and "cypher as far as the rule of three."
4. At the expiration of the indenture, in addition to the other stipulations, the master should pay to the apprentice $20 and furnish him with one good suit of clothes.
5. Illegitimate children could be bound out without their mother's consent if it were proved that she "disregarded their moral and mental culture and that she kept a house of ill repute, or lived in one."

Although these laws regarding the Master-Apprentice relationship remained in effect until the mid-20th century with few alterations, their application sometimes varied with court decisions. In different counties they seem to have been enforced with varying degrees of diligence. Only in Campbell County, in 1834, was evidence found of an annual accounting of indigent orphans; rather, they seemed to have been reported to the court at random by a JP or another interested individual, often the person to whom they were eventually bound. The mother's consent, when required and obtained, was not always recorded, leading at times to cancellation of the indenture.

Because copies of the indenture and accompanying bond seem to have vanished from most counties' archives, the Court Minutes are now the most complete record of these unfortunate children's fate. In some cases the complete documents were recorded in the minutes along with the order binding the child; other clerks simply recorded that the child was bound, without further detail.

Of course not all bound children were indigent or orphans. A parent or guardian might bind a child in order to have a boy taught a useful trade or a girl the art of homemaking. In a few cases, particularly in Knox County, financial arrangements were detailed in which the father was to receive annual payments for the son's services. It was occasionally stipulated in a will that an heir was to be bound out and to whom. Also, not all indigent children were bound. Those not felt to have the physical or mental capacity to make a productive apprentice were relegated to care in the poor house or in a private home at county expense. Many ordered to be brought for consideration of binding could not be found by the sheriff and were not produced in court.

The following pages contain records of apprenticeships in the counties of East Tennessee from the earliest surviving records until the practice became uncommon, usually the late 1870's. During the latter part of the Civil War few meetings of the County Courts were held, and it was not until after the war that apprenticeships again began to be recorded. The usual problems in handwriting interpretation were encountered, and names were spelled many ways, sometimes within the same document. Original spellings have been retained, but entries have been abbreviated and the names of the court officials and bondsmen omitted in most cases. In entries where the date of the original bond or indenture is not given, the information is from a later reference, such as the cancellation of the indenture.

When a name is found, it is suggested that the researcher consult the microfilmed minutes for several years before and after the event for further clues as to the parentage and circumstances of the child. Often an insolvent estate, provisions for pauper care or burial, a bastardy case, or orders to bring to court other family members may be found, supplying further information. A date following a fact in the notes points to the source of that fact. An asterisk after an entry or date directs the reader to a source for further data. It is hoped that these records will help researchers locate ancestors who, because they were penniless and often without living parents, might be recorded nowhere else.

Records were copied from microfilm obtained from the Tennessee State Archives with the exception of Vol. 4 of Grainger County and Vols. 9-15 of Jefferson County, which were found in the court houses. My thanks go to the staffs of the Tennessee State Archives, the Tennessee State Law Library, the County Clerk's offices in Rutledge and Dandridge, and the Dallas and Irving, Texas, libraries for their assistance and forbearance.

Anderson County

Name	Date	Age	Master	Notes
Miller, William	13Oct1812	15 yrs 3 mo	Miller, John	Blacksmith
Todd, Loe	12Jan1813	12 yrs	Patton, Robert	Hatter
Tipton, Jonathan	12Oct1813		Crozier, Arthur	Son of Brian Tipton
Henderson, Elizabeth	13Jan1814		Dixon, Sr, Thomas	
Wheeler, Aggy	10Oct1814		Leath, Willis	Orphan. Resc 14July1817
Wheeler, Polly	10Oct1814		Leath, Willis	Orphan. Resc 14July1817
Johnson, Robert	10Apr1815		Freele, Isaac	Illegitimate. On 11Oct1819 Freele ordered to show cause why indenture should not be rescinded
Craig, Thomas	10Apr1815	17 yrs on 23rd last mo	Hufstatler, David	
Brummet, Elizabeth	10Oct1815		Oliver, Charles Y.	Taken from Sam'l Worthington 11July1815
Wheeler, Polly			Williams, Alexander	Resc 9Apr1816
Tipton, Jonathan	9Apr1816	11 yrs on 4Apr1816	Sutherland, John	
Tipton, Sarah	9Apr1816	9 yrs on 11May1816	Noel, John	
Tipton, Minerva	9Apr1816	7 yrs on 29May1816	Noel, John	
Hasler,	14Apr1817		Hasler, Sen, Michael	Female baseborn child of Eve Hasler, Dcd
Duncan, John	15July1817		Freeman, Lewis	
Butler, John	12Oct1818	5 yrs next April	Horton, Nathan	
Harben, Jean	12Jan1819	13 yrs	Botten, Thomas G.	Female orphan
Harben, Arthur	12Jan1819	10 yrs	Bailey, Christopher	Orphan
Harben, Washington	12Jan1819	9 yrs	Morton, Quin	
Nance, Isham	12Apr1820		Hibbs, Amos	
Hutcheson, Johnson	9Oct1820	13 yrs next Dec	Ridenhour, David	
Nance, Isham	8Jan1821		Finch, Aaron	Resc 11July1821, Finch leaving county
Justice, Maria			Laughery, John	Ind resc 13Feb1824. Returned to Joseph Justice, father of Maria. Laughery leaving county
Wilson, Anderson	13Jan1824	12 yrs	Lett, Francis	Hatter. Resc as William Lett 12Apr1830, Wilson gone.

Name	Date	Age	Master	Notes
Frant, Tillitha J.	12Apr1824		Brown, Moses	
Cotton, Enoch	12July1824	5 yrs	Ross, Robert	Resc 11Apr1825, Ross deceased
Selvedge, James	12July1824	6 yrs on 1Jan last	Braden, Andrew	
Hutcheson, Margaret	11Oct1824	12 yrs	Miller, Esq, Isaac	
Murry, Thomas	11Apr1825	13 yrs on 30th last mo	Robbins, Samuel	
Cotton, Enoch	11Apr1825		Ross, James	
Hutcheson, Patsy	9Jan1825	8 yrs last Oct	Norton, James	
Hutcheson, Sally	9Jan1825	6 yrs	Norton, James	
Hutcheson, Polly	9Jan1825	3 yrs on 15June last	Norton, James	
Williams, Ephram	9Oct1826		Moser, Abreham	
Bennett, Benjamin	8Jan1827	13 yrs	Fox, George	
Bennett, Patsey	8Jan1827	15 yrs	Fox, George	
Sinclair, Mary Ann	9July1827	2 yrs	Sinclair, James & Abraham	Bond with Sarah Sinclair, mother of Mary Ann, sister of James & Abraham, who agree to support Sarah until her death. 8Oct1827*
Nance, Betsy			Kirkpatrick, Arthur	Ind resc 13Apr1829
King, Harriet E.	4Apr1829		Webb, William	Orphan
Ashurst, Elijah			Ashurst, J. M.	Resc 12Apr1830, Elijah refusing to live with J.M. 8Jan1821*
Ritter, Levi	12Oct1831	3 yrs 5 mo 4 d	Butcher, Hasten	Orphan
Cotton, Enoch	8Apr1833	14 yrs	Adkins, Elijah	
Van, Dixon	15Oct1833	17 yrs on 10Sep last	Noel, Jesse	
Miller, Eveline	14Apr1834	8 yrs	Miller, George	Orphan. Canc 1Aug1836
Poe, Joshua	14July1834	3 yrs on 27Oct last	Steuksbury, Jacob	
Voiles, Samuel	11Apr1836	6 yrs	Davidson, Samuel	Orphan
Cooper, William	2May1836	7 yrs on 2July next	Williams, Squire	
Viles, Henry	5Dec1836	11 yrs	Ashlock, Obediah	Orphan
Noel, Martha J.		8 yrs when ind resc	Shinliver, Frederick	Resc 6Mar1837, request of mother, Martha Noel
Stutt, Henry	3Apr1837	15 yrs on 25Dec next	Ross, James	Of color

Loftis, Pleasant	3Apr1837	8 yrs	Rucker, John	Orphan, son of Elizabeth Loftis 6Feb1837
Loftis, Polly	3Apr1837	7 yrs	Rucker, John	Orphan, dau of Elizabeth Loftis 6Feb1837
Weaver, Nancy	8Apr1845	13 yrs 2 mo	Davidson, James	Dau of Mrs Weaver.Sibs Nathan & John 7Apr1845
Weaver, John	8Apr1845	12 yrs	Siebers, John	Blacksmith. Son of Mrs Weaver. Sibs Nathan & Nancy 7Apr1845
Bandy, Manervy Catherine	8Apr1845	6 or 7 yrs	Norris, Alfred	Norris given right to rebind her
Weaver, Nancy	2Jun1845	13 yrs	Young, Samuel C.	Rebound
Hudleston, William W.	3Aug1846	4 yrs on 10 Jan1846	Tunnell, John	
Hudleston, Levi Croy	3Aug1846	6 yrs	Farmer, Nathan A.	
Bandy, Manervy	1Mar1847		Jackson, John	
Bandy, Malinda	1Mar1847	10 yrs	Smith, William B.	Taken from Smith 1Sep1851 for gross outrages on her morality. To care of David Hooks, a relative.
Garner, A. J.	1Mar1847	9 yrs on 13 Aug1847	Owen, R. G.	Waggon maker 3Nov1856. Canc 3Nov1856
Foy, James N.	4Oct1847		Harless, John	Newton ? Foy, 6Sep1847
Cornutt, James	4Oct1847		Wallace, Aaron	
Cornutt, William	4Oct1847		Berry, Samuel Stooks	
Cornutt, David C.	Nov1847	11 yrs 10 mo	Wallace, William	
Loveday, James	5Jun1848		Hedereck, Alfred	
Penny, Geoge	5Jun1848		Simes, John	
Van, N. P.?	2Apr1849	10 yrs	Vann, Daniel	
Viles, James?	2Apr1849	9 yrs	Jackson, Simon	Unnamed in minutes, name from census.
Vann, Martin V.	4Jun1849	8 yrs	Vann, Jesse	
Cooper, Eli	6Aug1849		Turner, Jacob	
Stewart, William	7Oct1850	5 yrs	Freels, Edward	
Longbottom, Lyhue	2Dec1850		Bonham, James S.	Resc 1Aug1853, Bonham deceased
Miles?, James			McAdoo, Willam G.	Indenture rescinded 6Jan1851
Vann, Jasper	6Jan1851	12 yrs	Tunnell, Samuel	
Gray, James	7Apr1851	5 yrs	Lamar, James	
Lovely, Charles	5Aug1851	12 yrs	Lovely, John P.	

Name	Date	Age	Master	Notes
Carnutte, Madison	5July1852	16 yrs 6 mo	Weaver, John	
Ruffian, James	2Aug1852	17 yrs	Foster, Joshua	Farming. Of color
Longbotom, Elihu L.	1Aug1853		McClure, William	
Beets, George	3Oct1853		Jennings, Elijah	
Sieber, Stephen	4Apr1854	6 yrs	Sieber, John	
Shelton, Henry F.	6Nov1854	10 yrs	Chapman, Samuel M.	
Braden, Wesly	4Dec1854		Wallace, William	Blacksmith. Resc 2Nov1863, as Wilie. Joined Federal Army
Braden, James	1Jan1855	8 yrs	Reader, B. W.	
Braden, Charles	1Jan1855	10 yrs	Prasise, Leanadan A.	Blacksmith
Fay, Nancy A.	1Jan1855	8 yrs	Webber, Elizabeth	Until age 21. Taken from Webber 1Oct1855
Gray, Henry L.	5Mar1855	6 yrs	Rhea, Eli	
Haskell, Jacob	5Mar1855	15 yrs	Lay, William	
Williams, Alexander	5Mar1855	11 yrs	Kirkpatrick, C. L.	Resc 7May1855
Stokes, William A.	2Apr1855	16 yrs	Dail, William	Canc 6July1857, Stokes having run away
Braden, Charles	2Apr1855	12 yrs	Maderis, Robert	
Braden, Mary A.	7May1855	8 yrs	Leinart, C. A.	Until 21 yrs. ? Child of color of Barton McKamy dcd. 7Nov1854 & 2Apr1855*
McKamy, Elizabeth C.	7May1855	14 yrs	Foster, Enoch	Until age 21. Child of color of Barton McKamy 7Nov1854*. Canc 1Oct1855, Elizabeth pregnant when bound
McKamy, Martha J.	7May1855	10 yrs	Cross, Mary	Until 21 yrs. ? Child of color of Barton McKamy dcd. 7Nov1854 & 2Apr1855*
Massy, Callaway	2July1855	5 yrs	Sweet, Vincen	
Braden, Charles	3Sep1855	12 yrs	Young, Samuel C.	Canc 7Apr1862. Braden in Army
Stokes, Elias	1Oct1855	9 yrs	Lienart, John	
Leath, A. J.	5Nov1855	11 yrs	Tunnell, John	Orphan of Joseph Leath, dec. 1Oct1855*
Haywood, James	7Jan1856	7 yrs	Devaney, B. J.	
Scarborough, Mary Jane	7Jan1856	8 yrs	Monger, G. G.	Until age 21
Horton, Screlda C.	7July1856	12 yrs	Freels, John T.	Until age 21. Female

Cooper, John G.	6Oct1856	8 yrs 6 mo	Chiles, J. C.	
Cooper, William R.	6Oct1856	2 yrs 9 mo	Prince, David	
Garner, A. J.	3Nov1856	18 yrs	Owen, R. G. W.	Terms changed. No waggon maker tools & trade
Massey, Caloway	7Apr1857	6 yrs 9 mo	Vann, William	
Massey, John	6July1857	3 yrs	Clark, Williamson	
Massey, Calaway	6Apr1858	7 yrs 9 mo	Smith, Moses	Resc 1Nov1858, as Calaway Duncan. [Smith decd]
Valentine, James Ruffin			Foster, Joshua	Previously bound, Valentine has now reached his majority 2Aug1858*
Davis, Alfred	7Feb1859	13 yrs 3 mo	Coward, R. H.	Orphan, of color. Canc 7Apr1862, taken by Confederate Army
Davis, William	7Feb1859	15 yrs 3 mo	Coward, Thomas J.	Orphan, of color. Canc 7Apr1862, taken by Confederate Army
Leath, Thelbert J.(Y?)	4Apr1859	14 yrs	Tunnell, Thomas C. W.	Orphan
Norman, Samuel	2May1859	6 yrs	Jennings, Elijah	Consent of father, Anthony Norman. Resc 6Apr1868, to father
Norman, William	2May1859	8 yrs	Jennings, Elijah	Consent of father, Anthony Norman. Resc 6Apr1868, to father
Scarborough, Mary J.	2Jan1860	12 yrs	Johnson, Noble	Orphan
White, Frances	4Jun1860	11 yrs	Braden, Hiram	Orphan
Massey, Calaway	2July1860	12 yrs	Steele, John D.	Orphan
Stokes, E. J.	2July1860	5 yrs	Thompson, G. W.	Female. Orphan
Massey, Josiah	6Aug1860	11 yrs	Leath, G. F. M.	Orphan
Stokes, Elias	6Aug1860	12 yrs 10 mo	Overton, Jr., Joseph	Orphan. Also called Elias Massey in records. Error?
Hale, M. C. H.	1Oct1860	14 yrs	Jones, Joel A.	Orphan
Brown, Ephram	1Oct1860	12 yrs	Bowling, H. B.	Orphan. Of color. Son of Zerelda Brown 3Sep1860*
Brown, Martha	1Oct1860	8 yrs	Bowling, H. B.	Orphan. Of color. Dau of Zerelda Brown 3Sep1860* Resc 7July1862
Brown, Mary E.	1Oct1860	7 yrs	Linert, Jacob	Orphan. Dau of Levaney Brown 4Jun & 3Sep1860* Resc 7Oct1867, Mary absconded
Brown, W. J.	1Oct1860	8 yrs	Dail, R. M.	Orphan. Son of Levaney Brown 4Jun & 3Sep1860*
Hall, Milly	7Jan1861	9 yrs	Hall, Richard	Orphan

Name	Date	Age	Master	Notes
McKee, Elizabeth J.	8Jan1861	13 yrs	Hank, L. C.	Orphan
Taylor, George W.	4Feb1861	10 yrs 8 mo	Freels, William S.	Orphan
Brown, Harrison	4Mar1861	17 yrs	Farmer, N. A.	Orphan. Of color. Son of Elizabeth Brown 4Feb1861. 6Feb1865*
Brown, D. A.	4Mar1861	15 yrs	Linart, John	Orphan. Of color. Dau of Elizabeth Brown 4Feb1861
Taylor, John	4Mar1861	7 yrs	Jackson, Claiborn	Orphan
Taylor, Orlena	6May1861	4 yrs	Rodgers, D. F.	Orphan
Brown, William	7Oct1861	11 yrs	Scaggs, Lewis	Orphan
Brown, Harrison	4Nov1861	17 yrs 8 mo	Farmer, Nathan A.	Orphan. Of color
Massy, Joseph	6Jan1862	7 yrs	Hibbs, Malan	Orphan
Davis, William	7July1862	18 yrs 8 mo	Young, D. K.	Of color
Brown, Martha	7July1862	9 yrs 9 mo	Large, A. V.	Of color. Resc 6Jan1863. Req of mother, Zerelda Brown
Brown, Martha	6Jan1863	10 yrs	Coward, R. H.	Of color. Dau of Zerelda Brown. Resc 2July1867, Martha having left
Kirkpatrick, Munsey	4Jun1866	6 yrs	Cross, William	Boy of color. Resc 7Aug1876, Muncy's conduct bad
Phillips, Nancy	8Jan1867	13 yrs	Moore, Samuel	Orphan
Phillips, Barthena	8Jan1867	7 yrs	Kincaid, Ritchey	Orphan. Female. Contract complied with 4Feb1878, cancelled
Philips, Samuel	5Aug1867	12 yrs	Galbraith, G. G.	Resc 3Apr1876. Phillips violent, unsafe for Gilbreath, a feeble old man, to keep him
Norman, James	2Mar1868		West, John	Resc 6Apr1868. To father, Anthony Norman
Elliot, Harrison	2Nov1868	10 yrs	Henderson, J. W.	
Daniels, Susan M. J.	6Jun1870	8 yrs	Moore, S. L.	Dau of Matilda Daniels 2May1870. Resc 3Feb1873
Daniel, Mary	6Mar1871	6 yrs	Lowe, C. R.	Dau of Matilda Daniels 2May1870. Resc 5Feb1872, Mary having left
Daniel, Jane	3Feb1873		Chopman, J. E.	Resc 1Apr1878, as Jennie Daniels
Taylor, Jane	7Apr1873		Crosier, C. G.	On petition of Jane, alias Jane Phillips
Scarbrough, William	3Oct1876	9 yrs	Peak, John A.	Orphan
Duncan, Alice	2Dec1878	5 yrs	Kincaid, Ritchey	
Graham, Alice	5May1879	6 yrs	Cross, Joe B.	

Bledsoe County

Name	Date	Age	Master	Notes
Coulston, Nathan	2May1842	18yrs on 31Dec1842	Green, Allen	Orphan. Canc 4July1842. Runaway
Cox, James	1Aug1842	18 on 25Sep next	Swafford, Aron	Orphan. Consent of mother
Kelly, Gilbreth	3Jan1843	11 yrs	Skillern, William	Orphan
Oneil, Anderson	5Jan1843		Thurman, John	Orphan. 2May1842*
Newby, John	6May1844	14 yrs	Curtis, Hesakiah	Orphan
Newby, William	6July1846	11 yrs	Batty, Edwin W.	Orphan
Rush, Joseph T.	4Sep1848	8 yrs 11 mo	Sherley, Hency?	Son of Cathrine Rush
Rush, Hugh Mc.	4Sep1848	6 yrs 3 mo	Sherley, Hency?	Son of Cathrine Rush
Blaylock, Benjamin Franklin	2Oct1848	12 yrs	Moyers, Thomas S.	Son of Margaret Blaylock
Blaylock, Allen	2Oct1848	9 yrs	Moyers, Thomas S.	Son of Margaret Blaylock
Slaten, Elisha	1Jan1849	13 yrs	Stranahan, Charles C.	Son of James Slaten, dcd
Smith, James	5Mar1849	18 yrs	Fain, L. R.	Taylor. For 3 years. Consent of mother, May Smith, widow
Raney, Josirah	2Apr1849	11 yrs	Owins, Robert	Consent of mother, Nancy Raney
Tabers?, Rebecka B.	3Dec1849	15 mo	Cannon, Mark M. C.	Domestik homewifery. Abandoned
Foster, Marten	8Jan1850	6 yrs	Gingery, Mikel	House carpenter. Son of Julyan Foster 7Jan1850.
Foster, William	8Jan1850	11 yrs	Leuis, Thomas D.	Taner & cover. Son of Julyan Foster 7Jan1850.
Foster, James Anderson	8Jan1850	15 yrs	Dabney, Paten R.	Saddler. Son of Julyan Foster 7Jan1850.
Raney, Martha	2Sep1850	7 yrs	Keedy, Sarah (Miss)	
Newby, William	7Apr1851	16 yrs	Swofford, John M.	Orphan
Stuart, George W.	1Mar1858	4 yrs	Roberson, Rufus B.	Orphan. Request of Milly Stuart, mother
Stuart, James L.	1Mar1858	1 yr 8 mo	Roberson, Rufus B.	Orphan. Request of Milly Stuart, mother
Bryson, James Momar	7Mar1859	8 yrs	Griffith, Mathew S.	Until age 20. Orphan
Bryson, Sarah Ann	5Apr1859	8 yrs	Schoolfield, James L.	Until age 16. Orphan. 6Dec1858*
Gilbert	4Oct1870	6 yrs	Swafford, Aron	Of color. No father or mother

Name	Date	Age	Master	Notes
Hill, John	5Jun1871	2 yrs 6 mo	Ward, John L. H.	Without father of mother
Ivy, James	5Jun1871	7 or 8 yrs	Higeons, H. M.	Without father or mother
Johnson, William	4Sep1871	8 yrs	Stout, John W.	Mother dead. Long since abandoned by father
Massey, James	4Sep1871	8 yrs	Swafford, John M.	Mother & father dead
Massey, Anna Jane	4Sep1871	6 yrs	Swafford, John M.	Mother & father dead
Loyd, John	5May1873	13 yrs	McReynolds, Isaac S.	Of color. Without father or mother
Wadkins, Henry Monroe	7Feb1871	3 yrs 20 days	Turner, John	Illeg son of Turner and Sarah Margaret Wadkins, a lude woman. Also adopted by Turner. Apprenticeship ordered, no bond or indenture recorded*
Clark, Thomas J.	2Aug1875	10 yrs	Billingsly, L. T.	Without father or mother
Hutcheson, Nick	2Oct1911	10 yrs	Cummings, Thomas	Abandoned by mother. Father, Malum Hutcheson, dead. Cummings is GF
Hutcheson, Sylvia	2Oct1911	8 yrs	Cummings, Thomas	Abandoned by mother. Father, Malum Hutcheson, dead. Cummings is GF
Hutcheson, Jake	2Oct1911	6 yrs	Cummings, Thomas	Abandoned by mother. Father, Malum Hutcheson, dead. Cummings is GF

Blount County

Name	Date	Age	Master	Notes
Hooks, Alexander	14Jun1796	11 mo	Hart, Sr., Joseph	Cooper. Orphan. Alias Alexander Hart
Smith, Charles	Dec1797	5 yrs last Aug	Wallace, Matthew	Shewmaker. Orphan. Resc 28Aug1802
McDonald(?), William	Dec1797		Wallace, Matthew	Orphan
Gibson, Robert	May1798		Wigans, Edward	Orphan. Alias Robert Tedford. Resc, as Eggins 28Aug1808
Write, John	May1800	3 yrs	Rogers, Benjamin	Orphan
Jester(?), Polly	26Nov1800	2 yrs	Six, Ambrose	Orphan
Jo___, Rebecka	23July1801	6 yrs	Mis___, John	Orphan
Lunn, Charles	24July1801	13 yrs	Jones, Francis	Orphan
Crowder, Nelson	26July1801	6 yrs	Shields, Robert	Orphan

Teel(?), Cindy	26July1801	4 yrs	Ore, Joseph	Orphan
Smith, Charles	28Aug1802		Gilmore, John	Orphan
Anderson, Robert	26Nov1802	16 yrs	Thompson, Andrew	For three years
Tilson, Jesse	5Mar1803	13 yrs	Sims, James	Orphan
Midleton, John	24May1803	6 yrs 3mo	Boyd, Robert	Orphan. Alias John Black
Fox, George	28Feb1804	9 yrs	Sloss(?), Joseph	By consent of father
Gentry, Jude	31May1804	13 yrs on 15June next	Pearce, Robert	Orphan
Strain, Allen	30Aug1804	17 yrs	Russle, John	
Gibson, Sally	26Nov1804	1 yr 6 mo	Cooke, Michel	Orphan
Richeson, Joseph	27Nov1804	11 yrs 4 mo	Cusack, John Black	Orphan
Richson, Drury	27Nov1804	7 yrs 4 mo	Cusack, John Black	Orphan
Griffey, Joseph	25Nov1807		Montgomery, James S.	Orphan, brother of Isoom 28Aug1807*, who died 9Oct1808. 2Dec1808*
Lauder, John	28Nov1807		Parrott, Henery	Orphan
Fox, George	28Nov1807		Lane, Samuel	Hatter. Formerly bound to James Gilmore
Griffin, William	26Feb1808		Taylor, William L.	Formerly bound to James S. Montgomery
Richardson, Drew(?)	27Feb1808		Cusak, John B.	Orphan
Thurman, Isah	27Feb1808		Logan, James	Formerly to James B. H. Porter
Richardson, Gideon	26May1808	13 yrs	McKee, Alexander	Orphan
Tedfor, Robert	28Aug1808		Licsenz (or Likenz), John	Alias Gibson. A prior indenture to Edward Eggins resc. Resc 1Sep1809
Carter, Benjamin	27Feb1809	16 yrs	Tucker, Samuel	Blacksmith
Thurman, Samuel	30Aug1809		Snider, Henry	
Tedford, Robert	1Sept1809		Henderson, Robert	
Anderson, Charlotte	1Sep1809		Debousk, Elias	
Jones, John	26Mar1810		Turk, James	Saddler. Resc 26Dec1810
Davis, Archibald	28Mar1810		Kelsoe, Hugh	Orphan, ordered brought from Tuckalicha 28Nov1807
Fox, George	25Sep1810		Wilson, Robert	
Snow, Reuben Smith	27Sep1814	11 yrs	Thompson, William	Orphan
Snow, Solomon	27Mar1815		Blackburn, Samuel	

Name	Date	Age	Master	Notes
Cooper, Burton			Malcon, John	Alias Beazly. Canc 25Sep1815, Cooper eloped
Wheeler, Ann	28Sep1815		McCully, John	
Gentry, Uriah	25Dec1815		McC____, Robert	Indenture between Susanna Gentry & McC_____
Hood, John Harvy	25Mar1816	6 yrs	Whittenbarger, Daniel	Farming
Yount, Ephrian	29Mar1816		Cummings, Thomas	Blacksmith
Jones, Nancy	23Sep1816		Jones, Francis	
Evins, Eli	26Mar1817	16 yrs	Smith, Michael	Orphan. Resc 24June1817, to care of mother, Barbara Evans
Evins, Vina (Lavinia)	26Mar1817	12 yrs	Cowan, Samuel	Orphan. Resc 24June1817, to care of mother, Barbara Evans
Yount, John	26Mar1817	16 yrs	Brown, Thomas	Orphan
James, John	27Mar1817		Love, Robert	
James, Jesse	27Mar1817		Garett, William	
Hood, Brison	23Jun1817	3 yrs	McCurdy, Robert	Orphan
Allen, Delilah	22Dec1817	12 yrs	Harris, John B.	Orphan
Allen, Thomas	22Dec1817	15 yrs	Strain, John	
Kibble, William	23Dec1817	7 yrs	Kibble, Sr., William	Orphan
Wallace, Green	23Mar1818		Turk, Esq., James	For 5 yrs
Jones, Charles	22Jun1818	5 yrs	Lane, Samuel	
Runyon, Loanie West	28Sep1818	17 yrs 6 mo	Turk, James & Archibald	Saddler
Weaver, Adam	3Oct1818	16 yrs 4 mo	Turk, James & Archibald	Saddler
Hood, Alexander	3Oct1818	12 yrs	Craft, Elias	Saddler
Hood, Brison	3Oct1818	5 yrs	Craft, Elias	Saddler
Stockton, James	3Oct1818		Agnew, Andrew	Saddler
Bowman, Josiah	3Oct1818	9 yrs	Maclin, William	
Aikman, Thomas H.	5Sep1836	14 yrs	McTeer, Jr., William	Resc 6May1839. Otherwise provided for
Aikman, Coffield T.	5Sep1836		McTeer, Jr., William	Tailor. For 7 years
Prestley, Charles	7Nov1836	16 yrs	Parham, F. A.	Printing. Prior ind to John Bonham rescinded
Brakebill, Sally	2Jan1837	8 yrs	Ewing, William	Resc 5Oct1840, Ewing leaving the state

Hitch, John	2Jan1837	14 yrs	Porter, Esq., Robert	
Arwood, John Madison	6Jan1837	14 yrs on 19July1836	Spencer, William A.	Tanning & currying
Bryant, Braxton	6Jan1837	17 yrs	Spencer, William A.	Tanning & currying
Pleasant, Wilson	6Jan1837	13 yrs	McLain, Andrew	Tanning & currying. Of color. Prior indenture to William Grigsby resc. Freed (time served) 5May1845
Adair, Calvin L.	6Jan1837	9 yrs	Alexander, Francis	
Greenfield, John	3Apr1837	2 yrs 4 mo	Parham, F. A.	Printing. Resc 3Dec1838, Parham having removed
McCullough, John	3Apr1837	8 yrs	Rankin, Thomas	Resc 6Jan1840. See John McCully
Greenfield, Campbell	3Apr1837	7 yrs	Wallace, Jr., Jesse	
Parks, James	1May1837	6 yrs 6 mo 24 d	Eagleton, John	
Farr, Eliza	1May1837	3 yrs 3 mo	McReynolds, Robert	
Farr, Alexander	1May1837	1 yr 11 mo	McReynolds, Robert	
Chambers, Charles	5Jun1837	11 yrs 2 mo	Hutten, Joseph	
Chambers, Isaac	5Jun1837	9 yrs 6 mo	Wood, Leonard	Resc 1Mar1841
Boyd, William	5Jun1837	7 yrs 2 mo 9 d	McReynolds, Stephen	Sadler. Resc 6Feb1843
Philips, Abner	5Jun1837	7 yrs 4 mo	Rorer, William	Resc 2Oct1843
Daily, Houston	2Oct1837	12 yrs last Aug	James, Will W.	
Dailey, Douthard	6Nov1837	10 yrs 3 mo	McFee, Thomas	
Dailey, Williamson	6Nov1837	8 yrs 9 mo	Kuntz, Adam	Resc 7Sep1840 (as William), Koontz deceased
Miller, William J.	1Jan1838	13 yrs 4 mo	McReynolds, Stephen	
Booth, David J.	1Jan1838	8 yrs	Lewis, William	
Booth, Jackson	1Jan1838	10 yrs	Mills, Benjamin	Resc 4Feb1844
Booth, Matilda	1Jan1838	11 yrs 4 mo	Lee, William	Resc 1Mar1841
Adams, Rebecca	1Jan1838	14 yrs 2 mo	Robertson, Jesse	
Bolen, John	2Apr1838	9 yrs 3 mo	Murrin, Sr., Robert	Resc 7Feb1848. Wm. McTeer app'td guardian
Bolen, Mitchell	2Apr1838	11 yrs 10 mo 12 d	Davis, George	
Farmer, Alfred			Parham, F. A.	Previously bound. 4June1838* Resc 1Oct1838*
Hammontree, John N.	5Nov1838	7 yrs 6 mo 5 d	Wayman, John	Blacksmith
Greenfield, John	3Dec1838	3 yrs 11 mo	Nance, James M.	Tailor
Lyle, William M.	7Jan1839	18 yrs 7 d	Spencer, William A.	Tanning & currying

Name	Date	Age	Master	Notes
Wolf, Jeremiah	7Jan1839	15 yrs 11 mo 23 d	Henry, James (of William)	Blacksmith
Hess, William	7Jan1839	15 yrs 5 mo	Henry, James (of William)	Waggon maker
Hammontree, William	7Jan1839	11 yrs	McCollum, Alexander	Son of Jesse Hammontree
Maupine, Harriet Maranda Jane	1Apr1839	11 yrs 3 mo	Jones, Joseph	Heir of Morgan G. Maupine, dcd. James Jones her guardian*
Maupine, Thomas Dewitt Finton	1Apr1839	6 yrs 21 d	Jones, James	Heir of Morgan G. Maupine dcd. Jones his guardian*
Maupine, Elbert Lafayette	1Apr1839	3 yrs 7 mo 13 d	Jones, Thomas	Heir of Morgan G.Maupine, dcd. James Jones his guardian*. Resc 4Oct1852
Pleasant, Reuben	1Apr1839	12 yrs 5 mo	Hair, Isaac M.	Blacksmith. Of color. Resc 3 July1843
Daily, Douthet	6May1839	11 yrs 10 mo	Koontz, Adam	Resc 7Sep1840, Koontz deceased
Mills, Maryann	6May1839	5 yrs	McFee, Thomas	
Ball, Margaret Jane	3June1839	2 yrs 9 mo 4 d	Parker, Henry	Resc 3July1848. Parker deceased
Henley, John	2Sep1839	13 yrs 8 mo	Wells, James B.	A prior indent to Samuel Houston canc. Resc 7Oct1839
Henley, John	7Oct1839	13 yrs 9 mo	Wright, Nelson	
Lankford, Jonathan	7Oct1839	16 yrs 6 mo	Scruggs, Moses & McClain, John	Tanning
Raynor, John	2Dec1839	15 yrs 11 mo 7 d	Harris, George W.	Blacksmith. A prior indent to Alexander Roddy canc
McCully, John	6Jan1840	11 yrs	Hall, Joseph	See John McCullough
Smith, William T.	4May1840	17 yrs	Garrard, Brittain	Waggon maker
Daily, Douthet	7Sep1840	14 yrs	Runnion, George	Brother of William Daily
Breakbill, Sally	5Oct1840		Rule, Henry	
Parks, James M.	4Jan1841		Love, William S.	
Webb, Arthur	4Jan1841		Stephens, Joseph	
Chambers, Isaac	1Mar1841	13 yrs	Thompson, John	Resc 2Oct1843
Greenfield, John	5Apr1841	6 yrs 2 mo	McTeer, William	Of color. Resc 3Feb1845
Chandler, Caroline	5Apr1841	8 yrs	McCallie, David E.	
Smith, William T.	3May1841	18 yrs	Cummings, John	
Maumpine, Benjamin T. H.	7June1841	3 yrs 6 mo 5 d	Kennon, Jeremiah	Heir of Morgan G. Maupine, dcd 1Apr1839* 5July1841* 6Sep1841*

Hitch, John	6Sep1841	18 yrs 7 mo	Young, Nathan M.	
Philips, Robert T.	5Dec1842	9 yrs	Limerly, Jacob	Resc 5Apr1852, H. T. Philips (sic) having run off
Shaver, Mary B.	5Dec1842	9 yrs 11 mo	Houston, John	
Boyd, William	6Feb1843	12 yrs 11 mo 21 d	Wells, James B.	Canc 1Apr1844
Rose, James F.	3Apr1843	13 yrs on 25Jan1843	Toole, William	Canc 4Jan1847 Frank Rose having run away
Ripley, Alfred E.	3Apr1843	13 yrs 6 mo	Anderson, Isaac	Mulatto, emancipated today on petition of Anderson
Dyer, Jacob	1May1843	11 yrs	Leboc, Henry	
Timmons, William	2Oct1843	17 yrs on 17Nov next	McClain, Andrew	
Chambers, Isaac	2Oct1843	15 yrs on 15Mar last	McTeer, James C.	
Philips, Abner	2Oct1843	14 yrs next Feb	Shields, Robert	
Boothe, Jackon	4Feb1844	16 yrs on 10th next mo	Henshaw, David	
Henry, Anderson	4Mar1844	2 yrs 2 mo	Law, Rufus	
Boyd, William	1Apr1844		Stout, David L.	Resc 6Oct1845
Shaver, William R.	6May1844	15 yrs 4 mo	McTeer, William	
McCawlie, John	6May1844	9 yrs on 8th this mo	Coulter, John	
McCawlie, William	6May1844	7 yrs in Feb	Coulter, John	
Woodard, John	3Jun1844	5 yrs	Stout, William S.	
Futtner, John W.	7Oct1844	14 yrs 7 mo	McReynolds, Stephen	Canc 4Jan1847, Futtner having run away
Huckaby, John	4Nov1844	10 yrs	Cochran, James	Resc 3May1852, Huckaby having run off
Miers, Rebecca	6Jan1845	12 yrs	Jones, Johnston	
Miers, Susan	6Jan1845	5 yrs	Bright, David	Resc 6Mar1854. Unruley
Greenfield, John	3Feb1845		Hunter, George	Of color
Myers, Jr., Philip	3Feb1845	14 yrs	Myers, Sr., Philip	
Myers, Robert	3Feb1845	16 yrs	Myers, Eli	
Daily, William	3Feb1845	14 yrs	Myers, Eli	
Reagan, Alexander	7Apr1845	9 yrs in June next	Lee, Jonathan	Resc 7July1845
McCawlie, James	8Apr1845	14 yrs	Loury, William	
Boling, Benjamin	5May1845	10 yrs	Kerry, John P.	
Boling, Caroline	5May1845	8 yrs	Headrick, John D.	

Name	Date	Age	Master	Notes
Boling, John A.	2Jun1845	5 yrs	Meginty, John N.	
Boyd, William D.	6Oct1845		Shown, Joseph L.	
Lawson, Robert	6Apr1846	1 yr	McGlothlin, Charles	Orphan in possesion of Daniel Yearout. 3Aug1846*
Myers, Elender	1Jun1846	11 yrs	Morton, Isaac W.	Dau of Matilda Myers 4&5May1846* Resc 4June1849
Handcock, James	3Aug1846	16 yrs	Lea, William	Orphan
Hix, Ann E.	5oct1846	14 yrs 8 mo	Hoyle, Andrew	Orphan
Brown, John	2Nov1846	6 yrs 1 mo	McFadden, David S.	Orphan
Boatman, Rebecca J.	7Dec1846	9 yrs 7 days	Bilderbeck, Thomas	
Moppin, Thomas Dewit C.	7Dec1846	14 yrs next March	Jones, Hezekiah	Resc 7July1851
Boatman, Nathan A.	7Dec1846	7 yrs 15 days	Henshaw, Zemri	Orphan. Resc 7Aug1848, request of mother, Sarah Boatman
Woodard, John	4Jan1847	7 yrs	Mingle, Rebecca	Orphan. Abandoned by Mingle 7Sep1857*
Paul, James	4Jan1847	14 yrs last March	Eagleton, John	Orphan
James	4Jan1847	10 yrs 2 mo	Henderson, James H.	Of color. Former slave of Thomas Hunter. Apprenticeship completed 1Feb1858*.
Hair, Isaac N.	7Jun1847	15 yrs 6 days	McTeer, Jr., William	
Webb, Arthur	7Jun1847	15 yrs	Parmer, James	
Williams, Emeline	5July1847	14 mo	Furguson, John C.	
Hackaby, N. A.	1Nov1847	8 yrs	Richey, Robert	Orphan
Paul, John L.	6Dec1847	9 yrs on 18Nov1847	McKenry, Samuel	
Paul, William B.	7Feb1848	12 yrs	Duncan, George	Resc 6Mar1854, as George Paul
Woolf, Cornelius	7Mar1848	7 yrs in May next	Kennon, Jeremiah	Orphan. Sibs William, Neal & Nancy 6Mar1848*
Dyer, Jacob	1May1848	15 yrs	Ritchey, J. H.	
Myers, Mary J.	1May1848	4 1/2 yrs	Emitt, Frederick	
Brooks, Hiram	3July1848	15 yrs	Pearson, Hiram	
Brooks, Polly	3July1848	13 yrs	Pearson, Hiram	
Brooks, Nancy J.	3July1848	11 yrs	Pearson, Hiram	
Hollingsworth, John	2Oct1848	7 yrs	Kidd, Robert	Resc 1July1850

Cryder, William	4Dec1848	19 yrs	Turk, William B.	
Myers, Elenor	4Jun1849	14 yrs	Bice, Lewis P.	
Daily, William	2July1849	16 yrs	Turk, William B.	Resc 6Aug1849
Page, William	6Aug1849	17 yrs 5 mo	Ambrister, Asa	For 4 yrs from 1 June last
Thurmon, Isley	3Sep1849	2 yrs	Thurmon, John	
King, Nathaniel W.	2Oct1849	3 yrs on 16 June last	Harvey, Michael	Nathaniel declared a pauper. Resc 3Dec1849
Key, William W.	5Aug1850	6 yrs in Oct1849	Moore, James	
Key, John A.	5Aug1850	9 yrs in Feb1850	Ballenger, Dempsey	Resc 1Sep1856. Ballinger leaving the state
Myers, Eleanor	5Aug1850	15 yrs on 8July1850	Waller, John	
Stuart, John A.	7Oct1850	15 yrs in Jan1851	Irvin, James B.	Wagon & carriage making. Minor heir of Joseph Stuart. Resc 4Feb1851, bad health of John*
Poplin, William T.	3Mar1851		Caldwell, George	Illegitimate. At request of mother, M. D. C. Poplin. Resc 1Mar1852, Poplin having run off
Folkner, James	7Apr1851	14 yrs	Barnes, James	
John	2Jun1851		Conner, William	Illegitimate. John and Conner of color
Brown, Solomon	2Jun1851		Cummings, William	
Brown, Elisha	1Sep1851		Cummings, William	
Poplin, George W.	6Oct1851		Billew, William	At request of mother Nolsey D. Poplin. Resc1Sep1856*
Tate, William	1Dec1851	8 yrs in May1851	Garner, Allen	Tate and Garner of color. Son of Celia Vance, dcd, by first husband.* Rebound to Garner 3May1852
Tate, Margaret Jane	1Dec1851	10 yrs in Oct1851	Garner, Allen	Tate and Garner of color. Dau of Celia Vance, dcd, by first husband.* Rebound to Garner 3May1852
Michael	5Jan1852		Conner, William	Michael & Connor of color
Garner, William	5Jan1852		Lamb. D. R.	Orphan, illeg chid of ____ Garner
Ragan, George W.	3Feb1852	9 yrs	Henry, James, of Bakins Creek	Orphan. Request of mother. Resc 2Apr1860, Reagan having left
Poplin, Anderson	1Mar1852		Mitchell, James	Orphan
Crye, John	5Apr1852		Walker, Hiram	Orphan
Cumming, Joseph	5Apr1852		Blanchord, Thomas J.	Orphan
Cumming, William H.	5Apr1852		Blanchord, T. J.	Orphan
Maupin, E. L.	4Oct1852		Allen, James C.	Moppin 21 yrs 7Sep1857*

Name	Date	Age	Master	Notes
Rainwater, Andrew	4Apr1853		McConnell, Isaac M.	Request of mother, Martha Rainwater. Resc 7Sep1857, McConnell leaving the state. On 3Dec1860 Andrew, now 21 yrs of age, paid $25
Rainwater, Thomas	4Apr1853		Edmonson, Wallace	Request of mother, Martha Rainwater. Resc 3May1858
Parker, C. M.	6Sep1853		Parker, Philena	Philena is GM. Father of bad character, mother dead*
Hubbard, Jane	3Oct1853		Keeble, Richard	Resc 2May1859, Jane having left Keeble
Parsons, Eli	7Nov1853		Lea, Sr., Ephraim	Orphan
Rowlet, Charles	6Mar1854		Blount, James F.	Orphan. Resc 4Feb1856
Poplin, Anderson	4Dec1854		Kenney, J. P.	Orphan. Resc 5Jan1858, Poplin left Kenney
Hatcher, J. W.	4Dec1854		Everett, Eppaphrodetus	Orphan
Stirling, Hariet A.	5Feb1855	8 yrs	Conor, William	Orphan. Both of color
Suthered, W. T.	5Mar1855		McIlherin, John	Orphan. Both moving out of state 7Sep1857*
Elder, Marian	2July1855	14 yrs	Dunlap, Aaron T.	Male orphan. Resc 6Feb1860, F. M. Elder a runaway
Lowry, Henry	2July1855		McCoy, J. C.	A prior indenture to J. W. Cochran resc. Canc 6Mar1866
Rainwater, Jackson	3Dec1855	Born 1Mar1845	Hudgeon, J. J.	Orphan. Resc 3Jan1859
Cope, Minda	3Mar1856	4 yrs 6 mo	Emmett, Frederick	
Tuck, Mary L.	5May1856	10 yrs on 18Nov1856	Hitch, James	Orphan
Tuck, William	5May1856	4 yrs on 5Sep1856	Hitch, James	Orphan. Resc 4Jun1860
Key, John A.	1Sep1856	16 yrs in Feb last	Miser, Joseph	Minor heir of William Key
Reagan, John T.	1Sep1856	6 yrs on 23Apr1856	Pugh, L. V.	Orphan. Until age 19
Blevins, Luny	7Jan1857	12 yrs on 28Dec1856	Kerr, Henderson	Request of father, mother dead. Kerr declined indenture*
Blevins, John	7Jan1857	9 yrs on 11May1856	Kerr, J. M.	Until age 18. Request of father, mother dead*. Resc 3Apr1858
Blevins, Nicholas	7Jan1857	7 yrs on 15Nov1856	Best, J. M.	Until age 18. Request of father, mother dead* Bro of Dills Blevins 1Apr1861* Resc 6July1863
Blevins, Isaac	7Jan1857	4 yrs on 15Jan1857	Best, Christopher	Until age 18. Request of father, mother dead* Resc 6Sep1858
Bird, Benjamin	7Jan1857	8 yrs in Feb1857	Townsley, James	Orphan. Until age 18. Request of mother, Mary Bird. Resc 3Oct1864, Bird absconded
McClure, John	1June1857	3 yrs	Yearout, J. N.	Until age 18. Son of John R. McClure, dcd.* 7May1857*

Elder, William L	13July1857	7 yrs	Taylor, Joseph	Until age 19. Abandoned by father, Daniel Elder. Resc 5Nov1860, Taylor leaving Tennessee
McCluer, Jane	13July1857	10 yrs	Hudson, J. C.	Until 17 yrs. Dau of John R. McCluer, dcd. 7May1857* 1 & 2Jun1857*
Pearson, Julia J.	3Nov1857	Unknown	Caldwell, J. M.	For 4 yrs 6 mo. Dau of John Pearson, dcd. Mother dead. 4Mar1861*
Pearson, George	3Nov1857	Unknown	Heart, Thomas	For 9 yrs. Son of John Pearson, dcd. Mother dead
Pearson, Sarah J.	3Nov1857	Unknown	Love, Jack	For 3 yrs. Dau of John Pearson, dcd. Mother dead
Brannum, S. E.	7Dec1857	10 yrs	Nuchol, Thomas	Until age 17. Female. Abandoned by mom, father dead or left the country. Resc 5Jan1858, Sarah ungovernable, ?idiotic
Caldwell, Sarah	7Dec1857	10 yrs on 31Jan next	Marshall. William	Until age 17. Illeg dau of Malvina Jane Caldwell Abandoned.* Resc 1Nov1858
Caldwell, James	1Mar1858	4 yrs on 8Jan1858	Caldwell, N. D.	Son of Malvina Jane Caldwell*
Bird, Ezekial B.	2Aug1858		Scott, R. H.	Son of John Bird 7June1858* 6Sep1858* Resc 4Jun1867, Houston Scott dead
Blevins, Isaac	6Sep1858		Carpenter, Samuel	Until age 18
Caldwell, Sarah	7Mar1859		Everett, Robert E.	Resc 7Apr1862, Sarah left
Davis, Samuel	7Nov1859	4 yrs in Sep1859	Freshour, Jac	
Kizer, George W.	6Feb1860	14 yrs in Mar1860	Blackburn, Thomas	Orphan. Resc 2Dec1861, Kizer having left
McCulley, J. W.	5Mar1860	2 yrs on 9Dec1859	Caruthers, H. C.	Until age 21. Orphan
McCulley, J. W. M.	5Mar1860	8 yrs on22Nov1860	Goddard, William	Until age 21. Orphan
Tuck, William	4Jun1860	8 yrs in Sep next	Hattox, James	
Moseley, Isaac	5Nov1860	14 yrs in Nov1860	Amburn, Bennet	Ind trans to Fanny Amburn on 3Mar1862, Bennet deceased. Resc 1Dec1862, Isaac having left.
Bird, Susan C.	5Nov1860	3 yrs in Aug1860	Suit, Gaston	
Elder, W. L.	5Nov1860	10 yrs in July last	Blackburn, R. H.	Until age 19
Lambert, Daniel P.	4Mar1861	9 yrs on 12Feb1861	Freshour, George	
Fultner, Asa L.	3Jun1861	7 yrs on 17Jun1861	Duncan, Benjamin F.	Request of mother. Resc 2Oct1865, Duncan dead
Nipper, Sarah M.	1Jun1863	11 yrs	Brown, John	Resc 4Sep1865, Sarah having left Brown
Smith, James	1Aug1864	8 yrs	Harvey, Michael	Orphan? of Jacob Smith*

Name	Date	Age	Master	Notes
Spears, Joseph T.	5Nov1865		Miser, Michael	Request of mother, Rebecca Spears
Carter, William M.	9Dec1865		Baker, Thomas	
Thompson, J. C.	5Feb1866	13 yrs	Walker, Jr., Elizah	
McCully, William	5Feb1866	5 yrs 11 mo	Means, William	
Kirby, Alice G.	4Jun1866		McPhaddan, Jane	
Kinnamon, James	3Sep1866		Wear, Dorcus	
Bird, J. C.	5July1858	4 yrs in Oct1858	Roddy, Calvin	Son of John Bird 7June1858*
Bird, S. E.	4Apr1859		Frow, J. R.	Female. Resc 9July1864, Frow dead.
Cox, Susan	2Apr1860	7 yrs on 25Dec1859	Taylor, Esq., Daniel	Of color. Request of father, Parm Cox
Cox, William	2Apr1860	5 yrs in May1860	Taylor, Esq., Daniel	Of color. Request of father, Parm Cox
Cox, Samuel	2Apr1860	9 mo	Taylor, Esq., Daniel	Of color. Request of father, Parm Cox
Key, Maston A.	2Apr1860		James, A. R.	Request of father, Joseph Key. Resc 6Apr1863*
Lambert, T. P.	1Apr1861	12 yrs on 16Mar1861	Tipton, J. W. H.	
Hall, J. M.	7July1862	6 yrs	Cox, John B.	
Johnson, Mary L.	6Oct1862	12 yrs in Jan last	Wright, Isaac	Resc 2Oct1865, Wright leaving the county
Johnson, Lydia	6July1863	11 yrs	Saffell, L. B.	
McCullough, W. A.	5Oct1863	3 yrs on 27May next	Anderson, William	Resc 4Apr1865, as Wm. Abraham McCully. Request of mother
Davis, Alfed	5Oct1863	5 yrs on 5Jan next	Jones, Emil M.	
Bird, Sarah E.	9July1864		Frow, T. J.	
Fultner, Asa	4Oct1865		Sandford, S. L.	Allowed to leave Co with Sanford 5Nov1866
Hollins, John	2Apr1866	13 yrs	Garner, Allen	
Bates, Thomas	6May1867	14 yrs	George, Isaac W.	At request of Bates
Bird, ____ [Ezekial]	4May1867		McCammon, O. P.	Orphan
Carter, Thomas J.	1Jun1867		McNutt, H. S.	Orphan. Req of mother. Resc 14Aug1871, Carter left
Sims, Sarah Ann	4May1868		Dugan, Mack	
Bolin, James A.	1Jun1868		Dunlap, Samuel P.	
Faulkner, William	3Aug1868	3 yrs	Kelly, William	
Price, William	7June1869		Byerly, Isaac	Of color. Request of mother

Gibbon, Nancy	2May1870	9 yrs	Gellespy, N. F.	
Hood, William [R.]	1Jan1872		Kinnamon, A. K.	Resc 1May1876, returned to mother, Jane Hood
Maynard, Mary Lucrecia	5Feb1872	9 yrs	Ferrary, Leo L.	Orphan
Jones, Milas Jefferson	7Oct1872		Jones, W. L.	
Jones, David	4Nov1872		Henry, John F.	Minor heir of Mary Jones, who gave consent
Rankin, Samuel B.	4Aug1873		Curtis, E. R.	
Fortner, Mary E.	2Mar1874		Allen, James	Security waived
Robison, James	2Mar1874		Henderson, R. P.	Request of mother, Easter Robison. Resc 2Nov1874*
Runnions, Elizah C.	2Aug1875		Miller, John D.	Orphan
Herrin, Granville	6Sep1875		Hutton, John N.	Orphan
Runnion, Malinda C.	1Nov1875	6 yrs 5 mo	Logan, John C.	Request of mother
Thomas, Martha J.	1Nov1875	14 yrs 8 1/2 mo	Hastings, W. P.	Parent unable to provide
Underwood, Nathaniel	5Aug1878	9 yrs	Griffiths, Esq., W. S.	Request of Underwood

Bradley County

Name	Date	Age	Master	Notes
Carter, Thomas	3Apr1865	9 yrs	Johnston, C. M.	Orphan. Resc 2Jan1872 as a guardian bond. Carter gone
Ezell, Thomas Lonzo	7Aug1865	9 yrs on 27Aug1865	Ezell, George	
Waller, Mary E.	4Sep1865	2 yrs	Russel, Thomas	
Ben	4Sep1865	9 to 10 yrs	Parker, George T.	Until age 19. Of color. Previously owned by Parker.
Huskisson, Thomas R.	3Oct1865		Willhoite, W. M.	Son of John Huskisson. Previously bound, bond burned
Taylor	6Nov1865	9 yrs	Campbell, James M.	Servant
Susan	6Nov1865		Campbell, James M.	Servant
Turner, Elijah Elsmore	3Jan1866	6 yrs	York, Abraham	Farming
Turner, Vincent	3Jan1866	8 yrs	Haynes, Lazarus	Farming. Orphan. Resc 4Sep1866
Philip	5Feb1866	10 1/2 yrs	Hall, Mary	Of color
Margaret	5Feb1866	9 yrs	Hall, Mary	Of color

Name	Date	Age	Master	Notes
Israel, Thomas O.			Israel, George	Previously bound to George Israel, his uncle. On 5Feb1866 returned to father, T. J. Collier. Mary Israel, mother, dead
Harris, William O.	2Apr1866	6 yrs on 13Dec last	York, W. C.	Resc 5Aug1867
Cockran, John L.	7May1866	10 yrs	Taylor, D. D.	Orphan. Destitute. Resc 8Jan1867, runaway
Columbus, George	3Sep1866	8 mo	Brown, James M.	
Read, Noah	3Sep1866	Born 25July1855	Lee, Thomas	Bound by father, John T. Read
Read, Mary Jane	3Sep1866	Born 14Oct1853	Lee, Thomas	Bound by father, John T. Read
Turner, Vincen	4Sep1866	8 yrs	York, Abraham	
Green, Thomas	3Dec1866	13 yrs	McGhee, James	
Arthur, John F.	9Jan1867	Born 7July1856	Blair, William	Orphan
Arthur, Willis V.	9Jan1867	7 yrs	Orme, Joseph	Orphan. Resc1July1867. To mother
Bradford, Samantha C.	1Apr1867	7 yrs	McNabb, Armstrong	Orphan
Barns, _____	2Apr1867	9 yrs	Dyson, J. W.	Of color. Bound by mother, Elizabeth Barns
Woods, Mary Jane	6May1867	11 yrs	Cate, G. B.	Bound by mother, Elizabeth Woods
Woods, Arena A.	6May1867		Julian, M. L.	Bound by mother, Elizabeth Woods
Johnson, Hetty	6May1867	8 yrs	Russell, H. B.	Servant. Of color
Sanders, James	3Jun1867	6 yrs	McAndrew, William	
Harris, William O.	5Aug1867	8 yrs	London, James M.	Resc 2Sep1867. To mother, Mary Harris
Hampton, Wade	7Oct1867	11 yrs	Traynor, John D.	Servant. Of color
Susan	2Dec1867	11 yrs	Donohoo, James	Of color
Hill, Wiley S.	2Dec1867	5 yrs on 9Aug last	Hughes, Thomas	
Stepherson, William	6Jan1868	14 yrs	Mahoney, William	
Hammontree, Jesse Franklin	5Jan1869	11 yrs	Smith, Isaac	
Alonzo	1Feb1869	8 yrs	Hall, Mary	Of color. Until age 20
Pettitt, James B.	5July1869	10 yrs	Swafford, Peter W.	Farming. Of color. Orphan
Clark, Andrew J.			Hall, Thomas	Resc 7Mar1870. Returned to mother
Edwards, E. E. Jane	3Oct1870	5 yrs on 1Apr1870	Edwards, G. W. & Matilda	Orphan

Edwards, Matilda Ann	3Oct1870	3 yrs	Edwards, G. W. & Matilda	Orphan
Cate, Ann	2Oct1871		Henderson, Delilah	Orphan. Both of color
Ray, James T.	2Oct1871		Newton, I. B.	Orphan
Harris, Lydia	2Oct1871		Barrett, S. S.	Orphan. 1Jan1872*
Harris, William P.	2Oct1871		York, Abraham	Orphan
Holder, Robert B.	7July1873		Smith, John H.	Consent of father, Poss Holder. Resc 6Oct1874
Tucker, Richard	1Sep1873	14 yrs	Blair, G. J.	Of color. Resc 5Jan1880, Richard having left
Holder, James	1Sep1873		Watenbarger, Adam	Son of Poss Holder
Airheart, Granville	4May1874		Tucker, J. R.	
Crumly, ____			Johnston, James	Resc 7Sep1874, returned to parents, Jane & Charles D. Crumly
Melton, Ellen Road	2Aug1875	3 yrs	Melton, G. W.	Parents unknown. Found near the house of Campbell Steed on abt 1July1875
London, Luther	3Oct1876	4 yrs	Smith, Anderson	
Holder, Bob	3Dec1877	10 yrs	Smith, D. H.	Farming. Orphan
Broaden, Lewis	8Jan1878	15 yrs	Newton, I. B.	Of color. Name ? Braden*
Hinkle, Anna Mindora	8Jan1878	4 yrs	Goodner, Caswell	Orphan, heir of Samuel Hinkle, dcd
Cate, Philip J.			Crews, Johnson	Resc 6Oct1879, Philip having left
Hinkle, Walter	7Mar1881		Cameron, William O.	No living parents. Cameron, of Polk Co, is uncle by marriage

Campbell County

Name	Date	Age	Master	Notes
Usrey, William	6Sep1814		Crag, Joab	Orphan
Anderton, James	6Sep1814	13 yrs 6 mo	Smith, Thomas, of Jacksborough	
Usher, John	6Dec1814	13 yrs on 15May1814	Moad, Loadermilk	Orphan. 6Sep1814*
Usher, David	6Dec1814	15 yrs 1 mo	Sharp, Joseph	Orphan. 6Sep1814*
Catchum, Polly	5Jun1816	7 yrs 8 mo	Cook, Michael	

Name	Date	Age	Master	Notes
Boyette, Jonathan	5Mar1817	6 yrs	Bratcher, John	
Boyette, Samuel	5Mar1817	13 yrs next June	Bratcher, Charles	
Lanum, John	2June1823	8 yrs on 4Feb last	Lanum, Joseph	
Gray, Letha	16Dec1825	1 yr 2 mo 27 d	Lanum, Joseph	Orphan
Rutherford, Campbell	8Sep1834	11 yrs	Clap, Henry	Orphan
Byran, Margaret Ann	10Mar1835	3 yrs	Boshears, Isaac	Orphan
Standley, Rueben	11Mar1835		McCoy, William	10Mar1835 ordered to court
Standley, Rhoda	11Mar1835		McCoy, William	10Mar1835 ordered to court
Burgess, Thomas	10Jun1835	14 yrs	Montgomery, Rufus K.	Taken from care of William Burgess 12Dec1834* A sister also ordered brought to court 10Mar1835*
White, Jimmy	14Sep1835	5yrs 6 mo	Richards, Thomas	Orphan
Brown, Christina	14Dec1835	14 yrs in Feb next	Archer, Enoch	Orphan
Brown, William	14Dec1835	8 yrs in May next	Archer, Enoch	Orphan
Marcum, Arthur	10Dec1835	7 yrs 4 mo	Fleming, Berd M.	Orphan
Godsey, Samuel	1Aug1836	4 yrs	Williams, Silas	Orphan. Resc 1Feb1841. Rebound as Sam'l Godfrey
Canter, Henry			James, Rollings	Ill used. Taken from James 5Sept1836
Canter, Jesse			James, Rollings	Ill used. Taken from James 5Sept1836
James, John	2Oct1837	11 yrs	Ballard, Richard	Orphan
Standley, F. H. Bratcher	4Dec1837	2 yrs on 1Jan1837	Stephens, Allen	Orphan. Assent of mother. Illegitimate. Resc 1July1844, req of mother
Cooper, Jane	5Feb1838	7 yrs	Vingant, George	Orphan. Resc 6Jan1840, request of mother, Barbary Cooper
Burgess, Charlott T.	5Feb1838	10 yrs	Vingant, George	Orphan. Taken from care of Tallufarro Butler
James, William	5Mar1838		Mars, James J.	
Godfrey, Samuel	1Feb1841		Lindsay, William	
Baxter, James	7Mar1842	12 yrs	Lindsay, Jr., William	
Campbell, Margarett Matilda Catherine	2May1842		Jacobs, Jesse B.	
Morgan, Frankling	3Oct1842	12 yrs in Aug1843	Hollingsworth, Daniel	Orphan

Newman, William	3Jan1843	9 yrs	Grant, James H.	
Newman, Polly	3Jan1843	7 yrs	Grant, James H.	
Kesterson, Martha	6Mar1843	4 yrs	Peterson, Calvin	
Peterson, George Washington	2Apr1844		Cole, Sampson D.	
Peterson, Andrew Jackson	5Aug1844	13 yrs in Nov1844	Stamper, Jesse	Tailor. Resc 3Feb1845
Peterson, Andrew J.	3Feb1845	13 yrs in Nov1844	Cary, William	Until 20 yrs. Resc 2Feb1846
Peterson, Andrew J.	2Feb1846		Crawford, William D.	For 2 years
Cooper, Sarah	2July1866		Bunch, David E.	Orphan of Peter Cooper
Cooper, Mary	2July1866		Bunch, David E.	Orphan of Peter Cooper
McKeehan, George W.	5July1869		McKeehan, William J.	Orphan
Roberts, Mary	2May1870		Price, Marcus F.	
Childress, James	May1872		Childress, Marvell	Orphan

Carter County

Name	Date	Age	Master	Notes
Lile, Ishmael	Feb1804	12 yrs	Humphreys, Jesse	
Wiliams, Jean			Wills, John	Prior ind resc 15Feb1804
Frazior, William	14May1805		Hendrix, Nathan	Agriculture. By John Frazior
Harris, Elizabeth	13Nov1805	6 yrs	Carter, Elizabeth	Sewing, Spining, kniting. Orphan
Canter, Ezekiel	14Feb1820	17 yrs	Harris, Benjamin C.	Hating. Orphan. Resc 12Feb1821
Jenkins, Jesse			Jenkins, Hugh	Indenture cancelled Feb1820
Jenkins, Jesse	14Feb1820		Williams, John	Blacksmith. Orphan. Resc 16Feb1821
Kelly, James	16Feb1820		Smith, George	House carpenter & joiner. For four years
Roberts, Allen	14Aug1820	6 yrs on 14 Oct next	Brown, George	Shoemaking. Orphan
Little, Elihu			Jones, William D.	Indenture cancelled 15Aug1820
Little, Elihu	15Aug1820		Tipton, Abraham	Resc 11Aug1824, as Elihu E. Little

Name	Date	Age	Master	Notes
Williams, Napoleon Bonapart	16Aug1820	15 yrs	Smith, George	Carpenter & House Joiner. Resc 19May1821, as Napoleon B. McCraw
Parnal, Vinea	19Aug1820	6 yrs	Carter, William B.	Female orphan
Parnal, Mary	19Aug1820	2 yrs	Carter, William B.	
Parnal, Jacob	19Aug1820	6 mo	Carter, William B.	
Duffield, George	19Aug1820	15 yrs	Taylor, Mary	Indian, brought from Creek nation in Apr1815
Jenkins, Larkin	14Nov1820		Buck, Isaac	Waggon wright
Jenkins, Jessee	16Feb1821		Mink, John	
McCraw, Napoleon B.	19May1821		Taylor, Joseph	Blacksmith. See N. B. Williams
Jackson, William	11May1825	9 yrs	Edens, James	Son of James Jackson, Dcd*. 9May1825*
Jackson, Andrew	9Aug1825	4 yrs	Edens, James	Son of James Jackson, Dcd. 11May1825*
Jackson, Nancy	9Aug1825	6 yrs	Edens, Nathaniel T.	Dau of James Jackson, Dcd. 11May1825*
Cates, Sarah	13Feb1826	13 yrs	Bogert, Jeremiah	Orphan. Dau of Nancy Cates. 14Nov1825*
Cates, Dixon	13Feb1826	4 yrs	Range, Johnothan	Orphan. Son of Nancy Cates. 14Nov1825*
Cates, Winney	13Feb1826	7 yrs	Range, Jacob	Orphan. Son of Nancy Cates. 14Nov1825*
Cates, Elizabeth	13Feb1826	9 yrs	Bogert, Samuel	Orphan. Dau of Nancy Cates. 14Nov1825*
Howard, William	13Nov1826	7 yrs	Ruen, Isaac	Orphan
Howard, Purlina	14Nov1826		Brown, George	
Howard, Isac	14Nov1826	5 yrs	Tipton, James J.	Orphan
Howard, Caroline	12Feb1827		Brown, George	
Howard, Isaac	12Feb1827	6 yrs	Lacy, Alexander	Orphan
Ward, Alfred	12Feb1827	2 yrs	Dugger, Julius	Orphan
Trusler, Joseph	15Feb1827	14 yrs	Gwinn, David	Orphan
Cassidy, William			Jones, William	Orphan. Resc 13Aug1827 at req of Thomas Paxton
Vann, Levi			Carver, Thomas	Resc 10Nov1828. Surety, David McNabb now dcd
Helton, Landon	9May1831	16 yrs last Easter	Cameron, Jacob	Sadler. Orphan. Consent of mother, Patty Helton
Scott, James	10May1831		Singletarey, Thomas	Taylor
Ford, Charlotte	8Aug1831	9 yrs 2 mo 7 days	Baker, Mathias B.	Orphan

Mange, William Hambleton	13Feb1832	6 yrs on 6March next	Williams, Calvin	Orphan
Mange, William Hamilton	13May1833		Bowers, Jr., Leonard	
Maines, Jackson	2Aug1836		Tipton, Abraham	
Hays, Daniel			Nair, Tennessee T.	Indenture rescinded 9Sept1836
Hays, Daniel	9Sept1836		Huffman, Moses	Wagon Maker or Millwright
Williams, Douglass	3Apr1837		Singletary, Thomas	
Hatcher, Leander A.	4June1838		Odell, David	
Redmon, Andrew	4June1838		Morton, Meredith Y.	
Mastin, George W.	1Oct1838		Hunt, Warrenton	Taylor
Goodwin, Lawson Laury	1Oct1838		Goodwin, Lawson	
Wagner, Calvin	1Apr1839		Woods, Uriah	Smith
Redman, Andrew	7Dec1840	10 yrs	Shook, Matthew	
Hodge, Lurana	7Dec1840	9 yrs	Smith, Nicholas	Female
Frasier?, Landon	6Sept1841		Allen, William	
Gourly, William M.	4Apr1842		Hess, David	Blacksmith
Hamrick, Joel H.	4Dec1843		Tilson, William	Farming. Son of David Hamrick. Ret to father 5May1845
Cook, Reuben P.	July1845		Hess, David	Blacksmith. Resc 8July1851*. Mother Delilah Philips
Bowes, Abraham J.	7Aug1848		Smith, Hamilton C.	
Februay, George	Oct1848	17 yrs	Patterson, Samuel B.	Capenter
Griffin, James	7Mar1853	Born 1Oct1851	Stout, David	Farming. Bastard child of Elizabeth Griffin. Of color*
Griffin, Lucinda	7Mar1853	Born 5Feb1851	Wilson, L. L.	Housekeeping. Bastard child of Sary Griffin. Of color*
Griffin, Andrew	Mar1853	Born 5Feb1852	Wilson, L. L.	Farming, Bastard child of Mary Griffin. Of color*
Greenway, James	8Feb1856	14 yrs	Slagle, Henry	Req of mother, Rachel Greenway
Carlton, Caroline			Taylor, Live	Ind resc 5May1856. Returned to mother
Carrell, Elizabeth	5Mar1860		Schuer?, William I.	Orphan. Of color
Lee, Jansey	5Nov1860		Crider, Jacob	Carpenter
Roberts, William	6Jan1868		Pattersen, Samuel B.	Carpenter
Love, Eliza	3May1869	3 yrs	Hughes, Sandy (of color)	Housekeping. Of color
Love, Samuel	3May1869		Hughes, Sandy (of color)	Farmer. Of color

Claiborne County

Name	Date	Age	Master	Notes
Cooper, William	6Sep1802	4 yrs on 5Apr1802	Hill, Joab	
Lard, Elijah	6Sep1802	8 yrs on 14May1803	Stubblefield, George	Resc 3Sep1804
Lard, Elijah	3Sep1804		Dodson, James	Orphan
Houseman, Nancy	3Sep1804		Cunningham, Thomas	Baseborn dau of Caty Houseman**Error! Bookmark not defined.**. On 2Jun1806 returned to mother
Simpson, Adam	3Dec1804	5 yrs last March	Damron, William	Son of Marjery Simpson
Staephan, Chappel Car	4Sep1805	6 yrs in March1805	Evans, Walter	Orphan, son of Sally Marshall
Cock, Leroy	3Sep1806	Near 2 yrs	Cock, John	Orphan, son of Susanna Cock
Houseman, Nancy	3Sep1806		Woodall, Bluford	Orphan, dau of Catherine Houseman
Wolf, Polly	25Aug1807	10 to 11 yrs	Bord, Esq., John	Dau of Jacob Wolf, Dcd. 25Feb1807*
Jones, Elisha	24May1808		Dobbins, Solomon	Son of Elijah Jones
Dobbs, Malinda	16Aug1816	3 yrs 2 mo	Cocke, John	Dau of Pheby Dobbs & ?Grimes Neal 16Aug1816*
Mundy, Wilson	14Feb1820		Mundy, William	14Feb1820*
Fields, Malin	8May1820	2 yrs	Collins, Elisha	
Moor, William	13May1822	2 yrs 8 mo	Whittaker, John	Orphan
Buice, William	21Jun1824		Marcum, Peter	Until 14 yrs. Orphan. 20Sep1824*
Buice, Sterling	28Jun1824	7 yrs	Bolinger, Frederick	Orphan. 20Sep1824* Resc 18Jun1827
Grady, Franklin			Vanbebber, James	Bastard of Frances Grady. Indent resc 18Dec1826
Cawn, Elizabeth	19Jun1827		Richardson, George	
Johnson, Jr., Hiram	19Jun1827		Johnson, Sr., Hiram	Name on indent changed to Hiram Private 17Sep1827
Gibson, Polly	19Dec1827		McCubbins, John	Resc 20Mar1832
Gibson, James	19Dec1827		McCubbins, John	Resc 20Mar1832
Tankesly, John	20Dec1827		Cooper, Archibald	
Tankesly, George W.	20Dec1827		Cooper, Archibald	Resc 21Sep1830
Woods, Stephen	17Mar1828		McBroom, James	Resc 30Dec1830, Woods having left
Langly, Joseph	17Mar1828		Graves, John	

McDowell, Livonia	17Jun1828		Huddleston, David	Orphan of Hetty Collins* Resc 15Dec1828, child having been taken from the state to parts unknown
McDowell, Julina	18Jun1828		Huddleston, David	Orphan of Hetty Collins 17June1828*. Resc 15Dec1828*, child having been taken from the state
Janeway, Farrow	15Sep1828		Dunsmore, William D.	Illeg child of Nancy Janeway 18Sept1828*
Brooks, Jesse	15Dec1828		Chapman, Joshua H.	
Keel?, Henry	17Mar1829		Vanbebber, Gabriel	
McCrary, William	17Mar1829		Spillers, William	Resc 21June1830
Ray, Luritha	21Sep1829	2 yrs	Pike, Jacob	
Brock, Bryor			Dunsmore, William D.	Indent resc 20Sept1830
Wallis, John Greenberry	21Mar1831	6 yrs on 25Dec1830	Fergerson, John	Assent of mother, Synthia Wallace. Abandoned by father, Goodwin Wallis. App by Wallis 24Mar1831*
Wallis, William Monroe	21Mar1831	4 yrs on 18May1831	Fergerson, John	Assent of mother, Synthia Wallace. Abandoned by father, Goodwin Wallis. App by Wallis 24Mar1831*
Wallis, Elizabeth	21Mar1831	1 yr	Fergerson, John	Assent of mother, Synthia Wallace. Abandoned by father, Goodwin Wallis. App by Wallis 24Mar1831*
England, Mariah Luisa	19Sep1831		England,Thomas	
England, Mary Ann Jana	19Sep1831		England, Thomas	
Baltrip, Frederick	19Jun1832		Harrison, Elias	18Sept1832* Resc2May1836
Hamilton, Elijah	17Dec1832		Hamilton, James A.	
Hamilton, Mary Ann	18Dec1832		Watson, Azariah	
Baltrip, Elizabeth	18Dec1832		Forgerson, John	? Dau of Elizabeth Battrip 18Dec1832*
Freeman, William	18Mar1833		Watson, Asariah	Resc 18Mar1834
Freeman, Sidny	18Mar1833		Watson, Asariah	Resc 18Mar1834
Freeman, Hugh	18Mar1833		Watson, Asariah	
Corron, Michael	16Dec1833	5 yrs	Debkus, Jr., Jacob	
Hamilton, Sidney	17Dec1833	6 yrs	Hooper, James F.	Female
Freeman, William	18Mar1834		Jenkins, Henry	
Freeman, Sidney	18Mar1834		Jenkins, Henry	
Murry, Polly Ann	17Jun1834		Murry, Permely	Mother Pleasant Murry 18Mar1834*
Murry, George	17Mar1834		Murry, Permely	Mother Pleasant Murry 18Mar1834*

Name	Date	Age	Master	Notes
Murry, Sabray	17Mar1834		Murry, Permely	Mother Pleasant Murry 18Mar1834*
Russell, Andrew	21Dec1835	7 yrs	Hodges, David M.	
Mize, Robert	21Mar1836		Hollandsworth, William W.	Of color
Unnamed	22Mar1836	5 yrs	Bunch, James	Twin. Of color
Unnamed	22Mar1836	5 yrs	Bunch, James	Twin. Of color
Russell, Willis H.	7Nov1836	3 yrs in May last	Meador, John	Farming. Illeg son of Meador (Meadow?) and Mary Russell, formerly of Campbell Co. Opposed by Uriah Honeycutt, SF*. 5Sept1836*
Venoy, William E.	6Nov1837		Jones, Daniel	Blacksmith
Graves, Lucy Jane	5Feb1838		Grave, Boston	Illeg dau of Sarah Graves
Nunn, Elisha	4Feb1839	10 yrs 5 mo	Fulington, David	
Miles, Sherrard	4Feb1839	16 yrs 6 mo	Fullington, Alexander	
Brooks, Nathaniel	6Jan1840	14 yrs	Campbell, George	Son of Armstead Brooks, Dcd. 7Jan1840*
Brooks, Levi	3Feb1840	12 yrs	Campbell, Charles	Son of Armstead Brooks, Dcd. 7Jan1840*
Brooks, Preston	3Feb1840	15 yrs	Campbel, James	Son of Armstead Brooks, Dcd. 7Jan1840*
Levi	3Feb1840	4 yrs?	Dobkins, Solomon	3Feb1840*
Clinton	3Feb1840		Dobkins, Solomon	3Feb1840*
Muceller	3Feb1840	11 yrs?	Dobkins, Solomon	3Feb1840*
Johnston, George	3Feb1840		Lanham, Joseph	Resc 4Apr1842. To mother, as George Marion Johnson
Nunn, Harvey	2Mar1840	13 yrs 4 mo	Evans, Newton A.	
Angel, Mary Matilda	1Jun1840		Rogers, Jr., David	Illeg dau of Nancy Angel*
Branson, John	4Oct1841		Mays, Jonathan	
Johnston, Fanny			Johnston, Hiram	Resc 4Oct1841
Johnston, Fanny	4Oct1841	4 yrs	Johnston, James	Resc 6Jan1845
Kelly, Thomas	1Aug1842	9 yrs	McMahan, John	Son of Sarah Kelly, formerly Sarah Dunnsmoore 4July1842*
Sherick, Mary Ann	3Apr1843		Beuford, John W.	Resc 1847, req of mother
Bolden, Wiley	3July1843	12 yrs	Davis, Abraham	Resc 1July1844, as Wiley Bauldwin

Johnson, Fanny	6Jan1845		Pornel, William J.	Brought by James Johnson
Johnson, Patty	6Jan1845		Pornel, William J.	Brought by James Johnson
Messer, Nuton A. Evans	6Jan1845		Townsley, Isaac	Bound by father, Hiram Messer
Hobbs, Thomas	8Apr1845		Gipson, Drury D.	Bound by mother, Litta Hobbs
Hobbs, Reubin	8Apr1845		Gipson, Drury D.	Bound by mother, Litta Hobbs
Woodson, Robirt C.	3Jun1845		Grubb, Nichlis	Tanning. At request of Woodson
Grubb, Thomas W.	7July1845		Smith, James B.	Resc 7Feb1859*
Simmermon, Elizabeth	7July1845		Jones, Phoebe	
Simmermon, Addline	7July1845		Jones, Phoebe	
Grubb, Lucinda Jane	7July1845		Smith, J. B.	
Parker, Martin V.	1Sep1845	2 yrs	Howins, Martin	
Smith, Amanda	6Oct1845	4 yrs	Hill, Abel	Dau of Nancy Smith
Sherrod, James M.	5Jan1846	4 yrs	Barnard, Sturlin J.	
Grubb, Milly W.	6Apr1846		Yoakum, Ewing	Dau of Nancy Grubb. Maltreatment alleged 1Jan1849* 5Feb49* 2Aug1852*
Willis, Milton T.	3Aug1846		Fullington, Alexander	Resc 6Nov1846, req of Elisabeth Willis
Willis, James M.	3Aug1846		Fullington, Alexander	Resc 6Nov1846, req of Elisabeth Willis
Willis, David	3Aug1846		Fullington, Alexander	Resc 6Nov1846, req of Elisabeth Willis
Worrick, Elisabeth	1Mar1847		Marcum, Gabral	
Park, Charity	5Jun1848		Hernel,L. L.	
Park, William	5Jun1848		Oursley, William	Resc 5Aug1850. Name given as William Nash
Willis, David	3Jan1849		Wornacutt, Washington	At req of mother
Willis, James M.	3Jan1849		White, F. S.	At req of mother
Lacock, John	2Apr1849		Barnard, P. W.	Orphan
Nunn, John	2Apr1849		Fullington, David	
Willis, Milton T.	6Aug1849		Burchfield, Josiah H.	Orphan. Consent of mother. Resc 1Dec1856
Dunsmore, Mary			Lane, Robert B.	Sally Dunsmore, mother. Ind resc 1Oct1849.
Brown, Lucy A.	3Dec1849	6 yrs	Vanbebber, Isaac	Of color
Nash, William	5Aug1850		Herrell, L. L.	Orphan. See William Park
Moss, Mary	2Sep1850		McKeehan, Western	Orphan. Resc 4Nov1850

Name	Date	Age	Master	Notes
Tucker, John	3Feb1851		Eppes, William	Orphan
Shelby, Anjaline	2Jun1851		Lynch, John	Orphan. Dau of Catherine Shelby 2Apr1851*
Welch, John	1Sep1851		Burchfield, Jeramiah	
Brooks, Auston G.	3Nov1856		Proffit, Auston	Orphan. Mother consents.
Unnamed	6Apr1857		Burchfield, Martin	Of color
Unnamed	6Apr1857		Burchfield, Martin	Of color
Unnamed female	1Jun1857	6 yrs	Buchanan, Isaac S.	
Hick, John	7Sep1857	5 or 6 yrs	Jones, E. E.	
Loues, Susan L.	3Dec1857		McNiel, G. R.	Dau of Jane Loues 2Mar1857*
Loues, John	3Dec1857	9 yrs	Walker, Jacob	Son of Jane Loues 2Mar1857*
Low, John	4Jan1858		Sharp, Mat	Orphan
Collins, L. William	1Feb1858		Vanbeber, Isaac	Orphan
Collins, Garrett	1Feb1858		Hayse, Calvin	Orphan
Dowell, John	5Apr1858	3 yrs	Simmons, Albert	
Overbey, William J.	4Oct1858	8 yrs	Shopsher, Walter	Orphan. Resc 1Nov1858
Overbey, John F.	4Oct1858	16 yrs	Ely, Annis	Orphan
Overby, William J.	1Nov1858	8 yrs	Johnson, Pleasant	Orphan. Resc 3Jan1859, taken to Poor House
Hutson, Hulda	6Dec1858	2 yrs	Jones, Thomas	
Loues, John	2May1859	11 yrs	McVey, Thomas C.	
Murry, Jessee	2May1859	3 yrs	Claud, G. B.	
Griffith, Wilson			Harvey, Pror	Resc 1Aug1859. Alias Wilson Collins
Griffith, Wilson	2May1859		Smith, George W.	Alias Wilson Collins
Ellison, Thomas	2May1859		Nun, Elizabeth	
Ellison, Joseph	2May1859		Nun, Elizabeth	
Overbey, William	3Oct1859		Pike, Benjamin	Resc 5Dec1859, maltreatment
Low, David	7Nov1859	12 yrs	Redmon, James	
Overbay, William	5Dec1859		Simmons, Albert	Orphan
Parker, Israel Ralley	7Nov1870	12 yrs	Hodges, William	
Robert, Joseph	1Jan1872		Carr, John H.	

Raler, Jasper	1Jan1872	14 yrs	Carr, John H.	At req of Raler
Peck, Elisha G.	6Mar1872	12 yrs	Scott, A. J.	
Crawford, Samuel Joseph	3Jun1872	14 yrs	Murphey, Pleasant	
Noe, Rufus	3July1872	12 yrs	Noe, Daniel	
Mullins, David	5Aug1872	3 yrs	Posey, Bill	
Mullins Susan M.	5Aug1872	5 yrs	Posey, Bill	
Collins, John M. D.	1Dec1879		Collins, J. L.	Orphan
Neil, Jepatha	6Sep1880		Hopson, J. M.	Consent of mother
Goins, Minnie Allice	5Feb1877		Ferguson, J. A.	Until 21 yrs. Consent of mother. No legal father
Davis, Martha	7May1877	6 or 7 yrs	Thomas, Joseph C.	No living parents
Davis, Ellen	7May1877	12 yrs	Moss, J. K.	No living parents
Pendleton, Cintha	7May1877		Fugate, Lee	Dau of Fany Pendleton. No legal father
Chorum, William	4Jun1877		Ellis, Elizabeth	No legal father

Grainger County

Name	Date	Age	Master	Notes
Holland, Wright	15Mar1797		Carrigan, Hugh	House carpenter
Hensley, Margaret	13Jun1797		Shaw, Benjamin	Orphan
Ingle, John Whitman	18Feb1799		Adams, John	
Short, William	20Feb1799		Burton, John	Taylor
Short, James	20Feb1799		Meriott, John	House Carpenter
Shaw, Charles	20Feb1799		Boatman, Henry	Cooper
McKinley, William	22May1799		Beaty, John	Orphan. On 22May1799 given to care of Henry Hawkins. Bound?
Simpson, James	17Nov1800	5 yrs 8 mo	Brown, James	Orphan
Smith, Nancy	15Feb1802	5 yrs	Reed, Esq., Phelps	Orphan. Dau of Sarah Smith 21Nov1799. 17Feb, 20May, 18Aug, 17Nov1800*
Simpson, Lewis	15Feb1802	8 yrs	Brown, James	Orphan

Name	Date	Age	Master	Notes
Young, Francis	23Feb1803	13 yrs	Cocke, Esq., John	Orphan
Martin, David	18May1803	2 yrs 8 mo	Martin, Isaac	
Smith, James		Over 14 yrs	Roddye, James (Col)	Orphan. Prev bnd by Samuel Smith, father 25May1804*
Alfred, John	19Nov1804	18 yrs	Mann, Thomas	Mill-wright. Orphan
Shaw, Joseph	21Nov1804	9 yrs	Easley, Miller	Orphan. Canc 16May1814. Shaw in US Army
Sartin, Lewis	19Nov1805	13 yrs	Huddleston, David	Orphan. Canc 22Feb1814. Sartin in US Army
Pucapile, David	19May1806	11 yrs	Bryant, William	Orphan. Canc 18May1812, as Purcupile
Wilson, Gidion	6Nov1806	5 yrs 6 mo	Wilson, Jacob	Orphan
Hammons, Sairah	16Feb1807		Hodge, Welcome	
Hammons, Baxter	16Feb1807		Hodge, Welcome	
Hammons, Martha	16Feb1807		Hodge, Welcome	
Holley, Mary	22Feb1809	Between 7 & 8 yrs	Moore, Rice	Orphan
Mitchell, Ruth	15May1809	6 yrs on 27Mar1809	Dyer, Sr, James	Orphan
McElhaney, Allen	17May1809	8 yrs 35 days	Bowen, James	Orphan
Henderson, John	24May1810	14 yrs 4 mo	McPheeters, John	Orphan. Canc 21Nov1814. Henderson in US army
Henderson, Harmon	24May1810	6 yrs 8 mo 19d	McPheeters, Andrew	Orphan
Chandler [Chambers], William	22Nov1810	15 yrs	Long, Joseph	Until 20 yrs. Canc 17Aug1813, Chambers having joined army
Chambers, Joseph	22Nov1810	11 yrs	Shirley, Balser	Canc 27Aug1816
Davis, Samuel	19Feb1811	14 yrs 6 mo	Boatman, Henry	
Sims, Elijah	20May1811	12 yrs	Stubblefield, Martin	Orphan
Davis, James	22May1811	9 yrs	Boatman, Henry	Orphan
Adkins, Jane	20Aug1811		Noe, Jacob	
Thomason, Frankey	18Nov1811	11 yrs 11 mo 2 d	Ezell, James	Orphan
Douglass, Younger	17Feb1812	9 yrs	Haily, Claiborne	
Rayl, Jr, William	17Feb1812	16 yrs 3 mo	Rayl, Sr, William	Orphan
Denson, Susanah	20Feb1812	13 yrs	Howell, Henry	
Thomason, Elisha	18May1812	11 yrs on 3July next	Isell, James	Orphan
Hale, Winefred	18Aug1812	13 yrs 8 mo	Bunch, Thomas	Male orphan

Kirby, Nancy	16Nov1812		Kirby, William	
Kirby, James	16Nov1812		Kirby, William	
Ivy, Hamilton	17Aug1813		Howell, Henry	
Ivy, Nancy	17Aug1813		Howell, Henry	
Ivy, Jenny	17Aug1813		Howell, Henry	
Buch, Charles	17Aug1813		Bunch, John	
Davis, Lewis	17Nov1813		Daniel, Francis	
Davis, John	17Nov1813		Daniel, John	
McVay, Thomas	23Feb1814		Bunch, Thomas	
Heckson, John	17May1814	13 yrs on 25Dec1813	Mays, John	
Heckson, Daniel	17May1814	15 yrs the last of next Aug	Mayes, Henry	
Gibbs, James	15Aug1814	4 yrs on 1July1814	Pullen, Leroy	Orphan
Walker, Nelly	16Aug1814	3 yrs	Lucas, Samuel	Orphan
Ails, William Preston	19May1815	7 yrs on 15Sep1814	Kline, Jacob	Tanning & curing leather. Canc 20Nov1816, as Preston Ailes
Blakley, Lewis	22Aug1815	7 yrs	Cox, Gale	
Dennis, Eli	22Aug1815	3 yrs	Jack, William	Canc 24Aug1815, request of May Dennis 23Aug1814
Dennis, Eli	24Aug1815	3 yrs	Dennis, John	
Ailes, Polly	26Aug1815	6 yrs		Ordered bound. Indenture completed?
Nelly	20Nov1815		Hickey, Joshua	Of color. Until 18 yrs. Nelly delivered of bastard child, bound for additional year 18Nov1819
Henry	20Nov1815		Hickey, Joshua	
Nancy	20Nov1815		Hickey, Joshua	Until 18 yrs
Frank	20Nov1815		Hickey, Joshua	
Richard	20Nov1815		Brown, John	
Mayse, Anderson	19Feb1816		Mayse, Sherad	Canc 16Feb1829. Absconded
Brender, Shedereck	19Feb1816		Smith, Henry	Permitted to remove to Knox Co 26Aug1816
Carrol, Patsey	19Feb1816		Griffits, Jane	
Boran, Abraham	20Feb1816		Dalton, Jr, Rubin	Canc 28Feb1816 on petition of Dianna Newkin

Name	Date	Age	Master	Notes
Jones, Jenny	20Feb1816		Daniel, Jr, Edward	
Bunch, John	22Feb1816		Thompson, Isaac	
Dobbs, Metilda	28Feb1816	3 yrs	Dobbs, Philip	Orphan
Taylor, Sally	21May1816	9 yrs	Moody, John	Orphan. Canc 15May1820
Moore, Rachel	19Aug1816		Hankins, William	
Moore, Patsey Self	19Aug1816		Hankins, William	
Moore, Stephen	19Aug1816		Hankins, William	
Moore, Thomas Mordecai	19Aug1816		Hankins, William	
Harrel, James	19Aug1816		Renshaw, John	
Bradley, George Curtis	21Nov1816		Thomson, Isaac	
Brown, Catharine	21Feb1817		Bull?, John	Master ?Beele, ?Brown
Brown, Lydia	21Feb1817		Bull?, John	
McVey, Charles			Bunch, Thomas	Indenture canc 22May1817
Eaton, Pleasant	20Aug1817		Robertson, Thomas	
Ivy, David	19May1818		Cassidy, James	Canc 23Feb1820
Cyrus, Elsey	17Aug1818		Moulder, Henry	Until age 18
Going, Rowland	18Aug1818		Lide, John W.	Resc 16Nov1818 on petition of John Gowin
Going, Anney?	22Aug1818		Tate, Edward	Resc 16Nov1818 on petition of John Gowin
Stone, Alexander	16Nov1818		Bunch, Josiah C.	Shoe & boot making. Ind proved by oaths of Wm. Parker & Isaac Thompson
Gowing, Henry	16Nov1818		Cocke, Stephen	Of color 21Feb1820. Canc21Feb1820, Cocke leaving county
Henshaw, Henry	16Nov1818		Trogden, Abner	
Eaton, William K.	17Nov1818		Eaton, William	Farming. Orphan of Andrew Eaton 17Aug1818. Resc 20Aug1821
Eaton, Joseph P.	17Nov1818		Eaton, William	Farming. Orphan of Andrew Eaton 17Aug1818. Resc 20Aug1821
Bean, Elizabeth Ann	19Nov1818		Bean, Robert	
Bean, William	19Nov1818		Bean, Robert	

Bean, Edmond	19Nov1818		Bean, Robert	
Bean, Jemima	19Nov1818		Bean, Robert	
Guein?, ____	19Nov1818		Millikin, William	
Guein?, Samuel	19Nov1818		Millikin, William	
Guein, Janny	19Nov1818		Millikin, William	
Going, Betsy	19Nov1818		Going, John	
York, Pleasant	15Feb1819		Wood, John	
Betsy	15Feb1819		Cock, John	Of color. Bound by mother, Molly, until age 18.
John	17Feb1819	4 yrs	Hickey, Joshua	Of color
Adkins, Barnet	17May1819	13 yrs	Dyer, George	Orphan. Canc17May1820
Whaleing, Pleasant	17May1819	12 yrs 3 mo	Field, Joel	Orphan. Pm't for transport of Anna Whaleing from Hawkins Co to Claiborn Co jail . Canc 19Feb1821
Davis, Janey			Boatman, Henry	Orphan. Canc 17May1819
Gowing, Henry	21Feb1820		Cocke, William	Of color
Holy, Woodson	18May1820		Howell, John	
Parker, John			Denning, William	Canc 21Aug1820
Findley, James	25Aug1820		Kline, Jacob	Bound by guardian
Ivy, Hamilton	21May1821	16 yrs	Cocke, John	Resc 19Nov1821
Ivy, Nancy	21May1821	14 yrs	Smith, Nathanial	Resc 19Nov1821
Ivy, Jensy	21May1821	12 yrs	Cocke, William C.	Resc 19Feb1827
Spoon, Abraham			Howell, Henry	Resc 21May1821
Spoon, John			Howell, Henry	Resc 21May1821
Gowen, Jr, Nancy	18Feb1822	8 yrs	Hicky, Joshua	
Davis, Lewis			Davis, Thomas	Resc 19Feb1822
Frances			Latham, James	Of color. Resc 20May1822
Frances	20May1822		McAnally, Charles	Of color
Wickliff, Pleasant	19Feb1823		Tate, Sr, David	Canc 10Nov1829
Ailes, Polly			Moyers, Frederick	Resc16Feb1924
Sword, William	16Feb1824	10 yrs	Atkinson, William L.	Orphan
Henry	16Feb1824	2 yrs	Counts, Jessee	Of color

Name	Date	Age	Master	Notes
Dinkins, Susan	15Nov1824		Cassedy, James	
Smissen, Adam	21Feb1825		Mitchell, Robert	Resc considered 23Aug1827, show cause ordered
Clark, William	16May1825		Coose, William	Canc 22May1827, abuse & neglect
Dinkins, William	15Aug1825		Dyer, Joseph	
Smith, Lidia	22Nov1825		Campbell, Charles	Resc 20Feb1826
Taylor, William	20Feb1826	16 yrs	Easley, Warham	Resc 21Aug1826
Smith, Willis	20Feb1826		Smith, Willis	
Smith, G____	20Feb1826		Smith, Willis	
McElhaney, Arch	15May1826		Fox, Samuel	
Toliver, John	16May1826		Roach, William	Resc 17May1828
Caits, Lewis	21Aug1826		Ore, Wilson	Resc 18Feb1828
Rush, Meridith	20Nov1826		King, John	
Atkins, Nancy	21May1827		Smith, John	
Atkins, Malinda	21May1827		Smith, John	
Toliver, Abraham	22May1827		Dyer, Joseph	Resc 18May1835
Clark, William	23May1827		Kirk, Armsted	
Moore, William	18Feb1828		More, Rice	
Benjamin	18Feb1828		Hackey, Joshua	Of color
Toliver, John	17May1828		West, James	
Phips, Rachel	17Nov1828	Over 3 yrs	Phips, James	Bastard. Alfred Norris reputed father 20Aug1828*
Dinkins, Susan	17Feb1829		Jones, Hugh	Mulatto
Smith, Green	19Aug1829	9 yrs in Feb last	Arnett, Jacob	Alias Green Arnett. Canc16Nov1829
Arnett, Green				See Green Smith
Smith, Green	16Nov1829		Smith, Willis	Sci Fa to W. Smith to show cause why Green should not be rebound 22Nov1831
Walker, Jackson	17May1830		Cocke, William E.	
Woods, John	17May1830		Hammond [Hommel], Henry	Sold into slavery by Hommel @ age 5 yrs 9 mo. Sheriff to take Hommel into custody 18May1835
Shipley, John	16Aug1830		Shield, Johnston, & Rice	

Goin, John	21Feb1831		Howell, Thomas K.	
Haun, Jacob	20Feb1832		Purkeypile, John	
John, alias Jack	20Feb1832		Hickey, Joshua	Of color
Holly, Woodson	21Feb1832		Cocke, Pleasant S.	Mulatto
Scott, Alfred	21May1832		Hammock, John	Resc 1Mar1832. Scott kept as one of the poor of the county
Johnson, Ephraim	21May1832		Moody, William M.	Canc 12Aug1834
Morgan, Rufus	21May1832		Cocke, Thomas S.	Resc 18May1835
Coward, William	19Feb1833		Millikin, Benjamin	
Curry, George	19Aug1833		Hazlewood, Joshua	
Lacky [Lacy], Leonard	19Nov1833		Tolbert [or Talbot], James S.	Cert of freedom to Leonard Lacy, 21 yrs, free man of color, on 4Nov1839. Apprenticeship completed.*
Anderson, William	19Nov1833		Jennings, Royal	Farmer 20May1835. Canc 17Feb1835
Bunch, Mahala	19Nov1833		Bunch, William	Resc 17Feb1835
Cutts, Coleman	18Feb1834		Dyer, Sr, James	
January, Benjamin	18Feb1834		Duff, Hugh A.	
Baker, Nathan D.	19May1834		Starnes, James H.	
Jones, William	18Feb1835	11 yrs on 1Jun1835	Malicoat, William C.	Resc 2Dec1844
Jackson, Wilson	18May1835		Bowman, Jeremiah	Resc 4Mar1839
Woods, John	19May1835		Moody, William M.	Resc 7Sep1846
Spriggs, July Ann	18Feb1836		Low, Abner	Spinning & weaving 5Jan1846. ?Child of Nancy Spriggs 6Jan1840.
Spriggs, Elizabeth	18Feb1836		Chiser,Thornton	?Child of Nancy Spriggs 6Jan1840
Spriggs, James	18Feb1836		Henshaw, Joshua	Ordered returned to court 6Feb1837. ?Child of Nancy Spriggs 6Jan1840
Spriggs, Mary	18Feb1836		Henshaw, Joshua	Ordered returned to court 6Feb1837. ?Child of Nancy Spriggs 6Jan1840
Perryhink, William	7Nov1836		Dyer, Joseph	Orphan
Witt, David	6Feb1837	12 yrs	Russell, Thomas	Orphan
Whitener, Pauline	5Jun1837	2 yrs	Bulcher, Isaac B.	Orphan
Mitchel, William	3July1837	4 yrs on 6Sep1836	Burket, George	Orphan

Name	Date	Age	Master	Notes
Edington, Allen	2Oct1837	9 yrs	Cates, Daniel H.	Orphan
Smith, Henry	6Nov1837	14 yrs	Roach, Sr, Absalon	Orphan. Resc 7Oct1839. Roach in poor health
Branson, Tilman	4Dec1837	3 mo	Watson, David	Orphan
Anderson, Rabecka	7May1838	9 yrs	Cocke, Thomas S.	Orphan. Resc 6Nov1843. Rebecca married to Jessee Solomon
Hudgins, Nancy	5Nov1838	13 yrs last October	Dunavant, John	Orphan
Jones, John Alford	5Nov1838	4 yrs 6 mo	McAnally, Charles	Orphan. Resc 7May1849
Jackson, Wilson	4Mar1839		Cocke, John	
Shropshear, Jane	3Jun1839	2 yrs on 7Feb last	Shropshear, Walter	Orphan. Resc 2Oct1848
Smith, Henry	7Oct1839	16 yrs on 1Nov next	Loyd, Robert	Orphan. On 3Dec1844 Smith's 21st birthday set as 7Oct1845. Resc 3Dec1844
Fry, Isaac			Loyd, Robert	Resc 7Oct1839. Runaway
Merchant, Louisa	3Nov1839	3 mo 10 days	Easley, John	Orphan
Claypole, Tabitha	3Feb1840	7 yrs	Stubblefield, Robert	Orphan. Dau of Rebecca Claypole 6Jan1840* Resc 5Feb1849
Claypole, Jeremiah	3Feb1840	9 yrs	Sunderland, James	Orphan. Son of Rebecca Claypole 6Jan1840*
Mitchel, James Calvin	5Sep1842	15 yrs 10 mo 10 d	Shipley, S. S.	Saddle making. Alias James Calvin Bibbins. Resc 7July1845
Bibbins, James Calvin				See James Calvin Mitchel
Sharp, Margaret	5Jun1843	3 yrs on 21Nov1842	Bethell, John	Orphan
Sharp, Airmatha Elizabeth	5Jun1843	2 yrs on 10Jun1843	Bethell, John	Orphan
Martin, John Wesley	2Oct1843	9 yrs on 3Feb next	Trott, James	Orphan. Resc 4May1846. To David Mincy, stepfather
Reynolds, Ann M.	3Feb1845	10 yrs on 20May next	Dyer, Charton [Charleton]	Orphan. Dau of Nancy Runnolds, dcd 1July1844* Resc 6Jan1851 as Ann Malessa Runnels
Yates, Alpheus	7Apr1845	3 yrs	Dunavant, John	Orphan. 7Apr1845* Resc 7Nov1854
Parker, Ann	7Apr1845	11 yrs	Turley, Thomas W.	Until 18 yrs. Of color. Orphan. Resc 5May1845
Gillett, James	5May1845	17 yrs last winter	Grantham, Willis	Orphan
Talbott, Lettitia	2Jun1845	1 yr 6 mo	Lea, Mary C.	Of color. Resc 6Nov1854. Returned to mother. Lea insolvent

Talbott, John	2Jun1845	6 yrs	Lea, Mary C.	Of color. Resc 6Nov1854. Returned to mother. Lea insolvent
Talbott, Jane	2Jun1845	4 yrs	Lea, Mary C.	Of color. Resc 6Nov1854. Returned to mother. Lea insolvent
Statsworth, Thomas	7July1845	5 yrs	Statsworth, John	Orphan
Statsworth, John	7July1845	15 yrs	McKinny, Daniel	Orphan. Resc 7Feb1848. Runaway
Statsworth, Elizabeth	7July1845	11 yrs	Gillmore, Samuel	[Orphan]
Statsworth, Samuel	7July1845	9 yrs	Vineyard, Daniel	Orphan
Bunch, Hamilton	7July1845	12 yrs on 1March last	Inglebarger, Lide	Orphan. Resc 5Aug1851
Statsworth, William	7July1845	13 yrs	Fielding, Willie	[Orphan]. Resc 7Sep1846
Amis, William	7July1845	11 yrs	Cocke, John	Orphan. Resc 4Sep1848 as William Amos
Bunch, James	4Aug1845	10 yrs	January, David	Orphan. Resc 1Feb1847. January deceased
Burden, Mary Ann			Eaton, Daniel	Bound by father, Lemuel Burden before 6Oct1845*
Burden, James			Eaton, Daniel	Bound by father, Lemuel Burden before 6Oct1845*
Burden, Katherine			Eaton, Daniel	Bound by father, Lemuel Burden before 6Oct1845*
Burden, Richard			Eaton, Daniel	Bound by father, Lemuel Burden before 6Oct1845*
Shelton, Eliza J.	3Nov1845	11 yrs	McBee, John	Orphan
Rowe, William			Moore, James	Resc5Jan1846
Rowe, William	5Jan1846		Moore, Rhoda	Rhoda widow of James Moore
Hughs, Nancy	6July1846	2 yrs 6 mo	Darling, George	Orphan
Jones, Nancy	6July1846	7 yrs	Daniel, Rabecca	Orphan
Statsworth, William	7Sep1846		McKinny, Daniel	Resc 7Feb1848. Runaway
Wood, John	7Sep1846		Holly, John	
Lafaett, Henry	5Oct1846	14 yrs on 26Oct1846	Kirkham, Jacob P.	Orphan
Mallicoat, Rhoda	7Dec1846	9 yrs	Dunavant, John	Orphan. Resc 3Jan1848
Bunch, James	1Feb1847	12 yrs in April next	Walker, James G.	Orphan
Statsworth, Nancy	1Mar1847	2 yrs 6 mo	Townsley, William	Orphan. Dau of Amos Statsworth, dcd 1Feb1847
Statsworth, Martha	1Mar1847	8 yrs	Smith, William	Orphan. Dau of Amos Statsworth, dcd 1Feb1847. Resc 5Jan1854

Name	Date	Age	Master	Notes
Right, Jane	6Dec1847	13 yrs 5 mo	Sparkman, George	Orphan. Jane ordered brought to court 3Sep1849. Resc 1Apr1850
Elkins, Susannah K.	6Dec1847	3 yrs	Vandagriff, Jacob	Orphan. Resc 4Aug1851. Mother's consent not had
Linear, Vanburin	4Jan1847	12 yrs	Rear, James B.	Orphan. Resc 6Oct1851
Beeler, Viny J.	7Feb1848	8 yrs	Wolfenbarger, Peter	Resc 4Apr1848. Returned to mother
Horner, James	5Jun1848	12 yrs	Tate, Sr, David	Son of David Horner, dcd 1May1848
Horner, McCarty	5Jun1848	10 yrs	Tate, Sr, David	Son of David Horner, dcd 1May1848
Bunch, Henry H.	7Aug1848	8 yrs in March last	Lane, Kennon	Orphan. Resc 3Sep1849
Amos, William	4Sep1848	14 yrs	Kline, James A.	Orphan
Shropshire, Jane	2Oct1848	11 yrs 8 mo	Noe. John J.	Orphan
Atkins, William	5Mar1849	14 yrs	Dyer, James H.	Orphan
Atkins, James	5Mar1849	16 yrs	Myers, George W.	Orphan
North, Eliza	3Apr1849	12 yrs	Goldman. Michael	Of color. Orphan. On 1Oct1849 Eliza North moved to quash indenture. Denied. Appealed to Circuit Court. Resc 2Apr1850
Jones, John Alfed	7May1849		McAnally, C. W.	Resc 3May1852, Jones having left McAnally
Graham, Samuel	7May1849	14 yrs	Tate, Edward L.	Orphan. Resc 2Oct1849
Andersen, Joseph	7Jan1849	4 yrs	McAnally, C. W.	Of color. Orphan. Resc 6July1852. Ret to mother. 1Nov1852*
Duff, H. T.	7Jan1849	12 yrs	Parrott, Joseph	Orphan. Resc 4Mar1850
Duff, Rufus	7Jan1849	8 yrs	Parrott, Joseph	Orphan. Resc 4Mar1850
Duff, Robert	7Jan1849	14 yrs	Mitchel, James R.	Orphan. Resc 5Aug1850
Duff, John	7Jan1849		Alsup, Henry	Orphan. Resc 1Aug1853*
Merrett, Leroy	4Jun1849	9 yrs 7 mo	Merret, John	Orphan
Merrett, Tandy	4Jun1849	7 yrs	Merret, John	Orphan
Simmons, Sarah	4July1849	12 yrs	Smith, C. C.	Of color. Resc 6Aug1849, as Sally Simmons
Duff, Temple	6Aug1849	7 yrs	Leng, James	Orphan*
Bunch, Henry H.	3Sep1849	9 yrs in March 1849	Yates, Hiram	Orphan
Daily, William	2Oct1849		Turley, Thomas W.	Of color

Harbin, Jane	5Nov1849	12 yrs 1 mo	Millar, Absalom	Orphan
Harbin, Jacob	5Nov1849	9 yrs 4 mo	Millar, Absalom	Orphan
Daily, John	7Jan1850		Cocke, William M.	Of color. On 7Feb Daily petitions for freedom under will of Charlton Dyer, Jr, dcd. Granted. 1Oct1849*
Shumate, George W.	4Feb1850	11 yrs	Simpsen, Barnett G.	Orphan
Turner, Thomas	4Feb1850	13 yrs	Lowe, Barten	Orphan. Alias Thomas Ivy
Ivy, Thomas				See Thomas Turner
Duff, H. T.	4Mar1850	13 yrs	Kline, James A.	Orphan
Duff, Rufus	4Mar1850	9 yrs	Cunningham, Bennet K.	Orphan. Resc 3Feb1851
Mallicoat, Rachel	1Apr1850	12 yrs	Roach, Absalom	Orphan. Resc6May1850. Absalon Roach, Jr released
Mallicoat, Rachel	3Jun1850	11 yrs	Lane, Samuel	Orphan. Resc 7Jun1851
Long, Eliza	3Jun1850	11 yrs	Fulkerson, Abraham	Orphan
Long, Isaac	3Jun1850	7 yrs	Lane, Samuel	Orphan. Resc 1July1850
Duff, Robert	5Aug1850	16 yrs 4 mo	Mitchel, Elijah	
Walden, Katherine Eliza	4Nov1850	14 mo	McCurry, James R.	Orphan
Collins, John	4Nov1850	12 yrs on 16March next	Clark, John	Orphan. Resc 2May1852, Collins having left Clark, Sr
Collins, George Hendersen	4Nov1850	6 yrs on 10Feb1851	Clark, John	Orphan. Resc 1Nov1852
Ivy, William	2Dec1850	15 yrs on 12Mar1851	Farr, Alfred H.	
Duff, Albert	2Dec1850	5 yrs 6 mo	Hipshear, Joshua	Orphan
Duff, Rufus	3Feb1851	10 yrs	Trogden, Solomon	Farming. Orphan. Resc 1Sep1851. Rufus diseased before bound. To care of James G. Walker, adm. of estate of Robert Duff, father of Rufus
Harris, Nathanial	3Feb1851	2 yrs	Bransen, Nathaniel	Orphan
Kitts, Lafaett	4Aug1851	3 yrs on 8May1851	Routh, Stephen	Orphan. Consent of mother, Lucinda Kitts
Kitts, Abraham Tillman	4Aug1851		Jennings, George W.	Orphan. Consent of mother, Lucinda Kitts
Linear, Vanburin	6Oct1851	16 yrs	Johnsen, Vincent	Orphan
Rush, James M.	7Sep1852	7 yrs on 2May1852	Shepherd, Henry	Consent of William D. Rush, parent. See Samuel Rush
Rush, Mary Jane	7Sep1852	2 yrs on 20Nov1852	Greenlea, Eli	Consent of William D. Rush, parent
Collins, George	1Nov1852		Bundren, Green	Orphan. Consent of mother. Resc 6Nov1854

Name	Date	Age	Master	Notes
Duff, Rufus	1Aug1853	13 yrs	Alsup, Henry	Orphan
Rush, Samuel	6Feb1854		Mincy, William	Consent of father, William Rush. Resc 7May1855, James [sic] having runaway
Hughs, Nancy A.	6Feb1854		Kinder, Jacob	
James, Wesley	6Mar1854		Bundren, Green	Of color. Destitute, child of Mary
James, Francis	6Mar1854		Hipshire, William	Of color. Destitute. Child of Mary 6Nov1854* Resc 2July1855, Hipshire dead
Kitts, William			Starnes, James H.	Resc 1May1854
Idol, John	5Jun1854	14 yrs	Wolfenbarger, John	Orphan
Idol, Mary	5Jun1854	12 yrs	Wolfenbarger, John	Orphan
Idol, Casten	5July1854	8 yrs	Sufferage, George	Orphan
Berry, William	2Oct1854		Sparkman, Henry	Resc 6Nov1854, as Archibald or William Berry
Right, Anderson	2Oct1854		Smith, Samuel	On 3Sep1860 Right given balance of time and paid full amount
Right, Millikan	2Oct1854		Smith, Samuel	
Westly, William			Bundren, Green	Resc 6Nov1854. ? same child as Wesley James
Wesly, William	6Nov1854		Mallicoat, William C.	Of color
Collins, George	6Nov1854	10 yrs	Harrell, Roadman	Of color
Berry, Archibald	6Nov1854		Kay, James	
Yates, William Alpheus	7Nov1854		Colison, John	Resc 2Oct1855. Collison deceased
Purkepile, Katharine	5Mar1855	9 yr 6 mo	Livingston, Jesse	
Idol, Barnabas	4Jun1855	4 yrs 3 mo	Idol, Chesley I.	Consent of Nancy Idol, mother
Idol, John	4Jun1855	15 yrs	Wolfenbarger, John	Until age 20. Court ordered over mother's objections.* 7May1855*
Idol, Mary	4Jun1855	12 yrs	Wolfenbarger, John	Court ordered over mother's objections.* 7May1855* Resc 2Jun1856
Frances Ann Elizabeth	2July1855	6 yrs 8 mo	Hipsher, Jacob	Illeg child of color, belonging to Mary
Nash, Thomas	3Sep1855	18 mo	Vittetoe, Thomas	Orphan. Consent of mother. Resc 3Mar1856. Illegally bound
Scott, Joseph	3Sep1855	7 yrs	Easley, John	Illeg child of color. Consent by mother

Scott, Andrew	3Sep1855	5 yrs	Easley, John	Illeg child of color. Consent by mother
Yates, William Alpheus	2Oct1855		Morgan, Allen D.	
Sterling	4Feb1856	12 yrs in March next	Evans, Hamilton	Of color. Consent by mother
Margaret	4Feb1856	7 yrs in Dec 1856	Evans, Hamilton	Of color. Consent by mother
Idol, Mary	2Jun1856	12 yrs	Idol, Adam	Illegimate
Wright, Silas	6Jan1857	9 yrs	Dyer, Lea	Of color
Casander, Margaret	6Jan1857	8 yrs	Dyer, Lea	Of color
Smith, John T.	4Jan1858	14 yrs	Starnes, James H.	By order of Circuit Court
Mefford, Rebecca	3May1858	10 yrs	Mefford, Harvey	Motherless. Neglected by father, Lilburne Mefford*
Smith, David Frankland	7Dec1858		Heath, David N.	Child of Nancy Smith. Sibs James & Mary*
Borden, William	6Dec1859	5 yrs 10 mo	Eaton, Daniel	Illeg child of color. Resc 7Aug1865. Eaton deceased
Borden, Lea	6Dec1859	3 yrs 11 mo	Eaton, Daniel	Illeg child of color. Resc 7Aug1865. Eaton deceased
Talbot, Martha	6Jan1862	13 yrs	White, C. S. (Mrs)	Of color
Talbot, Ann	6Jan1862	15 yrs	White, C. S. (Mrs)	Of color
Key, James	4May1863	9 yrs	Inglebarger, Lyle	Abandoned by father, mother dead
Vandagrift, Nancy A	3July1865	7 yrs	West, Thomas R.	
Vandagrift, Isaac	3July1865	2 yrs	Yates, Hyram	
Farr, Peter	4Jun1866	6 yrs	Farr, A. H.	Of color
Farr, Bell	4Jun1866		Farr, A. H.	Of color. Female. Until 21
Walters, George Washington	2July1866	6 yrs	Walters, Israel	
Watts, William Carter	5Nov1866	14 yrs 11 1/2 mo	Baker, Lucy	
Wyrick, James J.	4Feb1867	12 yrs 4 mo	Wallace, Riley	
Lewis	5Feb1867	5 yrs	Long, Nancy	Of color
Solomon, John	1Apr1867	9 yrs	McElhaney, N. H.	Resc 8Oct1867, Solomon having left
Lucy	7Oct1867	12 yrs	Shields, Samuel	Of color
Jackson, Henry	7Oct1867	6 yrs	Hillton, Alexander	Of color
Smith, Samuel	4Nov1867	9 yrs	Bird, Jacob N.	Orphan
Mayse, William	4Aug1868	14 yrs 8 mo	Roach, Absalem	

Name	Date	Age	Master	Notes
Roach, Jasper N.	6Nov1869	6 yrs	Roach, John	Son of John Roach, dcd. Mother remarried to William Martin. John Sr is GF of Jasper. 1, 2Nov1868* Resc 8Oct1873. Roach Sr dead
Croxdale, James	7Mar1870	12 yrs	Noe, Sr, David	
Carback, Eliza	5Dec1871	4 yrs	Jarnagin, T. J.	Of color
Semore, Larkin	6Nov1871	14 yrs	Yates, Anderson	Orphan. Desired by Larkin & his near relations. 7Nov1871*
Rucker, Cordelia	3Jun1872	12 yrs 4 mo	Hayse, Barnett	Father abandoned, mother, Matilda, not providing.* 3July1872*
Rucker, Emily	3Jun1872	15 yrs 11 mo	Dalton, Rubin	Father abandoned, mother, Matilda, not providing.* 3July1872*
Jarnagin, Orlena	3Jun1872	7 yrs	Morgan, J. M.	Mother, Jane Jarnagin, a partial lunatic 6May1872*
Jarnagin, Martha	3Jun1872	12 yrs	Duff, James	Mother, Jane Jarnagin, stated to be a partial lunatic 6May1872*
Rucker, Permelia A.	4Jun1872	14 yrs 8 mo	Kincaid, John W.	Dau of Matilda Rucker* Resc 4Nov1872. Kincaid not suitable
Rucker, Cornelia	4Jun1872	7 yrs 9 mo	Bird, J. N.	Dau of Matilda Rucker*
Rucker, Permelia	6Nov1872	15 yrs	Dalton, William	
Roach, Jasper	3Nov1873	10 yrs 9 mo	Roach, A. S.	Request of mother 7Oct1873

Greene County

Name	Date	Age	Master	Notes
Ray, John	Nov1783	13 Yrs	Ray, Benjamin	House carpenter. Orphan of Joseph Ray, dcd.* Cancelled Feb1796 at request of Susannah Ray, widow of Joseph
Dycher, Isaac	Feb1784	7 yrs	McCrossky, John	Skin dresser. Orphan of Jacob Dycher, dcd
Brabson, William	Feb1784	9 yrs next Apr	Fain, Robert	Weaver. Orph of John Brabson, dcd
Purciful, Peter	Aug1784	15 yrs	McAmos, James	Canc Feb1786. To care of Thomas Purciful
Coats, John	Aug1784	13 yrs	Newell, Samuel	Weaver. Orphan of Joshua Coats, dcd

Purciful, Martha	Nov1784		Crow, John	Weaver
Phillips, Elizabeth	May1785		Ward, John	
Parkison, John	Aug1785		Tadlock, John	Orphan of George Parkison
Purciful, Peter	Feb1786		Purciful, Thomas	Prior Indenture cancelled
Sutton, William	May1786		Kerr, Jr, Robert	Until 31 yrs [sic]
Kilgore, Nancy	May1787		Miller, Thomas	Sempster. Orphan
Trimble, James	Nov1787	13 yrs next May	Carson, John	Weaver
Trimble, James	5May1789	14 yrs	Carson, John	Weaver. Orphan of Jane Trimble
Wood, Dorcas	Nov1789	4 yrs on 15Apr next	Richey, Andrew	Linen Weaver. Dau of Sarah Wood
Tool, Michael	May1790		Boo, Rudolph	Shoe Maker. Minor of Michael Tool
Potts, Rebekah	May1790	11 Yrs	Calvert, Jane	Sempster. Orph of Nathan Potts, dcd
Berry, Hugh	Aug1790	11 yrs in Nov next	Jack, Samuel	Saddler. Orphan of Hugh Berry, dcd
Smiley, William	Feb1791		Richardson, James	Weaver. Orphan
Colvin, John	May1791	9 yrs	McCall, Robert	Weaver
Trimble, Sarah	May1791	7 Yrs on 15 July next	Henderson, Robert (Rev)	Sew, knit & spin
Edwards, George	7Nov1791	7 mo	Roan, Archibald	Baseborn mulatto
Mozier, Elizabeth Jones	May1792		Moore, Sr, Moses	
Drain, James	Nov1792	10 yrs	Ellis, Samuel	Blacksmith. Orphan
Bumpas, Elizabeth	Nov1792	8 yrs in May past	Broyles, Jacob	Spin, knit & sew. Orphan of Job Bumpas, dcd *
Bumpas, Lettia	Nov1792	4 yrs	Broyles, Jacob	Spin, knit,& sew. Orphan of Job Bumpas, dcd *
Bumpas, James	Feb1793	12 yrs last Sep	Jones, John	Weaver. Orphan of Job Bumpas, dcd *
Hopkins, James	Nov1793	18 yrs last July	Hopkins, George	Chair Making. Orphan
Kenedy, James	Feb1794	16 yrs 7 mo	Rodgers, James	Black Smith. Minor of Moses Kenedy
Walker, John	Feb1794	8 yrs on 1Sept last	Mauris, John	Wheelright. Orphan
Reynolds, Sarah	May1794	11 yrs	Hughes, John	Sew, knit & spin. Rescinded Aug1797
Kelly, Ruth	Aug1794	3 yrs on 3 Dec next	Henry, Robert	Sew, knit & spin. Orphan
McLaughlin, James	Aug1794	17 yrs on 1Apr next	Cole, Philip	Black Smith
Hopkins, David	Aug1795	13 yrs	Hopkins, George	Chair Making. Orphan
Goforth, Mary	May1796	11 yrs on 1Oct last	Lynch, Jesse	Orphan of John Goforth. Feb, May1796* Abuse alleged 8May1797*

Name	Date	Age	Master	Notes
Goforth, Miles	May1796	19 yrs on 16Nov last	Porter, Joseph	Orphan of John Goforth* Feb, May1796*
Bumpas, Sarah	Nov1796	5 yrs next Aug	Broyle, Jeremiah	Orphan of Job Bumpas, dcd *
Goforth, Jemima	13May1797	5 yrs	Goforth, Joseph	Sempstress. Orphan of John Goforth* Feb, May1796*
Goforth, Mary	13May1797	13 yrs	Holt, William (Dr)	Milner. Orphan of John Goforth* Feb, May1796*
Bogard, Benjamin	Aug1797	13 yrs on 10May last	Barnes, John Macksy	Blacksmith. Orphan
Barris, Abililah	Apr1798	4 yrs 6 mo	Wilson, William	Orphan
Lester, John	Apr1798	7 yrs on 24May next	Dobson, Joseph	Farming. Orphan
Dobson, Mary	Apr1798	7 yrs on 15Feb last	Dobson, Joseph	Spin & sew. Orphan
Bogard, Benjamin	July1798		Burris, John	Previously bound, abuse alledged *
Bryan, Eunice	July1798	6 yrs in Mar last	Johnson, Margaret	Knit, sew & spin. Orphan
Roberts, Amee	26Oct1798	7 yrs 4 mo 21 d	Williams, Benjamin	
Lester, Reuben	Apr1799	6 yrs on 25Jan next	Dobson, Robert	Orphan, natural born
Roberts, John	2Nov1799	8 yrs in Mar last	Frazier, Beriah	Orphan
Bumpas, Lettia	2Nov1799	7 yrs	Broyles, Elizabeth	Knit, spin & sew. Orphan
Kilgore, Hiram	Nov1799	14 yrs	Culburson, James	Wheelright. Orphan of Robert Kilgore, dcd
Craddick, William	Jan1803		Dodd, John	Son of Rachel Craddick, dcd
Craddick, John	Jan1803		Dodd, John	Son of Rachel Craddick, dcd
Craddick, Drucilla	Jan1803	4 mo	Jones, James	Dau of Rachel Craddick, dcd
Ireland, William	Apr1803		Edmundson, Solomon	Baseborn
King, Sarah	Apr1803	3 yrs	Williams, Alexander	Canc 30Jan1817, as Sally King
Carlisle, Robert	Apr1804	16 yrs	Dryden, Joseph	Orphan
Whittenberg, Rachel	29Jan1805	Over 14 yrs	Whittenberg, Margaret, John & William	Margaret also guardian
Whittenberg, James	29Jan1805	Under 14 yrs	Whittenberg, Margaret, John & William	Margaret also guardian
Wallace, Robert	23July1805		Patton, William	Tanner. Orphan
Burris, Abelilah	31Oct1805		Dobson, Jr, Joseph	Orphan
Roberts, William	27Apr1807	10 yrs	Clawson, Josiah	Hatter. Orphan
Love, John	27Apr1807	16 yrs	Porter, Stephen	Saddler. Orphan

Wright, William	28Apr1807	21yrs on 14Oct1812	Gordon, Robert C.	Orphan. On 25Oct1808 indent canc at request of Gordon and Daniel Dunnagan, Stepfather of William
Etter, John	29July1807	12 yrs	Etter, John	Taylor. Son of John and Mary Etter* Canc 24Apr1809
Etter, Elizabeth	29July1807	11 yrs	Guthrie, James	Housewife. Dau of John and Mary Etter*
Etter, Mary	29July1807	8 yrs	Guthrie, James	Housewife. Dau of John and Mary Etter*
Etter, Rebeckah	29July1807	9 yrs	Etter, John	Housewife. Dau of John and Mary Etter*
Etter, Daniel	29July1807	6 yrs	Rader, John	Waggonmaker. Son of John and Mary Etter *
Wright, Isaac	31July1807	8 yrs 2 mo	Maloney, Robert	Taylor. Orphan
Gardner, William	27Oct1807	9 yrs	Harrison, Joseph	House joiner & carpenter. Orphan
Kennedy, William	26Jan1808	16 yrs on 23Feb next	Caldwell, Thomas	Blacksmith. Orphan
Massa, John	30Jan1808	13 yrs on 12 Feb next	Edmondson, William	House carpenter & joiner. Orphan
Massa, William	30Jan1808	11 yrs on 11May last	Edmondson, William	House carpenter & joiner. Orphan
Helms, John	25Apr1808	14 yrs on 25Dec last	Murphey, Thomas	House joiner, carpenter. Orphan. Canc 26July1810
Cluts, Mary	26July1808	8 yrs in June last	Evert, Philip	Housekeeping. Orphan
Cluts, David	27July1808	12 yrs on 6Sept next	Murphey, Thomas	House carpenter & joiner. Orphan
Sevier, Henry	24Oct1808	11 yrs on 14Oct inst	Conway, Sr, Henry	Son of John Sevier
Sevier, Hundley	24Oct1808	6 yrs on 12Nov last	Conway, Sr, Henry	Son of John Sevier
Sevier, Elizabeth	24Oct1808	9 yrs on 10 Oct inst	Conway, Sr, Henry	Dau of John Sevier
Sevier, Sally	24Oct1808	4 yrs on 2Nov last	Conway, Sr, Henry	Dau of John Sevier
Sevier, Narcissa	24Oct1808	2 yrs on 30Oct inst	Conway, Sr, Henry	Dau of John Sevier
Sevier, Nancy	24Oct1808	2 yrs on 30Oct inst	Conway, Sr, Henry	Dau of John Sevier
Brown, Solomon	25Oct1808	15 yrs on 13May last	Babb, David	Blacksmith. Orphan
Etter, John	24Apr1809	13 yrs 9 mo	Maloney, Robert	Taylor. Orphan
Wright, Hannah	25Apr1809	9 yrs	Mosley, Jesse	Housewife. Cancelled 29April1809
Estip, Ibby	25Apr1809	7 yrs	Cross, Henry	Housewife. Orphan
Foashu, Joseph			Starnes, George	On 29Apr1809 indenture cancelled for abuse. Put in temp possession of Simon Weston
Gladden, Edward	25Apr1809	10 mo	Scott, John	Husbandry. Orphan. Canc 27Oct1809
Simons, Samuel	28July1809	18 mo on 23July inst	Simons, Leonard	Husbandry. Orphan, son of Betsy Simons
McKahen, George	29July1809	16 yrs	Farnsworth, David	Husbandry. Orphan

Name	Date	Age	Master	Notes
Porter, Ruth	25Oct1809	9 yrs on 26July last	McKemy, Robert	Housewife. Dau of Joseph Porter, abused *
Porter, Jinnsy	25Oct1809	5 yrs on I May last	McKemy, Robert	Housewife. Dau of Joseph Porter, abused*
Garnes, Peggy	25Oct1809	4 yrs on 5Jan next	Cavner, Hugh	Housewife
Jewel, George	27Oct1809	10 yrs	Porter, Stephen	Saddler. Orphan. Canc 29April1814, neglect
Gladden, Edward	27Oct1809	16 mo	Fellers, Abraham G.	
Cluts, Betsy	23Jan1810	11 yrs in April next	Gurtner, Rachel	Housekeeper. Orphan
Helms, John	26July1810	17 yrs on 25Dec next	Fester, Levi	Tanning & currying
Lane, Anne	31Jan1811	2 yrs 6 mo	Williams, Jr, Benjamin	Housekeeper. Orphan
Whitaker, William	23July1811	8 yrs	Coffin, Charles [Rev]	Orphan. Canc 28Oct1812
Orho, Christopher	25July1811		Winters, Christopher	Shoe & boot making. Orphan
Morgan, Robert	29Oct1811	11 yrs	Frazier, Abner	Orphan
Mahallow, John	29Oct1811	13 yrs	Gordon, George	Papermaking. Orphan
Jewell, Seburn	31Oct1811	12 yrs	Maloney, Robert	Taylor. Orphan
Kelly, David	31Oct1811	6 yrs on 7Feb last	Easterly, Philip	Blacksmith. Orphan. Canc 28July1823
Long, Anny	29Jan1812	1 1/2 yrs	Kirk, Joseph	Knit, spin & sew. Orphan
Kexia, Polly	28Apr1812	2 yrs on 30June1811	Myers, Jr, William	Knit, spin & sew Orphan. Canc 25July1814
Fernes, Sally	30Oct1812		Howel, Philip	
Carder, Jonathan	26Jan1813	15 yrs on 3June next	Collier, Thomas	Husbandry. Orphan
Carder, John	27Jan1813	9 yrs on 1Jan inst	Pope, Simon	Orphan
Haynes, Frankey	27July1813	1 yr on 27Feb last	Haynes, Abraham	Female orphan
Steel, Samuel	26Oct1813	3 yrs on 21Jan last	Register, Francis	Cooper. Bastard son of Mary Steel 30July1813* & ? of Francis Register 25Oct1814 & 27April1815*
Woods, Viney	26Oct1813	5 yrs on 22May1814	Rinker, George	Orphan dau of Polly Woods
Kinser, Sally	25Apr1814	4 yrs on 11Jan last	Lentz, Jacob	Orphan
Lyles, Delilah	26Apr1814		Evert, Philip	
Jewel, George	29Apr1814	15 yrs	Fields, David	Saddler. Canc 24Oct1815. James Patterson chosen Guardian
Woods, Samuel	25July1814	3 yrs 3 mo	Williams, Aaron	Farming. Orphan
Combs, Samuel	26July1814	7 yrs on 8Nov last	Dyke, Jacob	Orphan

Pope, Elizabeth	24Oct1814	14 yrs	West, William	Dau of Williamson Pope, dcd
Pope, Susanna	25Oct1814	12 yrs	Bell, John	Dau of Williamson Pope, dcd
Pope, John	25Oct1814	9 yrs on 10Sept1814	West, William	Son of Williamson Pope, dcd
Pope, Simon	25Oct1814	7 yrs on 22Nov1814	Smith, Frederick	Son of Williamson Pope, dcd. Canc 24Jan1820
Pope, Williamson	25Oct1814	4 yrs on 14Jun1814	Baley, William	Son of Williamson Pope, dcd. Canc 27July1815
Pope, Wiley	25Oct1814	2 yrs on 5Aug1814	Pope, Maryann	Son of Williamson Pope, dcd. Until age 6 yrs
Pearcen, Rachel	27Jan1815	6 yrs on 10Apr next	Robinson, John	Orphan
Carder, George	24Apr1815	5 yrs on 1Oct last	French, Henry	Coopering. Orphan
Lyles, Polly	26Apr1815	11 yrs 7 mo	Wampler, Michael	Cancelled 24July1815
Lyles, Holly	26Apr1815	3 yrs in Aug next	Wampler, Michael	Cancelled 24July1815
Lyles, Nancy	26Apr1815	6 yrs in Mar last	Cobble, John	Cancelled 28Oct1816
Lyles, Levi	26Apr1815	4 yrs in Oct next	Cobble, John	Stone Mason
Pope, Williamson	27July1815		Temple, Thomas	
Lyles, Holly	24July1815		Ervin, James	
Lyles, Polly	24July 1815		Ervin, James	
Armstrong, Preston	24Oct1815	3 yrs on 17Nov next	Dobson, Robert	Of color
Tidwell, Elizabeth	24Oct1815	7 yrs 3 mo	Hixon, Andrew	
Gray, John	25Oct1815	17 yrs on 17Sep last	Clawson, Josiah	Orphan
McBride, Amos	23Jan1816	14 yrs on 20Apr next	Delaney, Jr, John	Wheel Wright. Cancelled 30Jan1817
Steptoe, Alexander	25Jan1816		Gordon, George	Paper making
Porter, Lorenzo D.	22Apr1816	11 yrs in Aug next	Vance, William K.	Saddler. Orphan
Hood, Benjamin	22July1816	8 yrs	Newman, Jonathan	Farming. Orphan
Mills, Richard	22July1816	4 yrs on 9Apr last	Shirley, Adam	Coverlid weaving. Orphan, son of Elizabeth Mills *
Hutchison, Reuben M.	22July1816	15 yrs on 19Jun last	Robinson, James	Farming. Orphan
Lyles, Nancy	28Oct1816	7 yrs in Mar last	Baker, Jr, Isaac	
Kerr, Polly	27Jan1817	6 yrs on 28Aug last	Love, John	Orphan
Fields, Luke	27Jan1817	18 yrs on 15June last	Bible, John	Blacksmith. Orphan. 29April1814*
McBride, Amos	30Jan1817	15 yrs in Apr next	Ross, Jr, William	Waggon maker
Millhanks, Thomas	2May1817	14 yrs	Hays, James	Saddler. Alias Thomas Skaggs*. Taken from Aaron Parker

Name	Date	Age	Master	Notes
Mismer, George	28July1817		Sindser, Joseph	Wheelwright. Orphan
Weaver, Arthur	19July1817	15 yrs	Smith, George	House carpenter & joiner. Orphan
Shaver, David	30July1817	6 yrs on 1Sept next	Bible, John	Blacksmith. Orphan. Canc 28Jan1822, as David Shaner
Simpson, Henry	29Oct1817		McPherran, James	Orphan. Canc 29July1818. Simpson to leave county
Clutz, Sarah	26Jan1818	13 yrs	Kendle, John	
Rose, Levi	28Jan1818		Brabson, Robert	House carpenter & cabinet. Orphan
Ellis, Thomas	31Jan1818		Ellis, Jesse	Blacksmith. Orphan
Carbough, George	27Apr1818		Alexander, Stephen	Mill Wright. Orphan
Williams, William	27Apr1818		Hays, James	Sadler. Orphan
Rose, Robert	27Apr1818		Dinwiddie, James	Weaver. Orphan
Rose, James	27Apr1818		Dinwiddie, John	Shoemaker. Orphan
Mills, Christopher	2May1818	5 yrs	Cook, Jr, John	Blacksmith. Orphan, son of Elizabeth Mills 26April1816*
Faris, Jefferson	27July1818		Mauris, Esq, John	Orphan
Sands, Rachel	27July1818		Coulson, Thomas	Orphan of Doctor Sands 30Apr1818
Sands, Celia	27July1818	13 yrs on 9 Nov next	Coulson, Thomas	Orphan of Doctor Sands 30Apr1818
Liles, Levi	27July1818		Evert, Philip	Stonemason. Orphan
Hamlet, James	26Oct1818		Parker, Caleb J.	Orphan, commonly called James Magill
Farns, Polly Ann	25Jan1819	2 yrs on 16Oct last	Heartsuck, Peter	
Smilie, Hannah Jenny Helms	25Jan1819	9 1/2 yrs	Smelson, Joseph	Cancelled 25Oct1819
Porter, Thomas	26Jan1819		Vance, William K.	Orphan. Canc 23July1821
Milbourn, Betsy	28Jan1819	13 yrs	Millbourn, William	
Dennis, Hezekiah	26Apr1819	9 yrs on 19Aug1818	Johnston, William	Shoemaker. Orphan, bastard of Mary Moore, now Mary McAmish 29Jan1819
McNew, Jeremiah	26July1819		West, Richard	Farmer. Orphan
McNew, Shadrach	26July1819		Britten, Jr, James	Hatter. Orphan
Messimer, George			Smelson, Joseph	Indenture cancelled on 26July1819
Messimer, George	26July1819		Lince, Jacob	Wheelwright. Orphan
Thompson, Charity	26July1819		Swatzel, Peter	Orphan. Dau of Polly Thompson, dcd 27Apr1819

Carter, Jessee	29July1819	15 yrs on 26Jan last	Lincolen, Jessee & Mordecai	Shoemaker. Orphan
Hunter, John Standfield	25Oct1819		Standfield, Samuel	Linen weaver
Smilie, Hannah Jenny Helms	25Oct1819	10 yrs 2 mo	Reader, Jr, John	Orphan
Tidwell, Betsy	25Oct1819		Hexon, Andrew	Indenture cancelled
Tidwell, Betsy	25Oct1819		Willhoit, Samuel	Orphan
Shaw, David	24Jan1820		Ross, James	Blacksmith. Orphan
Youngblood, James	24Jan1820	7 yrs	Easterly, Abraham	Farming
Pope, Simon	24Jan1820		English, John	
Baxley, Zephimah	24Apr1820	7 yrs in Feb last	Lindsay, John	Cotton wheel making. Orphan
Falls, John	24Apr1820	12 yrs next August	Daley, John	Sadler. Orphan. ?Son of Elizabeth Falls 31July1818*. Canc 27Jan1823
Drain, Rebecca	25July1820	10 yrs	Maloney, Sr, John	Child of John Drain 24July1820*
Hood, Dutton	25July1820	8 yrs	Hendry, William	Weaving. Orphan, child of Keziah Hood 24July1820*. Trade changed to shoemaking 26Oct1829
Drain, John	26July1820		Brown, George	Bookkeeping. Child of John Drain 24July1820*
Drain, Thomas	26July1820	6 yrs	Perry, William S.	Tailor. Child of John Drain 24July1820*
Reid, Jr, John L.	23Oct1820	15 yrs on 30April last	Reid, Esq, John L.	Waggonmaking
Myers, Lucinda	23Oct1820	6 yrs	Ellis, Jonathan	Housewife. Taken from possession of John McCurry
Grubbs, Thomas	24Oct1820	3 yrs on 5Feb last	Dodd, Sr, John	Linen weaving
Massey, Polly	22Jan1821	8 yrs on 1Jan last	Rimell, Jacob	Housewife
Whited, William	22Jan1821	18 yrs on 21Nov last	Alexander, Stephen	Mill Wright
McGee, Robert	23Apr1821	10 yrs on 1May next	Bright, Charly	Linen weaver. Cancelled 24Oct1831
Miller, Nancy	23Apr1821	14 yrs on 1Jan last	McDaniel, William	Housewife
Youngblood, William	23Apr1821	16 yrs on 10April inst	Falls, Thomas	Papermaking
Youngblood, Alfred	23Apr1821	6 yrs	Falls,	Papermaking
Yarberry,William	23Apr1821		Falls, Thomas	Papermaking
Porter, Thomas	23July1821	13 yrs	Green, Evan	Cooper. Orphan
McNew, James	23July1821	16 yrs on 15Feb last	Alexander, Jr, Stephen	Mill Wright

Name	Date	Age	Master	Notes
Presley, Levi	23July1821	11 yrs in Aug next	Lane, Dutton	Shoemaker. John, Rebecca, & Matilda Presley also ordered brought to court
Walker, Rachel	22Oct1821	5 yrs 10 mo	Patterson, James	Housewife. Of color. Until 18 yrs. Canc 28Jan1822
Ingle, Bluford	22Oct1821	16 yrs	Haun, Christopher	Farmer
Shaner, David	28Jan1822	11 yrs in Oct next	Malony, Robert	Tailor
Kinney, Harmon	28Jan1822	12 yrs on 19May next	Pogue, Farmer	Farming. Canc 24July1826
Morris, Addison C.	28Jan1822	14 yrs 4 mo	Haymaker, John	Cooper & Tin Smith
Russell, Thomas	2Feb1822	16 yrs on 2June last	Malony, Robert	Tailor. Cancelled 30Oct1822
Cross, Elijah	28Oct1822	13 yrs	Bowers, Chresley	Tanner
Johnson, Wyly	29Oct1822	6 yrs	Dudley, Watson	Farmer
Law, William	27Jan1823	16 yrs 9July last	Law, Hugh	Blacksmith
Farner, John W.	27Jan1823		Farner, John	Blacksmith. 28Apr1823* See John Milton
Falls, John	27Jan1823	14 yrs last Aug	Clawson, Josiah	Hatter
Shannon, William	28Apr1823	17 yrs	West, Richard	Tanner
Myers, Sally	28Apr1823	Nearly 5 yrs	Moore, David	
Farnsworth, Thomas	1May1823	17 yrs on 1Aug next	Lincoln & Hieskell	Tanner
Milton, John			Farner, John	Prior ind (? as John W. Farner) canc on 28Apr1823. Son of Sarah Farner. Milton adopted by Peter Wilson 28Apr1823*, name changed to John Milton Wilson
Kelly, David	28July1823	18 yrs on 7Feb last	Wilson, Moses G.	
McCoy, Elisa	28July1823	5 yrs in Nov last	Kelly, David	Housewife
Sands, John	29July1823	20 yrs on 18Nov next	Gillespie. George T.	
Cross, Elizabeth	31July1823	6 yrs on 10Jan next	Craig, Jane J.	Canc 25Oct1825, as Betsy
Hood, John	27Oct1823	12 yrs on 1Jan next	Hendry, William	Shoemaker. Orphan
Coker, Esekiel	25Apr1825	12 yrs on last day next mo	Dailey, John	Sadler. Orphan. Ind Canc at request of Daily 26Apr1830
Coker, Nancy	25Apr1825	10 yrs 4th day present mo	Barkley, William	Housewife
Hunt, Rosanna	26Apr1825	7 yrs next June	Wilson, Moses G.	Housewife. Canc 28April1825
Halls, Ira	27Apr1825	16 yrs on 31July next	Clawson, Josiah	Hatter. Orphan. Canc 28July1825, as John Halls

Hunt, Rosanna	28Apr1825	7 yrs on 8June next	Hise, James	Housewife. Until 21 yrs
Shoemaker, Aurell?	28Apr1825	16 yrs	Myrick, Jacob T.	Blacksmith
Powell, Job	25Oct1825	14 yrs on 24Mar last	Boyle, George	Tailor
Cross, Betsy	25Oct1825	7 yrs	Kennedy, George D.	Housewife
Millstep, Sally	23Jan1826	3 yrs 3 mo	Matthews, Esq, John	Of color
Wilson, Auny	26Jan1826		Kesterson, John	Female
Swatrel, Jane	26Apr1826	3 yrs on 13 Nov last	Swatrel, Polly	
Goodman, Samuel	24July1826	2 yrs on 27Mar next	Sharpe, Thomas	Farming
Anderson, Peter	23Oct1826	3 yrs on 4Mar last	Harrison, Isaiah	Farming
Shannon, James	27Apr1827	16 yrs on 23Nov last	Malony, Robert	Tailor. Canc 23Jul1827. Maloney appeals to Circuit Ct.
Chidester, James	24Oct1827	17 yrs in June last	Lee, Thomas F.	Waggon maker
Rhinehart, Nancy	28Apr1828	10 yrs in Sept next	Whittenberg, John	Housewife. Rescinded 26July1830
Rhinehart, Polly	28Apr1828	9 yrs in Dec next	Leming, Robert	Housewife
Mills, Jonathan	2May1828	12 to 13 yrs	Lister, John	Brickmaking, laying & burning
Phares, Jefferson	28July1828	Upwards of 14 yrs	Fox, Isaac	Farming
Jones, Mary Ann	28July1828	7 yrs on 1Feb last	Jennings, Jr, William	Orphan of James Jones. 28April1828*
Jones, Peter	28July1828	11 yrs on 8June last	Jennings, Jr., William	House carpenter. Orphan of James Jones. 28April1828*
Jones, Cuseanna	28July1828		Haworth, West	Orphan of James Jones. 28April1828*
Baxley, Zephariah	28July1828	15 yrs in Feb last	Lindsay, Elizabeth	Chair & cotton wheel making. Orphan. Canc at request of Mrs. Lindsay 26Apr1830
Isom	31July1828	15 yrs	Ryan, Joseph	Farming. Mulatto boy
Dawson, Mehala	27Oct1828		Bird, Philip	Housewife. Orphan
McCoy, Dennis H?.	27Oct1828		Haworth, West	Farming. Orphan. For 5 yrs 1 mo 10 d (age 21 yrs)
Jones, Patsy	27Oct1828	9 yrs	Haworth, Mary (widow)	Housewife. Orphan of James Jones 28Apr1828*. Resc 26Jan1830
Troop, James	30Oct1828	13 yrs on 1Jan next	Maloney, Robert	Tailor. Orphan. Son of wife of Nehemiah Pettit, dcd. 27Oct1828*
Pettit, Polly Ann	30Oct1828	11 yrs on 25March next	Scott, James	Housewife. Orphan of Nehemiah Pettit, dcd. 27Oct1828* Canc 29Apr1834
Pettit, Susannah	30Oct1828	10 yrs on 27Sept last	Dyche, Christian	Orphan of Nehemiah Pettit, dcd. 27Oct1828*

Name	Date	Age	Master	Notes
Baxley, Sally	26Jan1829	9 yrs	Rader, Jesse	Orphan
Stoffle, Mary Ann	26Jan1829	18 mo	Stephens, Jr, Andrew	Orphan. Resc 25April1831
Wills, Minerva	27Apr1829	3 yrs	Dodd, Sr, John	Home wife. Orphan
Walker, Jesse	27July1829	6 yrs on 2Oct1829	Roberts, James	Farming. Orphan
Stuart, George	28July1829	3 yrs in May last	Phillips, Thomas	Farming. Son of Lucinda Stuart 27July1829*
Newberry, Lucinda	26Oct1829	7 mo on 1st of this mo	Rose, Alexander	
Balch, John	26Oct1829	16 yrs on 8Sep last	Rhea, Robert	Blacksmith. Canc 23July1832
Pettit, Alexander	29Oct1829	7 yrs on 27April next	Lister, John	Brickmaking & laying. Orphan. Agreeable to Will of father, Nehemiah Pettit, dcd. 26Oct1829. 25Oct1830* 22July1833*
Hicks, Mary	25Jan1830	11 yrs in Aug last	Ball, Esq, Lewis	Housewife. Orphan. Canc 23July1832
Dunham, William	27Jan1830	13 yrs on 29Nov1829	Barkley, John T.	Saddler. Orphan
Lard, Rebecca	26Apr1830	9 yrs on 10Apr1830	Matthews, James	
Lard, Sarah	26Apr1830	7 yrs on 19Mar1830	Kirk, James	
Barnes, Cornelius	26Apr1830	18 yrs on 3Aug next	Rhea, Robert	Blacksmith. Canc 28July1831
Barnes, Polly	26July1830	13 yrs	Wright, Jesse	
Rinehart, Nancy	26July1830	12 yrs in Sept next	Harrison, Josiah	Housewife
Dawson, Rachel	27July1830	2 yrs on 18Aug30	Bird, Philip	
Kerr, Thomas	28July1830	16 yrs	Ellis, Jesse	Blacksmith. Destitute boy
McNew, Catharine	25Oct1830	6 yrs	McNew, William	Orphan
McNew, John	25Oct1830	14 yrs this day	McNew, James	Mill Wright. Orphan
Walker, Ruthy	25Apr1831	3 yrs on 1May1831	Whittenberg, William	Resc 3Apr1837. To Henry Swatzell, blacksmith, who is intermarried with her mother, late Jane Walker
Stuffel, Polly Ann	25Apr1831	4 yrs on 14Aug1831	Burkey, Polly	
Williams, Thursey	22July1833	10 yrs on 30Mar last	Crawford, Sr, John	Orphan. Dau of Jane Williams 22Apr1833
Hicks, Mary	22July1833	15 yrs in Aug next	Wright, Robert	Housewife. Orphan
Basinger, Michael H.	28Oct1833	6 yrs on 9 Nov next	McBride, James D.	Farming. Resc 5Oct1846
Snider, George	29Oct1833	12 yrs present mo	Wade, John	Hatting. Destitute, deserted by father, Michael Snider
Hardin, Josiah R.	29Oct1833	7 yrs in Sept last	Etters, Frederick W.	Blacksmith. Destitute, deserted by father, George Hardin

Chursant, Jonathan H.	31Oct1833	16 yrs in June last	King, George	Cooper
Hardin, Sampson	31Oct1833	14 yrs in May last	Haun, Christopher	Blacksmith. Destitute, deserted by father, George Hardin
Halls, George	27Jan1834	14 yrs on 9Dec1834	Nelson, George W.	Blacksmith
Large?, Rebecca	27Jan1834	13 yrs on 10Apr1834	Trobaugh, William	
Houp, Edmund	27Jan1834	13 yrs on 15 Feb 1834	Hall, David	Farming
Snider, Adam	28Jan1833	10 yrs in Mar1834	Brannon, John	Waggon maker
Jackson, Jefferson	28Jan1833		Stone, Washington	Sadler
Jackson, John	28Jan1833		Marsh, James	Farming
Donahoo, Robert	29Apr1834	6 yrs in July 1834	Alexander, George W.	Farming. Baseborn son of Letty Donohoo* 23Oct1832. Canc 2Feb1846
Smith, Benjamin	28July1834	8 yrs	McNew, James	Mill Wright. William Smith app't adm of estate of John Smith, David Smith a security
Johnston, John	27Oct1834	10 yrs on 1Feb1835	Anderson, John	Little spinning wheel makingOrphan. Ind canc, as Johnson, 2Oct1843, fulfilled
Spurgeon, George	27Oct1834	4 yrs on 29Jan1835	Haworth, West	Farming. Resc 2Oct1848
Pettit, Alexander	27Oct1834	12 yrs on 27April next	West, Richard	Orphan son of Nemehiah Pettit* 22July1833. Resc 2Aug1841
Johnston, Mary Ann	27Oct1834	6 yrs on 10Sep1835	Davis, Thomas	
Kinser, Esther	25Jan1836	12 yrs	Reader, Andrew	Orphan
Russell, Emberson	2May1836	16 yrs on 16Mar last	Denwooddy, John	Orphan *
Russell, Thomas	2May1836	13 yrs on 18Nov last	Rankin, John	Orphan * Rescinded 6Apr1840. Of color. Adam Dunwody app't guardian 6Oct1840
Russell, Bembre	2May1836	5 yrs on 18Oct last	Earnest, Thomas	Orphan *
Russell, David M.	2May1836	13 yrs on 8Feb last	Dunwooddy, Adam	Orphan. Dunwooddy adm of estate of Carey Russell
Harrison, Abraham M.	4July1836	10 yrs on 11July last	Earnest, Jacob	Orphan. Indenture rescinded 7Sept1840
Morgan, Isaac	8Nov1836	6 yrs	Click, Martin	Orphan
Quinn, Edward	2Jan1837			Previously bound. William Barkley ordered to bring to court
McKeehen, Patrick	2Jan1837	10 yrs on 16Dec last	Maloney, John	6Mar1837*
Bradwell, James N.	6Feb1837	15 yrs	Rankin, Thomas C.	
Reeves, Robert	6Mar1837	12 yrs on 10Mar last	Reeves, John	

Name	Date	Age	Master	Notes
Dennis, Catherine	6Mar1837	6 yrs in Dec last	Jennings, George B.	Prob dau of Joshua Dennis * 1Aug1836
Basinger, Eliza Jane	6Mar1837	7 yrs on 24Mar last	Rader, William	Indenture cancelled 7Dec1840. 4Sep1843*
Basinger, William	6Mar1837	12 yrs on 28Nov last	Shields, John	Indenture cancelled 7Dec1840. 4Sep1843*
Basinger, Catherine	6Mar1837	9 yrs on 18Nov last	McBride, Martin	Indenture cancelled 5March1838
Thomas, Riley	7Aug1837	3 yrs on 14Apr last	Poe, William A.	6Nov1837*
Wells, George	7Nov1837	10 yrs	Williams, Robert R.	Of color
Harrison, Catherine	5Feb1838		Earnest, Jacob	Orphan. Indenture rescinded 7Sept1840
Smith, Harvey	5Mar1838	15 yrs	Laughlin, Alexander	
Tompkins, William E.	4Jun1838	11 yrs	Shaw, James	Orphan
Dennis, Mary	1Oct1838	4 yrs in May last	Balch, Kezekiah	Housewife. Orph. Prob dau of Joshua Dennis* 1Aug1836
Eddleman, James	5Nov1838	9 yrs on 21May last	Patty, Raffail W.	Tanning
Harris, Sarah	7Jan1839	7 yrs	Kirk, Alexander	Orphan
Reese, James	6May1839	12 yrs on 22Aug last	Good, Solomon	
Long, Samuel	4Nov1839	10 yrs on 23Jan last	Adams, David	Resc 4Aug1845, master now Samuel B. Adams
Bridewell, Margaret	4Nov1839	5 yrs on 25Dec next	Barkley, William	Orphan. Previously in possession of Philip Brobeck
Ward, James	2Mar1840	8 yrs	Cannon, Stephen	
Shanks, Mary Jane	3Mar1840	5 wks this day	Butler, Davis	
Harris[on], Abraham M.	7Sep1840	15 yrs on 11July last	Rankin, John	Orphan
Harris[on], Catharine	7Sep1840	13 yrs in July last	Rankin, John	Orphan
Gower, Ely	7Sep1840	5 yrs on 15Apr last	Davis, Ephraim	Orphan. Indenture rescinded 7Jun1841
Millstep, Susan	2Nov1840	11 mo on 15Oct last	Matthews, John	Of color
Reaves, Robert	2Nov1840	16 yrs on 10Mar last	Lightner, John	Blacksmith
Harrington, Asberry	4Jan1841	11 yrs on 27May last	Jones, Alfred H.	Resc 3May1847, as Asberry Wurts
Merida, Elbert	1Feb1841	10 yrs on 14July1840	Cook, Jonathan R.	Orphan
Rees, George	5Apr1841	8 yrs on 20Dec last	Rees, David	Orphan
Gass, Joseph G.	6Sep1841	14 yrs on 22Mar last	Harrold, James W.	For 4 1/2 years
Fulks, William B.	6Sep1841	7 yrs on 16Sep last	Self, Lewis F.	Prob. son of John Fulks* 1Nov1841. Canc 4Apr1842
Fulks, Andrew J.	6Sep1841	5 yrs in Dec last	Dunwody, John	Prob. son of John Fulks* 1Nov1841

Dudle, Bartley	1Nov1841	16 yrs on 22Sep last	Brown, George M.	Tanning & currying. Orphan
Grant, Richard	1Nov1841	10 yrs	Hardin, Cornelius B.	Farming. Orphan. Indenture cancelled 7Nov1842
Low, Henderson M.	6Dec1841	14 yrs on 19Nov last	Wilson, David	Waggon making. Orphan. 5July1841*. Resc 5May1845. John Morrow app't guardian 3Oct1842*
Low, Ruthy	6Dec1841	7 yrs on 6Feb next	Wilson, James C., of David	Housewife. Orphan. Resc 1Mar1847. 5July1841*. John Morrow app't guardian 3Oct1842*
Wilson, Nancy Emaline	3Jan1842	3 yrs on 26th instant	Squibb, John K.	Housewife
Gragg, John	7Mar1842	3 mo last day of Feb last	Gragg, James	Farming. Orphan. Resc 7Aug1844
Nichols, William	7Mar1842	15 yrs on 25Feb last	Trobough, George	Farming. Orphan. Ind canc 6Oct1845, absconded
Fulks, William B.	4Apr1842	8 yrs on 16Sept last	Brown, John	
Beach, John	5Apr1842	6 yrs on 5Feb last	Gooden, Lemuel	Farming. Orphan
Grant, Richard	7Nov1842	11 yrs	Murphey, Thomas	Farming. Orphan
Bridewell, Martin	2Jan1843	16 yrs	Britten, Daniel	Orphan
McKemy, Barney	6Feb1843	7 yrs on 20th instant	Dyke, Sr, Henry	Farming. ?lillig son of Rebecca McKemy *3July1843
Osborne, Sarah Jane	6Feb1843	6 yrs	Ailshire, John D.	Housewife. Dau of Margaret Osborne, a single woman 5Dec1842
Eddleman, William	6Mar1843	10 yrs in Aug last	Wright, John	Blacksmith
Jones, Jacob K.	3Apr1843	13 yrs 18Apr last	Price, Hiram T.	Brick making & laying. Orphan. Rescinded 7Aug1848
Gosnell, James Elbert	5Jun1843	4 yrs in Mar last	Rader, William, of Jno.	House carpenter & joiner. Orphan. Resc 5Aug1844
Low, James R.	5Jun1843	12 yrs on 30May last	Alexander, Thomas	Orphan. 5July1841*. Resc 1Mar1847 as Robertson Low. John Morrow app't guardian 3Oct1842*
Kesling, Christina	2Oct1843	13 yrs on 11Jun last	Andes, George	
McConnell, Franklin	2Oct1843	12 yrs in Feb last	Elliott, Robert	
Penland, Susan C.	6Nov1843	11 yrs on 8Nov last	Walker, Anderson W.	Rescinded 1Apr1844
Osburn, Sarah Jane	4Dec1843	6 yrs in Feb last	Ailshie, John	Housewife. Dau of Margaret Osborne, a single woman *
Penland, Susan C.	1Apr1844	11 yrs on 8Nov last	Russell, James	
Harrison, Ezekial	3Jun1844	11 yrs	Drake, Lewis J.	Orphan. Resc 4Dec1848, as Ezekial Harris
Keasling, Rufus	5Aug1844	10 yrs on 22Feb last	Knipp, Elias	Orphan
Gosnell, James E.	5Aug1844	5 yrs	Evans, James	Orphan
Gragg, John, of Polly	7Oct1844		Gragg, Thomas	

Name	Date	Age	Master	Notes
McNew, Joseph	2Dec1844	4 yrs on 23Jan last	McNew, William	
Pisby, James	7July1845	2 1/2 yrs this day	Anderson, John	Blacksmith. Orphan
Alexander, Hugh	1Dec1845	12 Yrs on 2May last	Rose, Alexander	Of color. Canc 7Dec1846
Keasling, Reuben	7Jan1845	10 yrs on 22Feb last	Rankin, Anthony	Orphan
Horn, Mary Jane	3Feb1845	3 yrs on 29Aug last	Gass, Mary, of James	
McKemy, Minerva	6Jan1846	7 yrs	Dyke, Nicholas	?Illig dau of Rebecca McKemy *3July1843
Donohoo, Robert	2Feb1846	17 yrs in July last	Alexander, George, of Wm.	Canc 4Jan1847
Payne, Francis A.	2Mar1846	17 yrs on 19Dec last	Lane, Jr, Thomas	
Dyke, William D.	2Mar1846	12 yrs on 20Mar last	Dyke, Allen	Rescinded 5Oct1846
Dyke, Hugh D.	1Jun1846	10 yrs in Mar last	Self, Claiborn	Orphan
Harmon, William R.	1Jun1846	6 yrs on 15Nov last	Black, Isaac	Orphan
McNeese, Nancy Ann	1Jun1846	4 yrs on 16Aug last	Linebaugh, Jacob	Orphan
Ausburn, Mahlon	7July1846	4 yrs on 17Jun last	Rector, George	Of color. Resc 2Jan1855, as Mahlon Osburn
Donohoo, George	5Oct1846	7 yrs on 10Mar last	Farner, Jacob	Rescinded 7Nov1853
Philip	2Nov1846	10 yrs on 8Mar next	Arnold, Esq, Thomas D.	Farming. Of color
Robinson, William	2Nov1846	1 yr on 8May last	Britton, Sr, James	Farming. Free boy of color
Alexander, Hugh	7Dec1846	13 yrs on 2May last	Feezel, Henry	Of color. Alias Hugh Miller
Debusk, Mary Ann	4Jan1847	5 yrs on 31Aug last	Debusk, Elisha	
Coleman, Eliza	1Feb1847	12 yrs on 15Mar last	Arnold, Thomas D.	Of color
Ruble, William A.	1Feb1847	6 yrs on 1Jan last	Reaves, George	Farming, blacksmith. Mother, Harriet, dead. Father, Joseph, not providing. Reaves is grandfather
Ruble, John C.	1Feb1847	4 yrs on 24Aug last	Reaves, George	Farming, blacksmith. Mother, Harriet, dead. Father, Joseph, not providing. Reaves is grandfather
Ruble, George D.	1Feb1847	2 yrs on 23Nov last	Reaves, George	Farming, blacksmith. Mother, Harriet, dead. Father, Joseph, not providing. Reaves is grandfather
Charlotte, Violet	1Mar1847	5 yrs	Robison, John	Of color
Evans, Mahala	5Apr1847	7 yrs in July last	Dameron, Abraham	Free girl of color. 1Mar1847*
Hatton, Sarah Jane	5Apr1847	4 yrs on 4Nov last	Morrison, James	Canc 4Apr1859

Petit, Richard	4Oct1847	7 yrs on 4Apr last	Haun, John	
Pinkston, Minerva	6Dec1847	7 yrs	Pinkston, Francis	
Burrus, Julia Ann	6Dec1847	2 yrs on 22Dec last	Halaway, Jeremiah	Of color
Meeler, Sarah Jane	6Dec1847	8 yrs	Morris, John	Rescinded 7Aug1848
Pinkston, John	3Jan1848	8 yrs	Drake, William W.	Rescinded 8April1856
Russell, Bluford	7Feb1848	10 yrs	Laney, John	Indenture cancelled 5Feb1849
Beach, Thomas A.	6Mar1848	7 yrs on 31May last	Dodd, Mary	Of color
Parker, Alexander	6Mar1848	15 yrs on 20Jun last	English, Allen	
Wolf, Joseph	7Mar1848	5 Yrs on 7Aug last	Dyche, Benjamin J.	Son of John Wolfe 5July1847* Canc 1Sept1851
Buster, Thomas	4July1848		Britton, James	Of color. Emancipated on 1Mar1847* by will of Isabella Buster, dcd, along with mother, Delilah, sibs Violet & Sarah Jane 4Jan1847*
Hatton, Sara Ann	4July1848		Dodd, Mary	Of color. Dau of Mary Hatton 5Feb1848
Meeler, Sarah J.	7Aug1848	8 1/2 yrs	Bird, David	Indenture rescinded 2April1849
Harris, Mahala	4Sep1848	14 yrs	Kidwell, John	Sibs John, Rose, William E. 4July1848. Canc 4Aug1851
Looney, William	4Sep1848	10 yrs in Feb last	Harrold, James W.	Indenture rescinded 6May1850
Harris, Rose	4Sep1848	9 yrs	Hutson, William B.	Until age 21. Sibs Mahala, John, William E. 4July1848
Harris, William E.	4Sep1848	7 yrs	McBride, John	Sibs Mehala, John, Rose 4July1848
Lucky, Rufus	2Oct1848		Gass, Charles	Indenture rescinded 2Oct1848
Reynolds, Joseph	6Nov1848	8 yrs on 23Jan last	McAfee, Archibald	
Winkle, William	6Nov1848	8 yrs on 9Apr last	Carter, John A.	Rescinded 7May1855
Thomas, William	1Jan1849	18 yrs on 5Aug last	Matthews, Esq, John	
Russell, Bluford	5Feb1849	11 yrs	Ottinger, Samuel	
Spurgeon, James M.			Simmons, Zachariah	Indenture rescinded 5Feb1849
Spurgeon, James M.	5Feb1849	16 yrs on 9Jan last	Smith, James	
Meeler, Sarah Jane	2Apr1849		Fillars, Douglass H.	Rescinded 6May1850
Noah, Richard	4Jun1849	6 yrs on 15th this mo	Lauderdale, Washington	
Dyche, Polly Ann	4Jun1849	3 yrs in Aug last	Foster, James H.	
Walden, Uriah T.	2July1849	8 yrs on 26 Aug last	Black, Joseph	Son of Betsy Walden 4Jun1849*
Jefferies, Andrew J.	2July1849	13 yrs in Sept last	Rodgers, Joseph	

Name	Date	Age	Master	Notes
Walden, Andrew	5Nov1849		Campbell, Jackson	Alias Andrew Gillet. Son of Betsy Walden 4Jun1849*
Walden, Margaret	5Nov1849	7 yrs	McMillan, Henry T.	Alias Margaret Gillet. Dau of Betsy Walden 4Jun1849*
Miranda	1Apr1850	4 yrs in Feb last	Stonesifer, John A.	Of color
Osburn, Alexander	6May1850	10 yrs in Jan last	Britton, Daniel	Rescinded 9Nov1854
Wolf, John	3Jun1850	6 yrs	Cobble, Joseph	?Son of John Wolfe 5July1847*. Resc 2Aug1852
Donohoo, Enoch	2Sep1850	14 yrs on 14May last	Campbell, Jackson	
Mohog, Willet	2Dec1850	3 yrs on 24Dec last	Cook, Jonathan R.	Rescinded 2Nov1857
Goodin, Matthew	7Apr1851	12 yrs on 15Feb last	Evans, James	
Looney, William	7Apr1851	13 yrs on 9Feb last	Crum, John	
Price, Hiram	7Apr1851	12 yrs on 8Mar last	Woolsey, James	
Gosnell, Mary Emily	1Sep1851	3 yrs on 17Nov last	Taylor, John W.	Alias Mary Emily Taylor. Petition to take her from Jesse Gosnell 6Oct1851* 5Jan1852*
Wolf, Joseph	1Sep1851	9 yrs on 7Aug last	Easterly, Jacob	
Evans, William	6Oct1851	7 yrs	Reaves, James G.	Rescinded 3Jan1854
Scott, Tabitha C.	3Nov1851	9 yrs on 31Aug last	Slater, Thomas J.	
Russell, James	2Feb1852	12yrs 6 mo	Johnson, William	Of color
Harmon, George W.	1Mar1852	9 yrs in Oct last	Prather, Jeremiah	
Russell, Thomas	1Mar1852	13 yrs on 10May last	Johnson, Joseph	Of color
Brown, Catharine	7Jun1852	4 yrs on 20Jun last	McCorkle, Samuel B.	Mulatto
Lauderdale, William Francis	7Jun1852	2 yrs in Jan last	Lauderdale, James	
Wolf, John	2Aug1852	8 yrs on 15Jun last	Hall, John	
Emmett, George	6Sep1852	8 yrs on 10Jun last	Self, Claibourn	
Lane, Viney	6Sep1852	11 yrs	Stone, Washington	Of color (mulatto). Permission to remove from Co under bond 3Apr1855, now aged 13 yrs on 1Nov last. To return at age 21. Freedom granted 5May1863
Simpson, John	2Nov1852	5 yrs in Apr last	Spencer, George M.	
Fouts, John Henry	7Mar1853	3 yrs in May last	Archer, Aaron	
Jones, Joshua	7Mar1853	16 yrs	Miller, Edmund B.	Joshua a cripple. To be rescinded if unable to work. Resc 8Sept1857

Sizemore, James	4Apr1853	7 yrs	Galbreath, James W.	Alias James King 6Dec1852. Resc 2Apr1866
Gosnell, Mary Emily	7Jun1853	4 yrs on 18Nov last	Gosnell, Jessee	Alias Mary Emily Taylor 6Jun1853. 1Sep, 6Oct1851*
Miller, Charles	5July1853	9 yrs in July1853	Masan, Robert	Complied with & canc as Robert Miller 3Mar1862
Warrick, Eli	1Aug1853	3 yrs on 10Aug1853	Kennedy, Jane	Both free & of color
Pettitt, Seymour	5Sep1853	6 yrs in Aug last	Kestersan, Uriah	
Brown, Elizabeth	5Sep1853	12 yrs on 1Sep inst	Boyce, William	Until 19 yrs. Rescinded 4Feb1856
Dunahoo, James	4Oct1853	9 yrs on 31Oct1852	Maloney, John	
Danahoo, George	7Nov1853	14 yrs on 10Mar last	Lowry, James M.	Blacksmith. Rescinded 6Dec1853
Donahoo, Susan	7Nov1853	6 yrs in Nov inst	Oliphant, Samuel R.	Until age 21
Brown, Martha Leticia	5Dec1853	10 yrs on 31May last	Rose, Mary Ann	Until 21 yrs. Rescinded on 4Feb1854
Miller, William Morgan	5Dec1853	10 yrs in Jun last	McLellan, William D.	
Dunahoo, George	6Dec1853	14 yrs in Mar last	Lowry, James M.	Rescinded 7May1855
Evans, William	3Jan1854	10 yrs	Wright, James	
Jackson, Edmund	4Apr1854	17 yrs in Jan last	Damron, Abraham	Of color
Williams, Alexander	1May1854	6 yrs on 11Apr last	Brunner, Joseph	
Brown, Martha Letecia	4Sept1854	11 yrs on 31May last	Mason, Robert	Of color
Nichols, William	6Nov1854	19 yrs	McCorkle, Samuel B.	Of color. Rescinded 3Sept1855
Osburn, Alexander	7Nov1854	14 yrs in Jan last	Dunwoody, Joseph R.	Resc 4Dec1854
Osburn, Alexander	4Dec1854	14 yrs last Jan	Britten, Margarit	
Osburn, Mahlon	2Jan1855	12 yrs on 17July last	Love, John S.	Of color. Bound as Ausburn 7July1846
Love, Livina	5Feb1855	6 yrs in Dec last	Brown, Charles F.	Of color
Love, Anderson	5Feb1855	6 yrs this inst	Brown, Charles F.	Of color
Coleman, Sally	6Feb1855	1 yr on 19Mar last	Arnold, Thomas D.	Of color
Hinkle, Josiah	6Mar1855	13 yrs on 6Feb last	Huff, Peter	Age corrected 3Apr1855. Ind resc 6May1861, request of John Hinkle, father of Josiah
Hinkle, John	6Mar1855	11 yrs on 7Jun last	Feazell, James H.	Age corrected 3April1855. Canc 8July1856
Hinkle, Elijah	6Mar1855	7 yrs on 8Jun last	Debusk, Jonathan	Age corrected 3April1855. Resc 7Sept1857
Hinkle, Harriet	6Mar1855	6 yrs on 18Aug last	Ren, Margaret	
Conzada	2Apr1855	16 yrs	Britton, Sr, James	Of color
Simpson, George Wash.	2Apr1855	6 yrs on 7Aug last	McMillan, Jeremiah	

Name	Date	Age	Master	Notes
Harris, Jane	2Apr1855	12 yrs	Maloney, John	Of color
Lowry, Mariah	2Apr1855	11 yrs on 6Apr1855	Doak, John W. K.	Rescinded 2July1855
Harris, Henry	3Apr1855	6 yrs	Chockley, Joseph W.	Of color. Rescinded 5May1857
Hinkle, Elizabeth	3Apr1855	9 yrs on 7Sep last	Rankin, Anthony	
Dunahooe, George	7May1855	16 yrs in Mar last	McLelland, William D.	Rescinded 2March1857
Lemmons, Robert	7May1855	8 yrs on 16Sep last	Reed, David	
Watkins, Henry	1Oct1855	9 yrs	Jackson, Thomas	Of color
Sawney, Smith	7Jan1856	8 yrs on 30Jun last	Rose, John W.	Of color. On 2 Aug1858, with sibs Frances Elizabeth & George W., ordered brought from home of Mary Rose, alias Mary Houston. Starving. See Smith C. Frishan
Brown, Eliza	4Feb1856	12 yrs in July last	Crawford, R. A.	Until 19 yrs
Redenhours, James	4Feb1856	15 yrs in July last	Redenhours, George	Rescinded 7Feb1859
Wolaver, Syrena	3Mar1856	13 yrs	Mason, John A.	Dau of Philip Wolaver, dcd 4Feb1856
Wolaver, Polly Ann	3Mar1856	12 yrs on 18May last	Mason, Robert	Dau of Philip Wolaver, dcd 4Feb1856. Resc 3March1862, as Letitia Wolaver
Wolaver, Isaac	3Mar1856	15 yrs on 1Aug last	McMillan, Jeremiah	Son of Philip Wolaver, dcd 4Feb1856
Frishan, Smith Colombus	4Mar1856	8 yrs on 30Jun last	Robinson, William B.	Of color. Alias Smith Sawney. Resc 1Jun1857
Hinkle, John	8July1856	13 yrs on 7Jun last	Wren, Margaret	
Heaton, James	8July1856	7 yrs in Feb last	Feazel, Jacob H.	7July1856*
McCulpin, George M.	4Aug1856	7 yrs	Prather, Jonathan	Alias George Holder
McCulpin, Thomas Alexander	4Aug1856	10 yrs	Brannon, John	Alias Thomas Holder
Brady, Marion	4Aug1856	12 yrs on 11Dec last	Headrick, Elijah W.	8July1856*. Rescinded 7March1864
McCulpin, Keziah	5Aug1856	4 yrs	Jackson, Charles	Female
Heaton, William	1Sep1856	3 yrs	Brumley, Alfred	
Charlton, Joseph E.	6Oct1856	14 yrs on 6Nov last	Hartman, Joseph	
Charlton, Victoria Adalaid	6Oct1856	7 yrs on 8Sep last	Hartman, Joseph	
Drayman, William Franklin	6Oct1856	4 yrs on 14Nov last	Nease, Joseph	Ind canc 7Feb1859*. Already bound in Cocke Co to Noah Renner
Harris, Franklin	6Jan1857	6 yrs on 1Jan1857	McCord, William B.	Of color

Heaton, James	2Feb1857	7 yrs in Feb1857	Easterly, Thomas C.	
Dunahoo, George	2Mar1857	18 yrs on 10Mar 1857	Rumbaugh, James H.	Of color
Coggburn, Livonia	4May1857	8 yrs	Ellenberg, Henry	
Harris, Henry	5May1857	8 yrs in Feb last	Rumbaugh, James H.	Of color
Hetton, James Frederick	1Jun1857	3 yrs on 6July last	Miller, Daniel Y.	Resc 5June1865 on testimony of Azor Koontz, Esq
Morrison, Isaac B.	1Jun1857	11 yrs in Oct last	Henry, Gabriel	Rescinded 1Dec1862, as Barten Morrison
Hinkle, Elijah	7Sep1857	10 yrs on 8Jun last	Biggs, James	Rescinded 7March1864
Pinkston, James Marion	2Nov1857	6 yrs on 2Mar last	Phillips, Gabriel	
Mahog, Willet	2Nov1857	10 yrs on 24Dec last	McGuffin, John	Mulatto boy
Woolhaver, Sarah M.	7Dec1857	2 yrs on 6Jun last	Rambo, Elbert M.	
Ellison, Ella Jane	8Dec1857	5 yrs in May last	Biggs, Elbert	
Brannon, Henry	5Jan1858	13 yrs in Dec last	Busky, John	
Parman, Nancy A. R.	6Jan1858	11 yrs in Sep last	Crawford, Robert A.	
Dennis, Theodore	1Mar1858	4 yrs on 1Oct last	Ottinger, Samuel	
Hester Ann	3May1858	8 yrs in Aug last	Baker, Henry B.	Of color
Carter, Abraham	7Jun1858	6 yrs in Jun 1858	Hankins, John C.	
Harris, Henry	5July1858	9 yrs in Feb last	Kingsley, Roswell E.	Of color
Crum, James G.	5Oct1858	11 yrs on 11Oct1858	Reeves, James G.	
Teague, William W.	1Nov1858	13 yrs on 16Oct last	Link, Ephram	
Manuel, Alpha	3Jan1859	10 yrs on 15Mar last	Johnson, William	Of color
Dennis, Lafayette	7Feb1859	5 yrs on 1Oct last	Harrison, Henry	
Lawson, Thomas Jasper	7Mar1859	10 yrs in Sep last	Wells, Henry E.	
Lawson, George Washington	7Mar1859	10 yrs in Sep last	Harmon, Alexander J.	
Ingle, Jacob	4Apr1859	8 yrs on 12Feb last	Hardin, Cornelius	Resc 3Dec1860. Rebound as Jacob England
Dennis, Dulciana	4Apr1859	7 yrs on 30Nov last	Broyles, James A.	
Irvin, Alexander	4Apr1859	15 yrs on 12Feb last	Caldwell, Thomas	
McCulpin, Hanna Jane	2May1859	8 yrs in Apr last	Brown, Richard W.	
Houlder, James Harmon	2May1859	7 yrs	Rite, Charles H.	
Houlder, William	2May1859	5 yrs	Harold, James W.	

Name	Date	Age	Master	Notes
Hinkle, John	6Jun1859	16 yrs on 1July1859	Kerr, Elizabeth	
Hinkle, Harriet Caroline	6Jun1859	9 yrs on 8Aug last	Kerr, Elizabeth	"Kinkle" in minutes.
McCulpin, Absalon T.	4July1859	3 yrs on 24May last	Alexander, Smith	
Morrison, John	4July1859	3 yrs on 5Apr last	Wolaver, George W.	
Cannon, Isaac	4July1859	11 yrs when bound	Mason, Robert	Of color. Bound by father, William Cannon, on 21Aug1858. Ind recorded.
Cannon, Wesley	4July1859	13 yrs when bound	Mason, John A.	Of color. Bound by father, William Cannon, on 21Aug1858. Ind recorded.
Cannon, Wesley	5July1859	14 yrs	Mason, John A.	Of color.
Russell, George	4Oct1859	16 yrs	Carter, Robert C.	Of color
McConley, James L.	5Mar1860	11 yrs on 4Jan last	Weems, James C.	
Morrison, John	7May1860	4 yrs on 5Apr last	Literal, Robert	
Riley, William	7May1860	5 yrs	Brumley, Alfred	Of color. A prior binding to Brumley rescinded
Feezel, Henry	7May1860	8 yrs	Feezel, Nancy Ann	
Harris, Mary	3July1860	7 yrs in Oct last	Guggenheimer, Henry	
Lawson, Newton McDonald	1Oct1860	15 yrs on 14Apr last	George, Michael	
Satts, Daniel N.	1Oct1860	7 yrs on 1Oct1860	Britten, William H.	
England, Jacob	3Dec1860	8 yrs	Carter, Hugh	Alias Jacob Ingle
Heaton, Thomas	3Dec1860	5 yrs	Brumley, J. C.	Rescinded 1July1867
Johnson, John	4Feb1861	4 yrs in Aug last	Britten, George G.	
Smith, Elizabeth	4Feb1861	10 yrs in Jun last	Hendry, Edward	
Ragsdell, Robert Hardin	4Mar1861	4 yrs on 17Jan last	Crozier, Samuel N.	
Cannon, Isaac	6May1861	13 yrs in Aug last	Mason, John A.	Of color
Morrison, George	2Sep1861	6 yrs	Russell, Thomas	Rescinded 3Feb1862
Waterford, Henn	2Sep1861	20 yrs this day	Hankins, J. C.	Of color
McFarland, William	2Sep1861	17 yrs	Britten, Sr, James	Of color. Bound by mother, Clara McFarland, free woman of color
McFarland, Andrew	2Sep1861	15 yrs	Britten, Sr, James	Of color. Bound by mother, Clara McFarland, free woman of color

Bensen, William	7Oct1861	5 yrs	Murphey, E. S.	
Henry, Oscar	7Oct1861	17 yrs on 14Oct last	Vestal, C. M.	Of color
Mathis, Calvin	7Oct1861	16 yrs on 1May1861	Creamer, James	Of color
Shannon, Harriet	7Oct1861	13 yrs	Vance, William K.	Of color. Ind resc 3June1862 as Harriet Showman
Manual, George	8Oct1861	19 yrs	Murphey, Thomas J.	Of color
Cavener, John	4Nov1861	8 yrs on 23May last	Cavener, William	
Coleman, Mary Adelaide	5Nov1861	8 yrs on 14Mar last	Arnold, Thomas D.	Of color. Age changed to 6 yrs on 6Jan1862
Coleman, Syntha Ann	5Nov1861	5 yrs on 16Mar last	Arnold, T. D.	Of color. Age changed to 3 yrs on 6Jan1862
Coleman, Henry Montgomerty	5Nov1861	Born 10Jan last	Arnold, T. D.	Of color
Henry, Clary	2Dec1861	6 yrs	Brumley, J. C.	Free girl of color. Resc 7Apr1862
Warrick, William	6Jan1862	14 yrs on 15July last	Morrow, Ebenezer	Of color. Resc 3June1867
Russell, Malen	7Jan1862	18 yrs on 6May last	Johnson, Abraham S.	Of color
Brown, William Alexander	3Feb1862	13 yrs on 10Apr last	Simpson, George B.	
McAlister, John	7Apr1862	7 yrs in Oct last	Campbell, Adam P.	Resc 6Jun1870
Showman, Harriet	3Jun1862	14 yrs	Fleming, James H.	Of color
Simpson, Lewis Richard	7July1862	4 yrs on 2Jun last	Ross, John A.	Rescinded 7Aug1866
Magee, Robert	7July1862	9 yrs	Creamer, George	Brother Andrew also ordered to Court 5May1862*
Harris, Elkanah	1Sep1862	10 yrs on 5Sep1862	Morrow, Ebenezer	Of color. Resc 3June1867
Peneriah?, Josiah A.	6Oct1862	12 yrs on 10Aug last	Hays, Thomas	
Walker, James	6Oct1862	14 yrs on 15Sept1862	Thomason, Thomas	
Deputy, John	6Oct1862	7 yrs	Beals, Daniel	
Deputy, James Franklin	6Oct1862	4 yrs in 1862	Beals, Daniel	
Evans, Moses	3Nov1862	7 yrs	Oliphant, William S.	Rescinded 5Feb1866
Fillers, Martha	1Dec1862	2 yrs	Wagner, Henry	
Evans, Richard	1Dec1862	4 yrs	Henry, Gabriel	
Magee, Anderson	5Jan1863	7 yrs	Hoyal, James O.	
Magee, William	5Jan1863	11 yrs	Cowan, John D.	
Heaton, James V.	2Feb1863	13 yrs on 10Feb1863	Russell, William H.	
Mitchell, Mary Ann	6July1863	12 yrs on 21July1863	Hacker, Jacob A.	

Name	Date	Age	Master	Notes
Shackleford, John D.	6July1863	9 yrs on 19May last	Henry, James	
Shackleford, Adaline	6July1863	7 yrs last Feb	Henry, James	
Dinsmore, George	3Aug1863	5 yrs in June last	Hannah, George	
Ashley, John	2Nov1863	11 yrs	Ervin, James C.	
Shackleford, Mitchell	1Feb1864	4 yrs	Evans, James	
Holland, Matilda	4Apr1864	9 yrs	Brumley, David	
Walker, Lee	5Sep1864	10 yrs on 17Sept1864	Lane, Samuel	
Swatzell, Joseph	4Dec1865	10 yrs on 9Dec present	Ervin, James C.	
Campbell, William C.	4Dec1865	7 yrs on 22May last	Wright, James	
Allen, Richard Alexander	1Jan1866	4 yrs on 7Feb next	Carter, James W.	Resc 1July1867 as John R. Alexander. Returned to mother
England, Jacob	1Jan1866	13 yrs in Feb last	Keny, William	
Swatzell, John A.	2Jan1866	12 yrs on 30Oct last	Lovitt, Charles	
Swatzell, Jacob	2Jan1866	14 yrs on 21Feb last	Lovitt, Charles A.	
Swaney, Joseph Bly	2Apr1866	4 yrs in July last	Winkle, John	
Smith, Andrew Johnson	7May1866	17 yrs on 6Sep last	Brown, William F.	
Brown, Joseph H.	7May1866	7 on 20Oct last	Brown, William F.	
Pickering, Mary Elizabeth	4Jun1866	6 yrs on 3Sep last	Beals, Jonathan	
Myers, John E.	4Jun1866	14 yrs on 20Apr last	Ball, Lewis B.	
Baker, John B.	2July1866	9 yrs in Oct last	Brubaker, Henry	Resc 2March1874. Ranaway
Jones, Rufus	1Oct1866	12 yrs	Bruner, Samul	
Fulkes, Augustus B.	1Oct1866	14 yrs	Westmoreland, N. B.	
Fulkes, Deaderick A.	1Oct1866	12 yrs	Westmoreland, N. B.	
Gooden, Mary E.	5Nov1866	6 yrs on 12Jan last	Brown, William A.	Resc 4Apr1870
Baker, Andrew J.	5Nov1866	4 yrs in Mar last	McCoy, William H.	Resc 1Apr1867, mother and McCoy agreeing
Fulkes, Nicholas N.	3Dec1866	8 yrs	Westmoreland, N. B.	
Adase?, Pinkney	9Jan1867	17 yrs	Farnsworth, Henry A.	Of color
Reynolds, Margaret	4Feb1867	6 yrs	Gentry, Lewis	

Reynolds, Mary Jane	4Feb1867	8 yrs	Gentry, Lewis	To be delivered to Lewis Gentry and Elizabeth Gentry, her mother
Small, William A.	4Mar1867	12 yrs on 6Jun last	Lewis, William V.	
Carter, James	2Apr1867	12 yrs on 1Jun last	Spencer, George M.	Resc 2Nov1868. Of color
Susong, John	1July1867	8 yrs	Susong, Alfred	
Richardson, John S.	2Sep1867	10 yrs on 1Jun last	Crawford, Isaac	Canc 7Feb1870, as John Richards. Mutually agreed
Hays, Thomas E.	4Nov1867	5 yrs on 26Oct last	Newberry, Joseph	Sparling Bowman, Security. See Elijah Hays
Keller, John	2Dec1867	14 yrs	Keller, Samuel	Of color. John Keller, security. 7Jan1868* Resc 5May1868, Samuel dcd
Keller, Betsey	2Dec1867	12 yrs	Keller, Samuel	Of color. John Keller, security. 7Jan1868* Resc 5May1868, Samuel dcd
Williams, John	7Dec1867	1 yr in 1867	Williams, Warren	
Jones, Rufus	6Apr1868	12 yrs	Smith, Cornelius	A. Smith, Security
Jones, Sarah Jane	6Apr1868	6 yrs on 4Feb1868	Anderson, Lewis	
Reeve, Samuel R.	1Jun1868	10 yrs	Dyer, John C.	
Ricker, William S.	6July1868	2 yrs on 28Jan last	Ruble, William J.	
Harrington, Newton Carroll	6Oct1868	10 yrs on 7Feb last	Butler, W. A. T. J.	
Farnsworth, Manning	3Nov1868	12 yrs on 18Aug last	Farnsworth, Henry A.	
Farnsworth, Elliot	3Nov1868	9 yrs	Farnsworth, Henry A.	
Farnsworth, Jason	3Nov1868	7 yrs	Farnsworth, Henry A.	
Sprinkle, Manning	3Nov1868	10 yrs on 13Aug last	Ripley, David S.	
Sprinkle, Charles W.	3Nov1868	7 yrs on 23May last	Ripley, David S.	Resc 5May1872. Ripley deceased
Pruet, James	4Jan1869	4 yrs	Susong, Andrew D.	7Dec11868*
Pruet, Martha	6Jan1869	8 yrs on 3May last	Woods, Levi	
Wilson, Henry	2Aug1869	17 yrs in Mar last	Smith, Nathan B.	
Mattocks, Joseph W.	2Aug1869	9 yrs on 22July last	Barnes, Leander	
Jones, Silva E.	5Oct1869	13 yrs	Brumley, J. C.	Female
Harrison, Levi	1Nov1869	15 yrs on 20Jun last	Lemans, Washington A.	Resc 3Jan1871. Ranaway
Harrison, Andrew N.	7Feb1870	12 yrs in Oct last	Kirk, James F.	Resc 5June1871, Ranaway

Name	Date	Age	Master	Notes
Grant, John	2May1870	3 yrs	Varner, Susannah	
Ludmilk, A. J.	6Jun1870	5 yrs in Apr last	Woodward, P. T.	Resc 5Dec1870. Ranaway
Mayfield, Noah	6Jun1870	12 yrs on 14Sep last	Huff, Barbara	
Carleton, William	6Jun1870	4 yrs on 15Nov last	Fresham, A. S.	
Morelack, Franklin	5July1870	9 yrs on 24Dec last	Morelack, Jerry A.	
Johnson, John	5July1870	2 yrs on 25Dec last	Clem, William T.	
Bible, Sarah A.	9Nov1870	4 yrs in Dec last	Ervin, James C.	Alias Sarah A. Ervin. Indenture voided, returned to father, George Bible
Woods, James L.	6Feb1871	10 yrs on 13Mar last	Dearstone, J. W.	Resc 2March1874. Ranaway
Dison, Sarah Jane	6Feb1871	3 yrs in Nov last	Gibson, Thomas	
Evans, George	3Apr1871	13 yrs in Sep last	Renner, John H. (or B.)	
Owens, William N.			Huff, Barbara	Resc 2Oct1871. Ranaway
Owens, George			Renner, John	Resc 2Oct1871. Ranaway
Deputy, James	1Jan1872	13 yrs	Dodd, W. J.	
Deputy, John	1Jan1872	16 yrs	Brooks, Marian W.	
Forsinger, George W.	2Jan1872	5 yrs on 26Jan last	Dicks, Henry	
Hays, Elijah	4Mar1872	11 yrs	Newberry, Joseph	Elias Newberry replaces Sparling Brown as Security
English, Franklin	1Apr1872	10 yrs on 25Dec last	English, Isam	
Foster, Susan	5Aug1872		Morrow, Adam	Of color. Ebenezer Morrow, security
Sprinkle, Charles M.	2Sep1872	12 yrs on 23May last	Wells, H. E.	
Blazer, Josiah	3Feb1873	5 yrs on 1Apr last	Blazer, William	
Fincher, Andrew	7Apr1873	11 yrs in Jan last	Stephens, B. M.	Prob son of Martha Fincher 2Dec1872*
Carter, William	7Apr1873	7 yrs on 26Jan last	Harmon, James R.	
Robinson, Charles	8Apr1873	5 yrs	Morris, Sillie	George Brown to turn over two trunks of Charles' clothes
Henegar, Charles	3Nov1873	9 yrs on 10Apr last	Gamman, Richard	William Gamman, Security
Cox, George W.	2Feb1874	8 yrs on 5Jun last	Davis, Thomas	
Bell, Millie	7Apr1874	4 yrs on 15Oct last	Arnold, Charles	
Pratt, Charles	4May1874	15 yrs on 8May last	Caldwell, Reuben	
Malaney, Harvey	5Oct1874	14 yrs in Mar last	Bible, David	

Malaney, Sevier	5Oct1874	4 yrs in Jun last	Bible, David	
Easterly, Francis M.	2Nov1874	7 yrs in Nov last	Saulsbury, James M.	
Smith, William	5Apr1875	16 yrs on 10Aug last	Morelock, Henry S.	
Henson, Mary Ann	4May1875	4 yrs	Thomason, Thomas	
Bailey, David	5July1875	13 yrs	Justice, D. K.	
Ruble, Marcus	6Sep1875	4 yrs on 16July last	Rambo, E. M.	
Brown, William	6Dec1875	14 yrs	Self, D. K.	
Landers, John	6Dec1875	3 yrs in Feb last	Sterm?, John F.	
Temple, Prince	8Feb1876	12 yrs	Smith, G. M.	
Patterson, William			Morelock, Henry S.	Indenture rescinded 6Mar1876. Runaway
Taylor, David			Justice, Daniel	Indenture rescinded 6Mar1876. Runaway
Bullington, Laura	6Mar1876	5 yrs	Morelock, Thomas	
Bullington, W. M.	6Mar1876	3 yrs	Morelock, Thomas	Male
Bowers, Davis	3July1876	9 yrs	Park, John A.	Son of Jacob Bowers, Jr, dcd 1May1876. Jacob Kyker, sec., released 4Aug1879
Coggins, Edward	3Jun1876	6 yrs	Grace, James K.	
Scudgon, Andrew			Bird, D. A.	Indenture rescinded 3July1876. Runaway
Ross, William	2Oct1876	11 yrs on 25Dec last	Hannah, John W.	
Ellenberg, John F.	6Nov1876	12 yrs on 7Jun last	Cox, William	
Fowler, Martha	8Nov1876	7 yrs	King, John H.	
Fowler, James W.	6Feb1877	9 yrs	Hunter, Rufus	
McLain, Daniel H.	2Apr1877	15 yrs on 25Feb last	Jones, Lafayette	
McLain, Joseph Grant	2Apr1877	14 yrs on 10Dec last	Wattenbarger, George A.	Enoch Wattenbarger, security. Resc 4Feb1878
Reynolds, Willam H.	2Apr1877	11 yrs on 3May last	Hartman, Joseph	
Reynolds, Ruth Malinda	4Jun1877	9 yrs on 27Dec last	Tucker, Lucretia	
Tipton, Robert C.	4Jun1877	6 yrs on 28Aug next	Helton, John L.	
Tipton, Elbert W.	4Jun1877	4 yrs on 12May last	Heilton, John L.	
Murrel, John	4Jun1877	8 yrs on 1Jan last	Pierce, A. H.	
Monroe, Houston	7Jan1878	3 yrs on 13Oct1877	Low, John R.	
Winters, Joseph	4Feb1878	5 yrs on 19Mar last	Gregory, A. C.	

Name	Date	Age	Master	Notes
Woods, William C.	6May1878	3 yrs on 17July last	Cooper, John T.	
Ruble, Perry W.	5Aug1878	6 yrs in Feb last	Reave?, Sophia	
Malone, Samuel	2Sep1878	5 yrs on 25Nov last	Weems, W. D.	J. D. Brown, J. R. Weems, securities
Smelcer, Frederick	2Dec1878	9 yrs on 1Mar last	Evans, James	
Smelcer, Joseph R.	3Feb1879	13 yrs on 7Feb next	Gosnell, J. E.	
Holley, George	3Mar1879	11 yrs in Apr last	McNew, John B.	
Elenbaugh, Edward	7Apr1879	7 yrs	Ottinger, W. A.	

Hamblen County

Name	Date	Age	Master	Notes
Brown, Isaac	8Nov1870	8 yrs	Kennon, Patsey	Both of color. Resc 2Jan1870, request of GF Abraham Crosby. Father living
Gill, Ben	3Jan1871		Flynn, M. P.	Waggon work. Until age 20
Carmichael, Richard	3July1871	13 yrs	Robertson, Samuel	Orphan, of African decent
Kenley, Nancy M.	1July1872	8 yrs on 9May1872	Pullen, E.	Until 20 yrs. Req of Mother, Mary D. Kenley
Wells, Andy	2Sept1872	9 yrs	Martin, R. B.	Req of father, Winton Wells
Golden, William	5May1873	16 yrs	Haun, Jacob	Orphan. Resc 3Nov1873, Golden having left Haun
Cobb, Alexander	6Oct1874	8 yrs	Cobb, Peter	Both of color
Hopkins, George C.	5Jan1876		Patterson, W. L.	
Miller, Ann	5June1876		Burts, M. L. (Mrs)	Of color
Nite, James F.	6Nov1876	5 yrs	Senter, D. W. C.	Abandoned by father, Doc Nite. Mother, Rachel L. Nite, a very poor person, assents
Tate, Ann	1Sept1879	9 yrs on 27Oct1879	Lonas, James H. & C. K. (wife)	Until age 21. Both parents dead.

Hawkins County

Name	Date	Age	Master	Notes
Chapman, William	6June1836	10 yrs last Feb	Wright, Daniel	
Chapman, John	6June1836	12 yrs last Christmas	Wright, Daniel	
Wright, Henry	5Sept1836	15 yrs 7 mo	Cain, Jr, Hugh	
Warren, Jacob	4Oct1836	15 yrs	Benson, Abraham L.	Orphan
Martin, Saloma	7Sept1857	4 yrs	Rogers, David S.	Female orphan
Smiley, Robert	4Jan1858	8 yrs	Gouldey, James N.	
Hill, Mary E. J.	1Feb1858	5 yrs	Braswell, John	until 21 yrs
Newcom, John	6Oct1858	6 yrs on 6May1858	Horton, Thomas	Farming. Son of Nancy Newcom*
Killingsworth, Joseph	1Nov1858	4 yrs	Young, James H.	
Davis, Amanda	1Nov1858	7 yrs	Williams, William	Female, until age 21. Resc 5Feb1866*
Jones, James	7Feb1859	15 yrs	Larkin, William	
McLaine, Warden	7Feb1859	2 yrs on 29July1859	Shropshire, James	
Jones, George	7Feb1859	13 yrs	Farmer, William N.	
Jones, Robert	7Feb1859	12 yrs	Davis, Payton H.	
Jones, David	7Feb1859	8 yrs	Davis, Payton H.	
Long, William Jasper	7Mar1859	14 yrs on 26Dec1858	Horner, H. B.	
Sanson, Amos	6June1859	1 yr 9 mo last 29May	Pearson, William I.	Req. of mother, Elizabeth Sanson
Hale, Mark	4July1859	16 yrs on 29 May last	Wells, George W.	Of color
Newcum, John	4July1859	6 yrs in April1859	Larkin, William	Of color.*
McLane, Gordon	5July1859	2 yrs on 29 July1859	Shropshire, James	
Courtny, Noah	1Aug1859	12 yrs	Miller, Jacob	Req.of mother, Sally Courtry
Russell, George	7Nov1859	16 yrs	Lee, William G.	Blacksmithing. Indigent, mulatto
Russell, Jim	5Dec1859	15 yrs on 1Sept1859	Hughs, Jr., Cornelius	
Russell, Matthew	5Dec1859	10 yrs on 29Nov1859	Beal, Elias	
Sam	6Dec1859	10 or 11 yrs	Parvil(?), George R.	Of color
Morris, John	2Jan1860	4 yrs	Walker, James C.	
Eaton, Robert	2Jan1860	8 yrs 5 mo	Anderson, David D.	

Name	Date	Age	Master	Notes
Sanson, Amos	6Feb1860	2 yrs in Sept1859	Pearson, William I.	Of color
Jewell, George	6Feb1860	14 yrs	McFarland, Oliver	
Burchan, Isaac S. G.	6Feb1860	6 yrs	Kinsinger, John	
Mabe, George	5Mar1860	14 yrs on 17May1860	Pearson, William I.	
Smith, Moses	5Mar1860	12 yrs on 3Dec1859	Starnes, John	
Frost, William Winfield?	5Mar1860	6 yrs in Jan1860	Cope, John W.	
Tawsey, Sam	5Mar1860	10 yrs	McKinney, Charles I.	Of color
Manis, Minerva	5Mar1860	15 yrs	Bussile, B___ W.	
Parker, Pleasant L.	2July1860	4 yrs on 6Jan1860	Charles, John N.	
Eaton, Samuel P.	1Oct1860	11 yrs	Hendrick, C. S.	
Breeden, John	2Oct1860	14 yrs	Shiffey, D. M.	Prev. bound to P. A. Cobb
Mitchell, Robert	2Oct1860	18 yrs	Peters, O___ W.	
Watts, Joshua W.	3Nov1860	11 yrs	Bewley, John W.	
Watts, George W.	3Nov1860	9 yrs	Bewley, John W.	
Ballard, Lucinda Catharine	3Nov1860	7 yrs	Wright, Elizabeth	Sibs. Richard, George. 1Oct1860* 5Mar1861*
Winegar, Nicholas	3Dec1860	6 or 7 yrs	Richardson, Eli	
Beckner, James Thomas	3Dec1860	10 yrs	Walker, James H.	
Jewell, George	3Dec1860	14 yrs	Arnold, William M.	
Bowman, Daniel	3Feb1861	10 yrs	Derrick, Enoch	
Manis, Minerva	1Apr1861	16 yrs	Burrell, B. L.	
Bowman, James	1Apr1861	10 yrs	Derrick, Nancy	
Eatons, James	1Apr1861	5 yrs 4 Mo	Anderson, David D.	
Pellifort, George G.	1Apr1861	1 yr 6 mo	Courtney, Jesse	Consent of mother
Dean, Eliza	1July1861	14 yrs	McFaddin, Joseph F.	
Hamilton, John	2Sept1861	7 years	Arnott, William M.	
Hartley, Floyd	2Sept1861	5 yrs	Herd, Elen	Bastard in possession of Nancy Shanks
Eaton, Samuel P.	2Sept1861		Arnott, Sally	

Courtney, Annis Rathbone	4Feb1861	6 yrs	Sizemon, Solomon B.	Until 21 yrs. Resc 2Sept1861
Courtney, Annis	2Sept1861	8 yrs	Courtney, Jesse	Until age 21. Female.
Mallett, Malvina	7Oct1861		Brown, O. M.	Until age 21. Req of Levi Mallett, father
Mallett, Mary Jane	7Oct1861		Sizemon, S. B.	Req of Levi Mallett, father
Mallett, John	7Oct1861		Sizemon, S. B.	Until age 21. Req of Levi Mallett, father
Mallett, Jane Amandon	7Oct1861		Bagley, John	Until age 21. Req of Levi Mallett, father
McGlaughlin, Lawrence	7Oct1861	6 yrs	King, William I.	
Hartley, Floyd	7Oct1861	6 yrs	Shanks, Jacob M.	
Wallace, Elkana	7Jan1862	10 yrs	Mitchell, Frederick E.	Male
Frazier, John	3Feb1862	14 yrs	Starnes, John	
Fawbush, James Harvey	7April1862	13 yrs	Sheppard, William	
Fawbush, Andrew J.	7April1862	11 yrs	Spears, James	
Mann, George	7July1862		Arnold, Harvey	
Bates, Henrietta Elizabeth	7July1862	5 yrs	Webster, Jr, John	
Spears, Sarah Elizabeth	3Nov1862	2 yrs 7 mo	Courtney, Jesse	Until age 20. Taken from James Spears, stepfather*
Wilson, Joseph	1Dec1862	5 yrs 6 mo	Charles, W. W.	
Fletcher, Andrew	2Feb1863	9 yrs	Derrick, Marvel	
McGloughlin, James L.	2Feb1863	7 yrs	Johnston, James	
Russell, John Morris	6Apr1863	13 yrs	Stacey, R. H.	
Smith, Mary Ellen	6July1863		Fry, Sarah	Until age 21. Req of Elizabeth Coldwell, mother
Hannah	8Aug1865	10 yrs	Morrisett, R. M.	Of color
Sally	8Aug1865	8 yrs	Morrisett, R. M.	Of color
Appleberry, Fernsil	8Aug1865	13 yrs	Phillips, Isaac	
Sally	8Aug1865	10 yrs	Chismette, Thomas H.	Of color
Charley	8Aug1865	11 yrs	Chismette, Thomas H.	Of color
Daniel	8Aug1865	15 yrs	Shanks, John	Of color
Julia	8Aug1865	14 yrs	Shanks, John	Of color
Matilda	4Sept1865	10 yrs	Payne, John G.	Of color

Name	Date	Age	Master	Notes
Sam	4Sept1865	8 yrs	Payne, John G.	Of color
Amanda L.	4Sept1865	14 yrs	Cockreham, D. H.	Of color
John	4Sept1865	11 yrs	Cockreham, D. H.	Of color
Susan	2Oct1865	7 yrs	Davis, Hezekiah	Until age 21. Of color.
Amanda	2Oct1865	7 yrs	Davis, Hezikiah	Until age 21. Of color
Esther	2Oct1865	5 yrs	Davis, Hezekiah	Until age 21. Of color
Frank	6Nov1865	15 yrs	Riley, John D.	Of color
George	6Nov1865	14 yrs	Riley, John D.	Of color
Fleming	6Nov1865	4 yrs	Riley, John D.	Of color
Margaret	6Nov1865	10 yrs	Dodson, Raleigh	Until age 21. Of color
Martha	1Jan1866	12 yrs	Hampton, A. P.	Of color
Sarah	5Feb1866	9 yrs	Simpson, Elizabeth (Mrs)	
Perry	5Feb1866	12 yrs	Simpson, Elizabeth (Mrs)	
Augustus	6Feb1866	7 yrs	Starnes, John E.	Freed slave
James	6Feb1866	10 yrs	Payne, John G.	Of color. Freed slave
Samuel	6Feb1866	8 yrs	Payne, John G.	Of color. Freed slave
Tildy	6Feb1866	10 yrs	Payne, John G.	Of color. Freed slave
Harlen, Benjamin	5Mar1866		Harlen, Thomas	Of color
Gallenwaters, Lucretia	5Mar1866		Gallenwaters, Polly	Of color
Edgar	7May1866	12 yrs	McCauley, Eliza	Of color
Morris	7May1866	10 yrs	McCauley, Eliza	Of color
Spears, Sarah E.	7May1866	8 yrs	Kensinger, William P.	Until age 21
Amanda	7May1866	10 yrs	Tomlinson, Thomas	Of color
Manis, May (?Mary)	4June1866	8 yrs	Sopers, Mary A.	
Jacob	4June1866	9 yrs	Rodgers, Matelar	Of color
Stuart, William	6Aug1866		Stuart, John C.	Of color
Stuart, Caledonia	6Aug1866		Stuart, John C.	Until age 21. Of color
Riley, Patton	6Aug1866		Beal, Joseph J.	
Johnson, Henry	3Sep1866	12 yrs	Johnson, A. D.	Of color

Blevins, William	4Jan1867	10 yrs	Blevins, John	Of color
Manis, James	7Jan1867	14 yrs	Bails, CarterM.	
Roark, James B.	7Jan1867	4 yrs 7 mo	Craver, William	
Griffin, Moses	5Feb1867	15 yrs	Critz, Philip & Kinkead, Philip C.	Of color
Baker, Andrew J.	3June1867	6 yrs	Amis, James A.	
Bailey, John	3June1867	8 yrs	Bails, A. W.	
Anderson, Nancy	5Aug1867	11 yrs		Until age 21.
Edson, Amister	5Aug1867	8 yrs	Starnes, Jackson J.	Of color.
Edson, Lawrence	5Aug1867	6 yrs	Starnes, Pleasant H.	Of color
Anderson, Elizabeth	2Sept1867	4 yrs	Shanks, John F.	Until age 21.
Jones, Tabitha	7Oct1867		Bailey, John B.	Until age 21, or until she marries.
Munsul, Martha	7Oct1867	6 yrs	Hanks, Franklin	Until 21 yrs. White
Anderson, Daniel	2Nov1867	13 yrs	Rogers, Harbert S.	
Bowman, Madison	2Nov1867	12 yrs	Brown, J. C.	
Winninger,	2Nov1867	13 yrs	Pace, James R.	Female. Until 21 yrs, unless sooner married.
Frausen, Anias	6Apr1868	8 yrs		Of color
Leroy, Ellen	6Apr1868	6 yrs	Vaughan, John	
Davis, Amanda	4May1868	8 yrs	Rice, J. W.	Of color
Leroy, Joseph	4May1868	7 yrs	Johnston, Joseph R.	
Manis, John	1June1868	12 yrs	Walker, Winton	
Wilden, James C.	1June1868	18 mo	Snyder, Robert	
Draper, Robert	2Nov1868	13 yrs	Cobb, P. A.	
Batey, Edward	7Dec1868	12 yrs	Davis, Henry	Of color
Milles, Mary E.	3May1869	10 yrs		Of color
Green, John	5July1869	14 yrs	Larkin, William	
Klepper, William	5July1869	10 yrs	Klepper, B. M.	
Klepper, Josephene	5July1869	8 yrs	Klepper, B. M.	
Mary Ann	2Aug1869	2 yrs	Netherland, John	Of color
Maddox, Levi H.	6Sept1869	13 yrs	Lynch, George W.	Of color

Name	Date	Age	Master	Notes
Kyle, Walter Scott	6Sept1869	14 yrs	Blevins, John	Of color
Moon, Daniel	6Sept1869	7 yrs	Bloomer, Isaac	
Dodson, Margaret	6Sept1869	14 yrs	Dodson, R.	
Dodson, Vina	6Sept1869	6 yrs	Dodson, R.	
Clarkson, Edward	4Octf1869	12 yrs	Etter, John	Of color
Mountcastle, Joseph	4Oct1869	4 yrs	Mountcastle, George	Of color
Hale, Silus	1Nov1869	12 yrs	Beal, Joseph	
Sizemour, Parolee	1Nov1869	4 yrs	Sizemour, James W.	Female
Cormichel, William	7Mar1870	8 yrs	Cormichel, Henderson	
Alex	4Apr1870	8 yrs	Charles, Sallie A.	Of color
Catharine	4Apr1870	7 yrs	Charles, Sallie A.	Of color
Sizemon, Rebeca J.	4Apr1870	9 yrs	Sizemon, Thomas P.	Until 21 yrears. ? Dau of William O. Sizemon 2May1870*
Harlin, Andy	2May1870	10 yrs	Gorgey, Gabriel M.	Of color
Unknown	3Oct1870	10yrs	Ketchum, B. F.	Name not filled in.
Hart, John	3Oct1870	8 yrs	Bradshaw, George	
Pippen, Robert	3Oct1870	5 yrs	Bradshaw, George	
Light, Reuben	6Feb1871		Murdock, Wright	
Campbell, Joel H.	6Mar1871	9 yrs	Crawford, Ellinor	
Anderson, William	3Apr1871	6 yrs	Larkin, Mina	
Lincoln, Israel	3July1871		Fry, Sarah	
Harrington, Pleasant	7Aug1871	12 yrs	Couch, Elinezer	
Proffitt, Amanda	2Oct1871	13 yrs	Proffitt, Lucy	Until age 21. Of color
Humphrey, Samuel	2Oct1871	11 yrs	Dyer, R. F.	
Bouman, Ellen	1Jan1872	7 yrs	Barrett, Thomas	
Parnell, Mary Ann	4Mar1872	5 yrs	Collins, S. D.	Until age 21
Robbins, Henry	6May1872	10 yrs	Lawson, McLellen	Of color. Resc 3June1872*. Stepfather, John Looney
Blevins, Henry Clay	6May1872	11 yrs	Blevins, John	
Humphrey, Jacob	4Nov1872	14 yrs	Williams, J. N.	Canc, request of mother, Susan Humphrey. 2Nov1872
Lawson, Charles	4Nov1872	8 yrs	Rogers, A. L.	

Humphrey, Samuel	4Nov1872	12 yrs	Wright, Jr, Joseph	Canc, request of mother, Susan Humphrey. 2Nov1872
Orrich, George	7Jan1873	10 yrs	Orrich, R. B.	
Allen, C. A.	7Apr1873	3 yrs	Parrot, Robert	
Mabs, Frank(?)	7July1873	16 yrs	Huntsman, G. W.	
Boyd, Lavidgo	1Sept1873	14 yrs	Anderson, Ampudia	
Luster, George	1Dec1873	2 yrs	Spears, E. M.	
Darter, John	5Jan1874	13 yrs	Davis, John	Of color
Lien(?), Israel	6Apr1874	7 yrs	Watterson, Richard	
Snapp, Harriet	1Jun1874	7 yrs	Charles, William	Child of George Snapps (?)*
Snapp, Sarah	1June1874	11 yrs		Child of George Snapps (?)*
Snapp, Jacob	1June1874	13 yrs	Powell, E. D.	Child of George Snapps (?)*
Snapp, Margaret	1June1874	9 yrs	Powel, Sam P.	Child of George Snapps (?)*
Lanson, Martin T.			Jenkins, Parson	Ind resc 7Sept1874, request of mother
Richards, Betsy	2Nov1874	7 yrs	Ball, Wiley M.	
Lawson, Ogen	2Nov1874	8 yrs 7 mo	Bloomer, William	
Burchfield, Samuel	1Feb1875	4 yrs	Shepherd, Thomas	
Hamblen, Orlena	4June1875	8 yrs	McCarty, Buina? V.	Orphan. Of color
Hamblen, Margaret	4June1875	11 yrs	Starnes, J. J.	Of color
Hamblen, James	4June1875	12 yrs	Powel, R. F.	Of color
Milburn, William E.	3Jan1876	10 yrs	Bryant, A. J.	
Smith, George	6Mar1876	1 yr 4 mo	Walters, John	
Petty, John	2Oct1876	7 yrs	Portrum, John	
Chambers, Cain	4Dec1876	11 yrs	Starnes, J. J.	Of color
Kyle, Jim	1Jan1877	7 yrs	Kyle, R. M.	Of color
Edens, Malissa	5Feb1877	6 yrs		
Madisen, Eldridge	7May1877		Patterson, John	
Manis,	7May1877		Manis, Elbert	
Belsher(?), Harvey	8May1877	11 yrs	Starnes, John E.	
Kersey, Elijah	6Aug1877	14 yrs on 25Sept1877	Tipton, A. D.	
Smith, John	5Sept1877	11 yrs 6 mo	Wells, Eldridge	

Name	Date	Age	Master	Notes
Lawson, Noah B.	4Feb1878	6 yrs on 8Nov1877	Charles, William A.	Approval of mother, Eliza Jane Lawson
Cagley, William D.	4Mar1878	11 yrs on 15Apr1878	Wells, William C.	Approval of mother [not named]
Tyra, William R.	4Mar1878	7 yrs	Morrisett, Richard M.	
Young, Charles	2Sep1878	7 yrs	Baines, John M.	Aband by Father, David Young. Mother, Rebecca, dead
Young, Sarah E.	2Sep1878	5 yrs	Baines, John M.	Aband by Father, David Young. Mother, Rebecca, dead
Young, Lenora	2Sep1878	3 yrs	Baines, John M.	Aband by Father, David Young. Mother, Rebecca, dead
Young, Augusta	2Sep1878	2 mo	Baines, John M.	Aband by Father, David Young. Mother, Rebecca, dead
Lawson, McLellan	3Mar1879	16 yrs 7 mo	Pearson, C. C.	
Everhart, Mary Laura	5Apr1880	6 yrs 3 mo	Smith, George	
Richards, William	6Apr1880	3 yrs	Odell, John	
Cline, Fred	10Sep1883	9 yrs	Charles, Jacob W.	
Hamblen, William S.	8July1884	14 yrs 11 mo	White, Robert	

Jefferson County

Name	Date	Age	Master	Notes
Tucker, William	12Aug1793	2 years	Morgan, Richard	
Drain, David	May1794	17 years	Graham, George	Gunsmith
Jones, Andrew	May1796	13 years	Carson, David	
Hamilton, Mary	Oct1799		Knabb, Jacob	Orphan
Givens, David	Oct 1799		Bradshaw, William	
Baily, Nelly	April 1800	8 years	Inman, Wiliam H.	Orphan
Black, Margaret	Jan 1798	6 years	McGuire, Cornelius	Orphan
Black, John	Jan 1798	9 years	Hunter, Samuel	Orphan
Going, Haulse? Ellis	Jan1801		Jones, John	Female
Beird, Rueben	Jan1803		Humpston, Edward	Orphan
Cox, Bartlett	Jan1805	7 years	Mitchell, Nathaniel	Hatter. Orphan
Jones, Isbell	21Jan1806	8 years	Laymon, Jacob	Orphan. Female
Halloway, Rachael	21Jan1806	12 years	Coons, Michael	Resc 24April1806
Williams, Nancy	18July1809		Moyers, David	Ind resc. Dau of Mary Williams

Glossup, Ruth	18July1809	7 years	Longacre Jr., John	
Jordan, Moses	19July1809	5 years	Coons, Jr., Michael	
Brown, John	10Sep1810	8 yrs	Ford, John	Orphan
Meredith, William	14Sep1813	3 years	Carson, John L.	Orphan. Resc 14Sept1829
Tredway, Isaac	14Sep1813	5 years	Duncan, John	
Tredway, Eliza	14Sep1813	3 years	Leith, Ebenezer	
Ryan, William	12Dec1814	11 years	McGee, James	Son of Elizabeth Ryan. Canc 13June1815
Petty, Eliza	12Jun1815	5 years	Hodge, Drury	
Bates, Calib	11Mar1816	15 years	Hayworth, Johnathan	*11Dec1817, 13Mar1818
Fairer, Henry	11Mar1816	16 years	Franklin, Lewis	Alias Gann. Son of Eliz. Gann 17Jun1815
Gann, Solomon	11Mar1816	12 years	Branner, Jr., Michael	Son of Eliz. Gann 17Jun1815
Fairer, Alexander	11Mar1816	18 yrs on 1 Dec last	Collins, Francis	Alias Gann. Son of Eliz. Gann 17Jun1815
Gann, Abraham	11Mar1816	10 years	Branner, Casper	Son of Eliz. Gann 17June1815. Resc 10March1824
Givans, James	11Mar1816	2 years last May	Coons, Michael	
Burket, Christley	11June1816	10 years	Sunderland, Solomon	Alias Christopher Burket
Bell, Jenny	9Sept1816		Findley, William	
Grace, John	9Sept1816		Ranken, Jr., Thomas	
Grace, Richard	9Sept1816		Ranken, John	Resc 11Sept1822. With Andrew McQuistion, guardian
Grace, Rebecca Morrow	9Sept1816		Bradshaw, Richard	
Grace, Jane Conway	9Sept1816		Bradshaw, Richard	
Patton, William Kelsey	10Sept1816		Mansfield, Thomas	Resc 9Sep1817
Ned	8Sept1817	16 years	Lowry, James	Of color
Wilkinson, Abner	8Sept1817	16 years	White, Thomas	Orphan
Moreur, Reuben	9Sept1817	17 years 6 months	Leper, Mathew	Resc 8June1818 as Reuben Morier
Henry, William	9Sept1817	12 years	Hickman, Henry	Resc13June1825
Kiles, Leannah	9Sept1817	9 years in April past	McSpadden, Esther	
King, Joseph K.	9Sept1817	16 years	Douglas, Alexander	Until age 19 years.
Hurley, Eliza	9March1818	10 years	Courtney, James	Bound by Wenny Murley(Hurley?)
Ellis, William	14Sept1818	4 years	Moyers, John	Orphan
Guinn, James	17Sept1818		Woodward, Abraham	Orphan
Lyle, Nancy	June1814		Sehorn, Levisca	Ind resc June1818. On 17Sep1818 Sehorn paid $48 for four year's care

Name	Date	Age	Master	Notes
Rice, Nianetta	16Sept1819		Hickle, George	Alias Nianetta Hickle. Resc 11Sept1820
Hodge, Andrew Jackson	13Dec1819		Sprowl, John	
Bonine, Jacob	12Sept1820		Turnby, John C.	Resc 10March1824
Thornton, Levi	14Dec1820		Doherty, James	Alias Levi Ward. Resc 10March1823
Nicholson, George	11Jun1821		Chase, Obed	Of colour
Ward, Michael	11Jun1821		Giger, George	
Jourdan, Mary	11Jun1821		Coons, Michael	
Anderton, William			Hanes, William	Ind resc 11June1823, restored to mother. 9Jun1823*
Thornton, Levi	8Sep1823		Bragg, John	Alias Levi Ward. Resc 9Dec1833
Gann, Abraham	10Mar1824		Turnby, George	
Rhoda	14Jun1824		Henderson, Noden & Lewis, C W	Of colour
Bear, Letty	14Jun1824		Kirkpatrick, Jacob	Of colour
Webb, Anna	14Jun1824		Webb, Jessee	
Morse, Marion	14Jun1824		Arnold, Holbert	Male
Middleton, Patience	14Jun1824		Sellars, Samuel	?Dau of Smallwood Middleton* Resc 12June1827
Middleton, Nancy	14Jun1824		Rickats, John	?Dau of Smallwood Middleton* Resc 13Dec1824
Middleton, Selenia	14Jun1824		Pierce, Robert	?Dau of Smallwood Middleton*
Middleton, Polly	16Jun1824		Caldwell, Anthony	?Dau of Smallwood Middleton*
Middleton, William	13Sep1824		Brazelton, William	?Son of Smallwood Middleton 14June1824*
Morgan (?Morris), William	14Sep1824		Bonine, Smith	Ind to George Seahorn rescinded*
Middleton, Able Lewis	14Mar1825		Hill, William	Rescinded 13Mar1828
Stover, Joseph	14Mar1825	14 yrs	Snodgrass, Isaac	
King, Penelope	12Sept1825	11 yrs	Turnley, George	
Stephens, Joseph	12Sept1825	17 mo	Linsey, John	
Webb, Reuben	12Sept1826		Carter, Peyton	Son of William Webb. 11Sept1826*
Webb, William Lea	12Sept1826		Moyers, Jacob	Son of William Webb. 11Sept1826*
Webb, Eliza Ann	12Sept1826		Moyers, Jacob	Dau of William Webb. 11Sept1826*
Webb, Mary	12Sept1826		Dickey, James	Dau of William Webb. 11Sept1826*
Middleton, Patience	12June1827		Rankin, Thomas	
Shepperd, Mary Ann	14June1827		Frank, William	Dau of Hiram & Elizabeth Shepperd*

Shepperd, Betsy Ann	14June1827		Frank, William	Dau of Hiram & Elizabeth Shepperd*
Shepperd, Nancy	14June1827		Frank, William	Dau of Hiram & Elizabeth Shepperd*
Burnett, Edward P.	14Jun1827		Stiff, Edward	Resc 11Mar1828
Mosegy(?), John	14Jun1827		Stiff, Edward	
Elder, Mary	14Sep1827		Elder, Charles	
Cole, Joseph Alexander	12Mar1828		Dick, Henry	
Cole, Sampson David	12Mar1828		Dick, William	
Cole, Patsy David	12Mar1828		Caldwell, Jr., Anthony	
Whorley, Willis	12Mar1828		Rice, Augustus	
Cole, A. L.	13Mar1828		Bragg, John	
Bok, Betsy	9Jun1828	13 yrs	Myrik, John	
Worley, Job	9Jun1828	13 yrs	Mansfield, John	
Mount, Isiah	9Jun1828	10 yrs	Mills, James	Orphan 11Dec1827*
Quarle, William	9Jun1828	15 yrs	Thompson, Vandenburgh	
Poll, Greenebury	8Dec1828	2 yrs	Ayres, John	Resc 11Mar1833
Quarles, James	9Mar1829	14 yrs	Thompson. William	Resc 14Sept1829
Cole, Catherene	8Jun1829		Newman, [Jr.], Aron	Resc 4Oct1836
Meredith, William	14Sep1829		Thornburgh, Ai	
Chambers, William McCullen	14Dec1829		Bicknell, Daniel E.	
Sasseen, Edward R.	13Jun1831	10 yrs last December	Bruckner, Charles F.	Until age 20.
Wright, John	13Jun1831	5 yrs	Minter, Mathias	
Smith, George W.	8Mar1830	17 yrs on 23Aug last	Gibbs, Obediah	
Ryan, Elliston	8Mar1830	14 yrs on 16Feb past	McGee, James	
Ryan, Wyly	8Mar1830	17 yrs this day	McGee, James	
Ryan, James	8Mar1830	12 yrs on 22Feb past	McFarland, John	
Campbell, Eli	8Mar1830	17 yrs on 29Aug next	Moyers, Jacob	
Henry, Isaac A.	12Sep1831	3 yrs on 19June last	Carmon, Calib	Resc 5Apr1847, as Anderson Henry
Locust, Auston	12Sep1831	9 yrs on 22Jan next	Howell, Patton	
Hays, Joseph. C.	13Dec1831	7 months	McClister, John	McAlister adm of est of Joseph Hayes 12Mar1832
Hays, Frances Matilda	13Dec1831	7 yrs	McClister, John	McAlister adm of est of Joseph Hayes 12Mar1832
Kerr, John	11Jun1832	13 yrs on 2Mar past	Howell, Patton	

Name	Date	Age	Master	Notes
Rhoda	13Dec1830		Moyers, William	Of color
Johnson, Hannah	10Dec1832	10 yrs	Kimbrough, Thomas	Dau of Lydia Johnson 11Sept1832*
Johnson, William	10Dec1832	5 yrs	Kimbrough, Duke W.	Son of Lydia Johnson 11Sept1832*
Johnson, Thomas	10Dec1832	7 yrs	Patton, Thomas C.	Son of Lydia Johnson 11Sept1832*
Johnson, Robert	10Dec1832	11 yrs	Mills, Samuel	Son of Lydia Johnson 11Sept1832*
Pool, Greenebury	11Mar1833	6 yrs	Woodward, Abraham	
Hays, Delila	11Mar1833	7 yrs	Moyers, Alfred I.	Resc 5Dec1836 at req of Moyers*
Wright. Benjamin	4June1838		Hickman, James	Prior indenture cancelled. Canc 3Jan1842
Anderson	10Jun1833		Coons, Joseph	
Davis, Alfred	11Jun1833	16 yrs on 15Jan last	Clemmons, George W.	Resc 10Sept1834
Garner, James	9Sep1833		Carter, Peyton	
Middleton, Lewis	9Sep1833		Bradshaw, John P.	Resc 8Dec1840
Garner, John	9Sep1833		Landrum, Robert M.	Resc 1Oct1838. Abuse alleged
Branson, Obed	9Sep1833		Gatlin, Radford	
Thornton, Levi	9Dec1833	18 yrs in Mar past	Branner, Jr, Michael	Alias Levi Ward
Doherty, David Harrold	9Dec1833	14 yrs on 29Nov past	Powle(?), Henry	
Hays, Levisca Emeline	10Mar1834	5 yrs	Helm, Henry	
Branston, Harriett	10Mar1834		Hodges, Zelpha	Dau of Rebecca Branson 11June1832*
Branson, Thomas	10Mar1834	6 yrs	Hodges, Zelpha	Son of Rebecca Branson 11June1832*
Quarles, Polly A.	12Mar1834	11 yrs	Tumly, George	Dau of Betsy Quarles 10Mar1834*
Quarles, Joseph	12Mar1834	4 yrs	Tumly, George	Son of Betsy Quarles 10Mar1834*
Roberts, Thomas Bradford	12Mar1834	13 yrs	Tankersly, William	
Quarles, William	12Mar1834	3 yrs	Tumly, George	Son of Betsy Quarles 10Mar1834*
Brooks, William P.	12Mar1834	7 yrs on 15Oct1834	Ferguson, William	
Johnson, Thomas	9Jun1834	9 yrs	Bradford, James	
Taff, Susannah Melvina	9Jun1834	6 yrs on 8Jan last	Denton, Jacob	Dau of Elizabeth Taff*
Taff, Infant	10Jun1834		Boyd, John W.	Child of Elizabeth Taff*
Auston, Minerva	10Jun1834	10 yrs on 15Aug	Talbott, Williston	
Auston, Jane	10Jun1834	8 yrs in Sep next	Talbott, Williston	
Auston, Rachel	10Jun1834	4 yrs on 14Jun inst	Talbott, Williston	

Auston, James	10Jun1834	3 yrs on 3July next	Talbott, Williston	
Gann, Ranson	8Sep1834		McSpadden, Milton A.	Resc 7Dec1846, McSpadden deceased
Gann, Matilda	8Sep1834		McSpadden, Milton A.	
Quarles, Joseph	8Dec1834	6 yrs	Daily, John	Son of Betsy Quarles 10Mar1834*
Taff, Nancy Jane	8Dec1834	1 yr 9 mo		
Quarles, William	9Dec1834	4 yrs	Fain, Josiah	Son of Betsy Quarles 10Mar1834*. Resc 9Mar1835
Quarles, Polly Ann	9Dec1834	11 yrs	Whittington, John	Dau of Betsy Quarles 10Mar1834*
Davis, Ned	10Dec1834		Branner, George	Father, Baker Davis, appealed. Of color*
Davis, Jack	10Dec1834		Moyers, Jacob	Father, Baker Davis, appealed. Of color* Resc1844*
Davis, Margaret	10Dec1834		Woods, Johnathan	Father, Baker Davis, appealed. Of color*
Davis, Mariah	10Dec1834		Branner, Jr, Michael	Father, Baker Davis, appealed. Of color*
Davis, Katy	10Dec1834		Denson, Thomas	Father, Baker Davis, app. Of color* Resc 6Nov1843
Quarles, William	9Mar1835	4 yrs	Davis, Thomas	
Webb, Wesley	9Mar1835	10 yrs in Jun next	Hale, Stephen A.	Resc 2Aug1841
Reons, Henry	9Mar1835	16 yrs on 26Jan1835	McGee, James	
McCrarey, Thomas W.	9Mar1835		Riggs, Lewis	Bound by Ann McCrarey. Indent canc 14Sept1835
Carr, Whelem Lilburn	16Sep1835	11 yrs	Elliott, George	
Wright, Benjamin	16Sep1835	5 yrs	Thornburgh, Richard	Stepson of Wm Wright 11June1832* 14Sept1835* Son of Jane Wright. 15Dec1835*
Wright, William	16Sep1835	12 yrs	French, Loffard	Stepson of Wm Wright 11June1832* 14Sept1835* Son of Jane Wright. 15Dec1835*
Riggs, John	14Dec1835		McGee, James	Canc 3June1844, "Biggs" having absconded
Ketteral, Terrersa	17Mar1836	14 yrs on 19Jan1836	Moyers, William	
Newman, Ewen Jefferson	Jun1836	5 yrs in May last	Newman, Samuel	? Resc 2Jan1837 as _____ Ballard
Clemmons, Jackson	3Oct1836	9 yrs	Graham, David R.	
Johnson, Robert	3Oct1836		Howell, Patton	
Davis, Mariah	3Oct1836	15 yrs	Stephens, George	Both of color
Striplen, John	7Nov1836	17 yrs on 9Aug next	Gregory, Sr, George	Resc 6Mar1837
Hays, Delilah	3Dec1836		McClister, John	
Trott, Gillispie	6Feb1837	15 yrs in Oct past	Jeaneway, Daniel	Resc 3Apr1843
Biggs, Willis	6Mar1837	17 yrs 11 mo	Guinn, William	Consent of father (unnamed)
Thomas, Mary	4Dec1837	13 yrs on 25Dec inst	Owens, Richard	

Name	Date	Age	Master	Notes
Flemm	4Dec1837	11 yrs on 26Dec inst	Watkins, Osborne R.	Male, of color
Maples, Jackson	4Dec1837	12 yrs in Aug past	Martin, Jr, Lewis	
Sampson, William	5Feb1838	17 yrs	Chaney, William	
Gillett, Noah	7May1838	15 yrs	Curenton, Robert	
Todd, John	3Sep1838	6 yrs	Odle, Samuel C.	Maltreatment alleged 6Feb1841* Resc 5Apr1841
Parks, Elizabeth	3Sep1838	9 yrs in Jan next	Lively, Beverly	Resc 3Sept1838
Chilton, Joshua	3Sep1838	10 yrs	Branner, Benjamin	Resc 7Aug1843, "Shelton having run off"
Parks, Elizabeth	3Sep1838		Leaper, Matthew	Resc 6Jan1840
Chilton, Isabella	5Nov1838	12 yrs	Fain, John (of Muddy Creek)	
Wright, Addeline	7Jan1839	16 yrs on 10Sep past	Routh, John	Prior ind canc. Dau of Polly Wright 11June1832*
Birdwell, Andrew Jackson	1Aug1839	6 yrs in Mar last	Taylor, Hugh W.	
Park, George G.	7Oct1839	10 yrs on 10July past	Graham, David R.	
Parks, Elizabeth	6Jan1840		Love, James T.	
Cates, Malaena	6July1840	6 yrs	Swann(?), John	Female
Shepherd, Nancy Ann E.	3Aug1840	15 yrs	Shelton, Nelson N.	
Shepherd, James William	3Aug1840	13 yrs	Shelton, Nelson N.	
Franklin, Sarah	5Oct1840	12 yrs	Thornburgh, Montgomery	
Jabez	2Nov1840	18 yrs	Neff, David	Of color. Resc 7June1841
Middleton, Lewis	8Dec1840		Green, John O.	
Scarlett, John	8Dec1840	10 yrs	McGass, Samuel G.	Son of Ruth Scarlett 6July1840* Resc 5Apr1847
Scarlett, Lewis	8Dec1840	15 yrs	Bailey, Carr	Son of Ruth Scarlett 6July1840*. Resc 1Sept1845
Scarlett, Abraham	8Dec1840	5 yrs	Bailey, Joseph M.	Son of Ruth Scarlett 6July1840*
Todd, John	5Apr1841		Lotspeich, William	Resc 3Feb1845
Kelley, Joshua P.	5Apr1841	12 yrs	Newman, Madison	Resc 7Oct1845
Jabez	7June1841	18 yrs	Dankins, Abner	Resc 5Apr1842
Webb, Wesley	2Aug1841	16 yrs	Neff, David	Resc 6July1842
Cross, George W.	6Sept1841	3 yrs	Blackburn, Andrew A.	Consent of parents
Adams, George			Hoskins, Charles C.	Ind canc 7Sept1841, to return to father, Wyley Adams
Ball, Mary Jane	6Dec1841	7 yrs	Lewis, Fanny	
Ball, Peter	6Dec1841	4 yrs	Dunwoodie, John	

Wright, Benjamin	3Jan1842	13 yrs in Mar next	Baker, William	Of color. 6June1842* 5Oct1846*
Jabez	5Apr1842	19 yrs	Hickman, James	Of color
Webb, Wesley	6July1842	17 yrs on 4Jun last	Temples, Joseph C.	
Parks, Martha	3Oct1842	9 yrs on 21Feb last	Doan, John	Dau of Cassandra Parks 6Sept1842* Resc 3Feb1845
Trevillion, John C.	5Oct1842	7 yrs on 18Apr1842	Churchman, Reuben	
Hays, Jasper	8Nov1842	17 yrs on 15Mar1843	Mitchell, James	Resc 6Jan1843
Hays, John J.	5Dec1842	13 yrs in Jan1843	McSpadden, Milton H.	Resc 1June1846, as John Hays. McSpadden dcd.
Trevillion, Rhoda R.	5Dec1842	6 yrs on 20Sep last	Reese, Joseph B.	
Trevillion, Pleasant N.	5Dec1842	9 yrs on 7Aug last	Jones, George W.	
Calyer, Pharoah C.	6Feb1843	11 yrs on 2Apr1842	Hutcheson, James	
Todd, Gillaspie				See Gillispie Trott
Jarnagin, Aaron	1May1843	12 yrs in Aug last	Chaney, William [of Grainger Co]	Son of M___ and Elizabeth Jarnagin. 3Apr1843*
Jarnagin, David	1May1843	13 yrs	Walker, John	Son of M___ and Elizabeth Jarnagin. 3Apr1843*
Trevillion, Joseph	1May1843	4 yrs	Daniel, Edward	Twin. Son of John Trevillion, Dcd. 3Apr1843*
Trevillion, Joab	1May1843	4 yrs	Daniel, Edward	Twin. Son of John Trevillion, Dcd. 3Apr1843*
Jarnagin, Sarah	5Jun1843	9 yrs in July next	Gregory, Isaac	Dau of Eliz. Jarnagin 2May1843*. Resc 4June1849* Sarah having left without consent
Moody, William	3July1843	10 yrs on 17Mar last	Gregory, Isaac	Resc 1July1850
Sartin, William	5Feb1844	16 yrs	Walker, John	
Todd, Martha			Lotspeech, William	Ind cancelled 1Apr1844
Todd, Martha	2Apr1844	14 yrs	Gross, Daniel P.	
Biggs John R.				See John Riggs
Hays, John W.	1July1844	12 yrs	Caldwell, Robert	Until age 17 yrs*
Hayse, James, of Cyrus	1July1844	10 yrs	Eckel, Sr, Peter	Until age 17 yrs* Canc 7Sept1846
Alderson, Stephen	5Aug1844	15 yrs on 8July1844	Monset?, John	
Hays, Amos N.	2Sep1844		G___t, John	Until age 17 yrs*
Sellers, Joseph	4Nov1844	17 yrs	Woodson, William T.	
Edgar, William J. J.	2Dec1844	8 yrs in Apr1844	Balch, James P.	
Sellers, Caroline	6Jan1845	12 yrs	Hoskins, Thomas A.	Until age 21 yrs. Resc 1Sept1845
Parks, Martha	3Feb1845	11 yrs	Dawson, Thomas	Until age 21 yrs
Todd, John	3Feb1845	12 yrs in spring,1845	Caldwell, William A.	

Name	Date	Age	Master	Notes
Sellers, Mary	3Feb1845	10 yrs	Bales, William	Until age 21 yrs. Resc 7July1845
Lanning, Jemima	3Feb1845	9 yrs on 10May1845	McClane, Robert A.	Until age 21 yrs
Richards, Edward	3Mar1845		Blanchard, Thomas J.	For 4 yrs from 23Aug1844
Sellers, Mary	7July1845	9 yrs	Thornburgh, Richard	Until age 21 yrs. Resc 1Sept1845
Jones, Pleasant A.	4Aug1845	5 yrs	McCuistian, James	Resc 7Oct1850
Hays, Amanda(?)	4Aug1845	4 yrs on 18Mar1845	Bettis, Jacob W.	Resc 5Nov1849
Jones, Eliza J.	5Aug1845		Helm, W. C. F.	Dau of Nancy Jones 7July1845*
Newman, Granville			Hudson, William L.	Resc 1Sept1845
Kyle, Bradley	6Jan1846	7 yrs	McMahan, John	Resc 4May1846, "Coil" having been given to father
Copeland, Joseph	6Apr1846	10 yrs in Oct next	Elliott, George M.	
Denson, Margaret	5May1846	8 to 9 yrs	Branner, Michael T.	Dau of Thomas Denson, dcd 5May1846* Resc 7Feb1848. Until age 21
Jones, Margaret	6July1846	6 yrs	Mansfield, Thomas	Until age 21. Dau of Nancy Jones. 7July1845*
Hays, Sarah	8July1846	9 yrs	Sharp, Lacky M.	Until age 21. Resc 4Sept1854, to care of brother.*
White, John H.	3Aug1846	15 yrs on 21Aug1845	Hickman, James	
Hays, James, son of Cyrus	7Sept1846	12 yrs	Eckel, Thomas R.	Until 17 yrs*. Resc 7Feb1848
Kimbrough, John	4Jan1847	3 Yrs in Mar next	Kimbrough, Thomas	Applcation by mom to have rescinded 1Mar1847*
Harrison, Joshua	1Mar1847	6 yrs on 13 inst	Bettis, John	
Hightower, Nancy A.	1Mar1847	10 yrs on 14Feb last	Bettis, Simeon	Until age 21 yrs
Coffee, Eli L.	1Mar1847	7 yrs on 20Jun1846	Garner, John	
Coffee, Sarah E.	1Mar1847	3 yrs on 10Oct1846	Garner, John	Until age 21 yrs
Scarlet, Stephen			M____t, John	Indenture cancelled 6Dec1847
Conner, Chloe	7Feb1848	12 yrs	Scarlett, John	
Hays, James	7Feb1848	14 yrs in July1847	Dick, Henry J.	
Miller, David R.	7Feb1848	4 yrs on 18Jun1847	Walker, Thomas	Resc 2Nov1863, Miller in Confederate Army
Asberry	5June1848	2 yrs 6 mo	Thornburgh, Montgomery	Of color
Lackey, Obediah	7Aug1848	14 yrs	Marshall, Benjamin	Son of Catherine Lackey. 3July1848*
Turnley, Elizabeth M.	3Oct1848	10 yrs on 1June last	Houseley, John W.	Dau of George Turnley* 2Oct1848*
Turnley, Joseph F.	3Oct1848	2 yrs on 15Dec1847	Graham, Joseph	Son of George Turnley* 2Oct1848*
Turnley, Adeline	1Jan1849	5 yrs	Helm, Henry	Dau of George Turnley* 2Oct1848*

Nelson, Martin L.	5Mar1849	11 yrs next May	Neal, John	
Denson, Andrew J.	5Mar1849	7 yrs on 11Jan1849	Denton, Camden C.	
Brizendine, John	4Jun1849	11 yrs in Dec1848	Brizendine, Thomas	
Brizendine, James	4Jun1849	1 yr on 16Nov1848	Brizendine, Thomas	
Dafferon, Edward C.	1Oct1849	12 yrs	Branner, John	
Frazier, William	4Mar1850	10 yrs on 18July1850	Baker, John	Son of Fanny Frazier 8Jan1850*
Frazier, Andrew	4Mar1850	11 yrs on 29Mar1849	Lann____, Johnathan	Son of Fanny Frazier 8Jan1850*
Frazier, James	4Mar1850	13 yrs on 29Aug1849	Hammon, John C.	Son of Fanny Frazier 8Jan1850*
Terry, John	4Mar1850	9 yrs in June 1849	Patile, William	
Turnley, Isaac	3Jun1850	2 yrs in Feb1850	Hickman, James	Son of Esther Turnley, dcd*. Of color. Resc 7July1851
Jones, Pleasant A.	7Oct1850	10 yrs	Canary, James	
Stafford, Margaret	6Jan1851	7 yrs	Wright, John	Until 21 yrs
Lethco, Ritta	5May1851	7 yrs on 1Apr past	Barnett, William R.	Until age 21 yrs
Lethco, James	5May1851	3 yrs on 7Mar past	Barnett, William R.	
Copeland, Joseph	5May1851	15 yrs	Copeland, James G.	
Turnley, Isaac	7July1851	3 yrs last Feb	Blackburn, Andrew A.	Of color
Amos, Elvina	4Aug1851	14 yrs	Gray, James F.	Until age 21 yrs
Taylor, George	1Dec1851	3 yrs last Sept	Evans, Jesse R.	Son of Prudence Taylor. 3Nov1851*. Resc 2Feb1852
Taylor, Emeline	1Dec1851	6 yrs last Sept	Moore, George R.	Second dau of Prudence Taylor*
Manley, Luena	2Feb1852	2 yrs	Watkins, A. R.	Of color
Wall, Chester	2Feb1852	12 yrs in Aug1851	Finley, William T.	
Taylor, Margaret D.	1Mar1852	10 yrs	Case, John	Dau of Prudence Taylor. 3Nov1851*
Mary	7Jun1852	5 yrs on 25Dec next	Moffett, William W.	Assent of mother, Narcissa Fin. Of color
Nathan	7Jun1852	4 yrs	Williams, L. D.	Assent of mother, Narcissa Fin. Of color
Martha Jane	7Jun1852	7 yrs on 1Feb1852	Williams, L. D.	Assent of mother, Narcissa Fin. Of color
Harriet Emilly	7Jun1852	11 mo	Williams, L. D.	Assent of mother, Narcissa Fin. Of color
John Thomas	7Jun1852	2 yrs on 1Apr1852	Williams, L. D.	Assent of mother, Narcissa Fin. Of color
Williams, Charles	5July1852	10 yrs	Pryor, Andrew J.	
Murry, Pleasant	6Sep1852	6 yrs	Willock, Wilson	Farming & agriculture. Bound by mother, Jemima Murray on 19Apr1852
Murry, Samuel	6Sep1852	4 yrs	Willock, Wilson	Farming & agriculture. Bound by mother, Jemima Murray on 19Apr1852

Name	Date	Age	Master	Notes
Hays, Amos Napolion	1Nov1852	17 yrs	Hoskins, George C.	Blacksmith
Hickey, Theodrick B.	6Jun1853	3 yrs on 4th day this mo	Hickey, Thomas D.	Son of William P. Henson. 3Oct1859* 2Jan1860*
Roena			Reese, George A.	5Sep1853 to mother, Nancy Rann or Spoon. Of color
John			Reese, George A.	5Sep1853 to mother, Nancy Rann or Spoon. Of color
Angeline			Reese, George A.	5Sep1853 to mother, Nancy Rann or Spoon. Of color
Bill			Reese, George A.	5Sep1853 to mother, Nancy Rann or Spoon. Of color
Coffe, Sarah Eveline	7Nov1853	11 yrs	Rainwater, Miles W.	
Flinn, William D. M.	6Mar1854	3 yrs on 16Sep1853	Tucker, John	
Flinn, John J. H.	6Mar1854	1 yr on 5Oct1853	Tucker, John	
Prudence, Visa	5Apr1854	6 yrs	Pryor, A. J.	Of color. Resc 5Feb1866*
Laben	5Apr1854	3 yrs	Pryor, A. J.	Of color. Resc 5Feb1866*
Smith, Thomas	5Apr1854	8 yrs	Lebolt, John	
Adams, Malissa Jane	1May1854		Lively, Beverly	Until 21 yrs
Curry, Thomas Alexand	1May1854	4 yrs	Caldwell, Robert	
Curry, David Simpson	1May1854	6 yrs in Aug next	Line, Joab	Resc 4Jan1859. To care of father, George Curry
Curry, Margaret Adaline	1May1854	2 yrs	Line, Joab	Resc 4Jan1859. To care of father, George Curry
Hancoke, J. N.			Bettis, Simeon	Ind canc 4Dec1854, Hancocke having left
Taylor, Joseph	5Mar1855	16 yrs in Mar1855	Turnley, John C.	
Childers, Jackson	2July1855	6 yrs on 4Apr1856	Seabolt, John	White
Poe, William Hastin	3Sep1855	8 yrs last June	Poe, Login J.	Resc 1Oct1855. Returned to mother
Poe, Sarah Elizabeth	3Sep1855		Poe, Login J.	Resc 1Oct1855. Returned to mother
Carmichael, Thomas J.	1Oct1855	1 yr on 17 inst	Carmichael, Lemuel	White
Witt, William Senter	4Feb1856	11 yrs	Witt, William K.	White
Bias, Doctor Hoy	3Mar1856	11 yrs	Chandler, William	
Bias, Elisha Hampton	3Mar1856	16 yrs on 1Dec1856	Loyd, Anderson	Until age 21
Bias, Malissa Jane	3Mar1856	8 yrs on 14Jun1856	Loyd, Anderson	Until age 21
Hodges, Thomas	7Apr1856	5 yrs	Dick, Jacob	Alias Thomas Lamore. White
Murry, Thomas A.	7Apr1856	6 yrs	Housley, J. C.	White
Bias, Elliott Smith Chambers	5May1856	14 yrs next Oct	Loyd, William	Canc3Mar1862, Elliott having joined army

McBride, Samuel E. H.	5May1856		Milligan, L. D.	Son of Marcus McBride
Walden, Prissilla			Beason, Benjamin	Indenture canc 5May1856
Wooten, John Key	3Aug1857	9 yrs	Chaney, William	Resc 2Nov1863, Wooten in Federal Army
Coiler, Alexander	3May1858	16 yrs on 10Mar last	Cox, James	White
Oaks, Jacob	7Jun1858	7 yrs	Hodge, James C.	
Trogden, John William	5July1858	14 yrs last June	Bettis, Emsley	
Branson, Levi	2Aug1858	12 yrs	Dunkin, Isaac A.	White. Resc 11Jan1862. Returned to mother
Stone, William Preston	4Oct1858	11 yrs last June 9	Warren, Charels W.	Resc 5Mar1866, Stone having absconded
Griffin, Catharine	5Oct1858	7 yrs on 20Jun last	Dick, Henry J.	Until age 21 yrs. Mulatto
Huett, Sarah	5Oct1858	8 yrs	White, I. B.	Until age 21 yrs. Mulatto
Huett, William	5Oct1858	7 yrs next Jan	Provence, William	Mulatto. Resc 8July1868, to mother during rebellion
Huett, Margaret	5Oct1858	12 yrs	Provence, William	Mulatto. Resc 8 July1868. Dead
McBride, Eliza Ann	2May1859	10 yrs last Dec	Balch, James P.	White
Mills, William Henry	6Jun1859	6 yrs	Gass, Samuel E.	White
Mills, Deborah Elizabeth	4July1859	4 yrs	Peirce, Albert	White
Huett, Sarah	5Jan1859	8 yrs	White, Isaac B.	Mulatto
Taylor, Sally	7Feb1860	4 yrs	Dunkin, Isaac A.	White
Manis, Duke	7Feb1860	15 yrs	Sharp, James B.	White
Whitson, James	8Feb1860	14 yrs	Seabolt, John	Son of James Whitson, Dcd. 2Jan1860* Resc 7Apr1863*
Whitson, Jesse	8Feb1860	12 yrs next April	Copeland, Jacob T.	Son of James Whitson, Dcd. 2Jan1860* Resc 10Jan1861
Whitson, Zacheriah	8Feb1860	6 yrs	Zerkle, Benjamin	Son of James Whitson, Dcd. 2Jan1860*
Whitson, Caroline	8Feb1860	8 yrs	Nicely, Jacob J.	Dau of James Whitson, Dcd. 2Jan1860*
Moore, Henry	6Mar1860	15 yrs	Drinnon, William H.	White
Right, Nancy	3Apr1860	14 yrs	Martin, Robert	Mulatto
Colyer, Richard B.	7May1860	3 yrs on 10 June next	Neff, David	White
Colyer, William	3Sept1860	8 or 9 yrs	Walker, Samuel	White
Bias, Doctor Hoy	1Oct1860	15 yrs in June 1860	Loyd, Anderson	White
Huet, Sarah	4Dec1860	10 yrs	White, Isaac B.	Mulatto
Whitson, Jesse	10Jan1861	11 yrs	Whitson, Baxter	Bricklayer. Ind also recorded 4Feb1861
Byrum, Samuel Henry	10Jan1861	12 yrs	Lam, W. J.	Blacksmith. White. Resc 11Feb1861. "Boy is run off"

Name	Date	Age	Master	Notes
Howard, Mahlen	4Mar1861	15 yrs 2 mo	Elmore, Thomas A.	White
Merritt, William Alexander	1Apr1861	6 yrs on 3Apr1861	Chaney, James W.	White
Merritt, Margaret Ann	1Apr1861	5 yrs next Oct	Chaney, James W.	White. Resc 5Feb1866, Chaney having left county
Hickey, Theodric	1Apr1861	11 yrs	Kidwell, J. J.	White
Muller, Lu	2Dec1861	10 yrs	Bell, Edmund	Mulatto
Whitson, Zacheriah	7Jan1862	8 yrs	Alderson, Isaac	White
Evans, Mary Jane	3Feb1862	5 yrs on 27Mar next	Bewley, Jacob M.	Of color
Shields, Susan Jane	3Feb1862	11 yrs next September	Bewley, Jacob M.	Of color
Shields, Lovina	3Feb1862	8 yrs	Bewley, Jacob M.	Of color. Sister of Susan Jane
Conway, Mariah	4Mar1862	15 yrs	Bewley, Jacob M.	Of color
Conway, Laura	4Mar1862	12 yrs	Bewley, Jacob M.	Of color
Madison	4Aug1862	9 0r 10 yrs	Newman, James C.	Of color. 6Oct1862*
Newman, Samuel N.	7Oct1862	13 yrs on 13May last	McGuire, Thomas A.	White
Newman, Rebecca Jane	7Oct1862	7 yrs on 20Jan last	Ballard, Eleanor H.	
Newman, John A.	7Oct1862	11 yrs on 11May last	McGuire, Silas A.	Resc Feb1865
Madison	6Jan1863	10 yrs	Maner, Mashah	Of color
Thornburgh, John	7Aug1865	12 yrs	Thornburgh, J. M.	Of color
Hurt, William	3Oct1865	3 yrs	Henderson, Thomas	Orphan
Province, William M..	4Oct1865	16 yrs	McGuire, Silas	Son of John Provence. Both parents dead. 1Sept1865* Resc 2Oct1871, runaway
Province, Isaac	4Oct1865	13 yrs	Baker, William R.	Son of John Provence. Both parents dead. 1Sept1865*
Provence, Samuel D.	4Oct1865	15 yrs	Baker, Gideon	Son of John Provence. Both parents dead. 1Sept1865*
Provence, Isaac	4Dec1865	13 yrs	Jacobs, James W.	Prior indenture rescinded
Bishop, William Porter	4Dec1865	5 yrs on 10Jun next	Bettis, John	
Hobby, Alexander Zacharia Taylor	5Dec1865	6 yrs 10 mo	Nicholson, James M.	Orphan
Woolard, David Thomas	1Jan1866	8 yrs next Sept	Woolard, James	Renewed 6Feb1866
Nichols, James	5Feb1866	9 yrs	Cline, E. H.	White. Resc 7July1873 (as Hanry Cline). Runaway
Davis, William	2Apr1866	2 yrs on 13Feb last	Bascom, Reuben J.	Farming. White
Hobby, Joseph J. G.	2Apr1866	5 yrs in May next	Weldon, William E.	White
Hurt, Susan	7May1866	10 yrs	Meek, M. D.	White

Dan, Samuel Lorenza	7May1866	9 yrs	Walker, Thomas	White
Tyra, Dianah	8May1866	9 yrs last Feb	Greer, A. J.	White. Resc 3Nov1866
Fain, Monroe	7Aug1866	13 yrs	Fain, Sam N.	Of color
Fain, Henry	7Aug1866	12 yrs	Fain, Sam N.	Of color
Fain, William	7Aug1866	10 yrs	Fain, Sam N.	Of color
Hobby, Eliza Ann	3Sep1866	13 yrs	Edgar, William J. J.	White
Doughty, Benjamin	3Sep1866	6 yrs	Doughty, Benjamin	White
Mitchel, George	3Sep1866	13 yrs	Turnley, John C.	Of color
Goan, David P.	5Nov1866	12 yrs on 28Jan1865	Stratham, Elizabeth	White
Lizie	5Nov1866	1 year	Bradford, Anthony	Of color
Blevens, William M.	3Dec1866	8 yrs	McGuire, Silas M.	Resc 2Oct1871. Mother took boy & emigrated west
Hobby, Eliza Ann	2Sep1867	14 yrs	Riggs, Edward C.	White
Cutts, William	2Sep1867	13 yrs	Fry, George W.	White
McKInney, George W.	2Sep1867	12 yrs	Fry, George W.	White
Roach, John	4Nov1867	6 yrs	Webb, Andrew J.	White. Rescinded 7Jan1873
Nooncaper, Rebecca Ann	5Nov1867	11 yrs	Swann, James P.	White. Until age 21 yrs
Nooncaper, Andrew J.	5Nov1867	12 yrs	Swann, James P.	White
Whitacre, Arnold	4Feb1868	11 yrs	Corbet, Shadrack P.	White
Tyra, Parmeanus	3Mar1868		Williams, James H.	Son of Elizabeth Tyra 3Feb1868*. Resc 7July1868
Whitson, Jesse	7Apr1868		Seabolt, John	
Hamilton, Hannah A.	4Jan1869	11 years	Hill, Robert D.	
Hamilton, Lucinda	4Jan1869	13 years	Galbraith, Joseph P.	Resc Jan 1870
Sarah	5Jan1869		Blackburn, David R. N.	
Ellison, Joseph N.	8Jun1869	6 years 7 mos	Burchfield, Robert	Son of Margaret Ellison*
Payn, George W.	7Feb1870	11 yrs on 19Mar next	Hiley, William A.	
Meadows, Richard	7Mar1870	10 years	Line, Alfred M.	
Glossip, John Henry	1Jun1870	4 yrs on 12Apr1870	Smith, David	p. 94 Bk of Indenture Bonds
Barnes, Teressa D. D.	7Nov1870	13 yrs 6 mo	Edmonds, William	Until age 21
Barnes, David H.	7Nov1870	8 years	Poe, W. O. H.	
Whitaker, Arnold	5Jan1871	14 yrs on 3Feb1871	Lyle, Dr. J. Nat	
Branner, Samuel	6Feb1871	10 yrs	Rankin, Samuel	Both of color. Resc 2Jun1873, gone to parts unknown
Lyle, Elbert	5Jun1871	14 years on 1Feb1871	Bell, Jacob	

Name	Date	Age	Master	Notes
Philips, William	4Sep1871	9 yrs 2 mo	Swann, N. B.	Son of Polly Philips* 6June1871
Mason, Frank	4Sep1871	11 years	Walker, Samuel	
Gann, Uriah	2Jan1872	18 mo	Bell, Uriah	
Fry, W. C.	4Mar1872	10 years	Fry, Henry	
Philips, Mary	2Dec1872	11 yrs 6 mo	Bell, Edmond	
Unknown (not entered)			Williams, S. D.	Ind resc 3Mar1873. Mother took child.
Nichols, James			Cline, Harvey	Ind resc 7July1873. Runaway
VanDyke, William M.	1Dec1873	11 yrs on 4Dec1873	Philips, Samuel	Resc 6April1874
McNish, Joseph W.	5Jan1874	8 yrs 4 mo	Lewis, Absalom	
Peck, Sandy	2Nov1874	13 years	Tittsworth, Charlotte	Male child of color
Roten, Effy	2Nov1874	9 years	Webster, A. H.	Child of color
Satterfield, Su	1Sept1875		Bailey, John M.	Son of Eliza Satterfield

Johnson County

Name	Date	Age	Master	Notes
Manes, Godfrey	Dec1836	12 yrs 10 mo	Moore, Rufus	Shoemaker. Illegitimate
Shuffield, Nathaniel	Oct1838	9 yrs	Smith, Alexander D.	Hammerman. Of color. Sept1838*
Asher, Larkin	Nov1841	10 yrs	Stout, John L.	Orphan
Cress, Daniel N.	Jan 1843		Farmer, Jessee	Consent of mother, Uree Cress. Son of David Cress, Dcd.* Uree and N. L. Cress, Adms.of Estate
Forgason, Sarah Ann	1June1846	6 yrs on 28Oct last	Carlisle, Elisha	Orphan
Hockada, Wilburn	7Oct1850	3 yrs	Cable, Casper T.	Of color. ?Son of Sally Hockaday, now Longworth. 4June1849*
Helmstetler, William H. H.	1Mar1852	11 yrs last October	Osborn, J. K.	Orphan. 5Jan1852*
Canter, William A.	6Sept1852	14 yrs	Greyson, James W. M.	Orphan.
Ruston, Calvin	6Feb1854	11 yrs	Johnson, Thomas	Mulatto
Canter, Allen	4Jan1859		Greyson, J. W. M.	Prior binding to William S. Williams resc. Mistreatment
Head, Rachael	2May1859	8 yrs	Crosswhite, A. C.	Orphan of William and Mary Head
Head, George W.	6Feb1860		Land, A. J.	

Wilson, Almos M.	7May1860	15 yrs	McQuown, J. N.	
Rankins, William L.	7May1860	3 yrs	Perdeue, Robert	
Adams, James C.	4June1860	15 yrs	McQuown, J. N.	Carpenter
Tilly, Albert N.	7Nov1864		Bradfute, Archibald	Orphan of John C. & Elizabeth Tilley. 7Aug1865*
Stone, Andrew P.	7May1866	4 yrs 5 mo	Mullins, Absalem	Son of Ellen E. Johnson, formerly Ellen E. Stone. Canc 2July1866
Smith, Rufus	7Oct1867	11 yrs 9 mo	Smith, William L.	Of color. Son of Eliza Smith
Marefield, Samuel	2Dec1867	8 yrs	Harris, William J.	Blacksmith. Until age 20. Son of William Marefield
Cress, Eliza J.	6July1868		Wilson, William L.	Until age 21. Dau of William W. Cress (pauper). 4Feb1867* Pm't for coffin for William Cress 7Apr1873
Wilson, William L.	3Aug1868	2 yrs	Greever, C. T.	Consent of mother, Martitia ____, formerly Martitia Wilson.
Cumby, Minerva	7Dec1868	11 yrs	Gregory, Giles	Pauper
Lee, William J.	5Apr1869	8 yrs	Shown, E. A.	Son of Rhoda Lee, destitute
Walker, James D. E.	4July1870	2 yrs on 9Dec1869	Braswell, W. A.	
Barry, Charles	3Feb1873	12 yrs	Moore, Rufus	Orphan. Mother unable to provide. 8Apr1873*
Warden, Margaret C.	8Apr1873	8 yrs in March	Potter, Enoch	Father dead, abandoned by mother
Taylor, David S.	2Mar1874	6 yrs	Snider, Andrew	Orphan, or abandoned by father

Knox County

Name	Date	Age	Master	Notes
Fillson, Polly	21Jan1793	6 yrs	Sims, James	Orphan
Turner, John Fothergill	6Aug1793		Roulstone, George	Printing
Hanley, Alexander	7Feb1794	16 yrs	Stone, John	Orphan
Ogden, David	5May1794		Woodward, Thomas	Orphan
Pharo, George	8May1794	6 wks	Dyer, John	Orphan
Pharo, Elizabeth	8May1794	5 yrs	Dyer, John	Orphan
Bond, Joseph	28Oct1795	16 yrs	Hinds, Samuel	Orphan
Bond, Benjamin	28Oct1795	14 yrs	Green, Solomon	Orphan

Name	Date	Age	Master	Notes
Bond, Isaac	28Oct1795	11 yrs	Hinds, Joseph (son of Levi)	Orphan
Bond, Joel	28Oct1795	11 yrs	Hinds, Sr, Joseph	Orphan
Bond, William	28Oct1795	6 yrs	Hinds, Levi	Orphan
Bond, Elizabeth	29Oct1795	8 yrs	McAmy, John	Orphan. Canc 2Feb1797
Hood, John	30Oct1795	16 yrs	Roulstone, George	Orphan
Doyl, Catharine	25Apr1796	15 yrs 7 mo 16 d	Carrick, Samuel (Reverend)	Orphan
Sharp, Sarah	29July1796	9 yrs 20 d	Hines, Levi	Orphan
Joe	31Oct1796	6 yrs	Montgomery, John	Orphan
George	31Oct1796	2 ys	Montgomery, John	Orphan
Sharp, Elizabeth	3Nov1796	11 yrs	Hinds, Samuel	Orphan
Box, Hessiah	30Jan1797	3 yrs	Hellum, William	Orphan. Female. On 31Oct1796 taken from possession of Thomas Halmark. 1Feb1797*
Bond, Elizabeth	2Feb1797		Chapman, Thomas	Orphan
Heburn, John	Jan1800	4 yrs 10 mo	McNeil, John	Orphan
Heburn, Henry	Jan1800	3 yrs on 5Feb next	McNeil, John	Orphan
Brady, Jesse	Apr1800	14 yrs 6 mo	Kannon, Bartlett	Orphan
Thrasher, Rebecca	18Oct1800	18 yrs on 9July1807	Formwalt, John & Eve, his wife	Orphan
Gibbons, William	18Apr1801	16 yrs 6 mo	Roddy, Moses	Orphan
Bush, Nancy	18Apr1801	3 yrs 6 mo	Brooks, Joseph	Orphan
Dean, James	12Oct1801	3 yrs 6 mo	Dunlap, William	Orphan
Dean, John	12Oct1801	1 yr 11 mo	Dunlap, William	Orphan
Hood, William	15Jan1802	18 yrs 3 mo	Wetzell, John	Orphan
Ogden, Francis	11Oct1802	15 yrs 6? mo	Leigh, George	Orphan
Hill, William	16Oct1802	12 yrs	Lindsey, John	Orphan
Caldwell, Willis	11Jan1803	5 yrs 3 mo	Kerr, William	Orphan
Flinniken, Samuel	15Jan1803	7 yrs	Anthony, John	Orphan

Epps, James	15Jan1803	18 yrs 10 mo	Anthony, John	Orphan
Lambert, Hugh	15Jan1803	5 yrs 6 mo	Anthony, John	Orphan
Fortis, Isaac	15Jan1803	19 yrs 15 d	Wetzel, John H.	Orphan
McConnell, James	15Jan1803	16 yrs	Craighead, Robert	Orphan
Lambert, John	15Jan1803	9 yrs 7 mo	McAffy, Terrence	Orphan
Brown, Polly	15Jan1803	5 yrs 6 mo	Kearns, Nicholas	Orphan
McConnell, Thomas	14Oct1803	15 yrs 6 mo	Craighead, Robert	Orphan
Veal, John	14Oct1803	13 yrs	Webb, John	Orphan
Denny, Nancy	9Apr1804	5 yrs on 10Oct next	Norton, George	Orphan
Cunningham, Samuel	8Oct1804	5 yrs	McAmy, John	Orphan. Resc 11Oct1804. McAmy not a Knox Co resident
Cunningham, Samuel	11Oct1804	5 yrs	Barclay, William	
Roddy, Philip	19Jan1805	14 yrs	Webb, John	Orphan
Lambert, Hugh	10July1805	7 yrs	White, Andrew	Orphan
Pellum, John	17Jan1806	19 yrs	Dawks, John	Orphan
Wills, William	19Apr1806	17 yrs	Long, William	Orphan
Crippen, George	19Apr1806	14 yrs	Majors, Smith	Orphan
Herron, William	19Apr1806	16 yrs	Booth, Edwin E.	Orphan
Ward, Jesse	17July1806	8 yrs 9 mo	Taylor, William	Orphan
Howard, Meredith	17July1806	4 yrs	Roane, William	Orphan. Resc 1July1816. Roane dead
Clap, Phoebe	17Apr1807	7 yrs	Trout, George	
Peterson, Hyram	17Apr1807	12 yrs	Bowan, William	
Wood, Sarah	14Jan1808		Love, Joseph	
Delancy, Hiram	6Jan1812		Gamble, John N.	Orphan. Resc 5Apr1816. To mother
Fleshart, Joseph	6Jan1812		Hewlett, Edmund	Orphan
Malaby, Jane	4Jan1813		Clarke, John	Orphan
Neathery, Robert	5Apr1813		Donoven, Andrew	Orphan of Thomas Nethery, dcd.* Resc 10Apr1817
Neathery, Samuel	5Apr1813		Roberts, Samuel	Orphan of Thomas Nethery, dcd.*
McGhee, Jr., James	6July1813		Dardis, James	Orphan
Fleshart, Francis	6July1813		Cain, Thomas	Orphan

Name	Date	Age	Master	Notes
Neathery, Thomas	5Oct1813		Gamble, Samuel	Orphan of Thomas Nethery, dcd. 5Apr1813*
Risedon, Fletcher	3Oct1814		Lindsey, Moses	
Brock, Allen	3Apr1815		Craighead, Thomas	Orphan
Norris, Patsy	3July1815		Caruthers, Andrew	Orphan
Smart, Rosetta	3July1815		Saunders, John	
Smart, John	3July1815		Saunders, John	
Norris, Nelson	3July1815		Caruthers, Andrew	
Miskell, Charles	2Oct1815		Kennedy, Walter	
Miskell, Robert	2Oct1815		Kennedy, Walter	
Bonizer, David			Hood, John B.	On 3Oct1815 Hood ordered to show cause why indenture should not be rescinded
Brown, Gabriel			Howell, William L.	Canc 3Oct1815
Brown, Robert			Howell, William L.	Canc 3Oct1815
Brown, Gabriel	3Oct1815		Bartholomew, Joseph	
Brown, Robert	3Oct1815		Mitchell,	
Watkins, John	1Apr1816		McCullen, John	
Watson, James H.	1Apr1816		McCullen, John	
Moore, George	1Apr1816		Wilson, George	
Handley, Lardner	1Apr1816		Donovan, Andrew	
Watkins, James	1July1816		McCampbell, John (Minister)	Orphan
Brown, David	1July1816		Wilson, George	Orphan
Howard, Meredith	1July1816		Rigney, William	Orphan
McEldry, Edmund			Ramsey, Samuel	Reported mistreated 1July1816
Ayles, William Preston	7Jan1817	10 yrs	Murray, Thomas D.	Orphan. 7Oct1819* Canc 7Oct1819
Coyle, Craven	7Jan1817	13 yrs	Cullen, John M.	Carpenter. Orphan. Resc 1Jan1821
Miller, William	7Apr1817	14 yrs	Thrasher, Benjamin	Orphan

Delancy, Hiram	9Apr1817	14 yrs 11 mo	Garner, Griffin G.	Orphan
Netherly, Robert	10Apr1817	17 yrs 6 mo	Bell, David	
Childers, Lotan	7Oct1817	7 yrs 6 mo	Bell, David	Orphan
Polson, William	7Oct1817	14 yrs	Dearmon, Sr., John	Orphan
McBride, William	5Jan1818	16 yrs 6 mo	McCaffry, Terence	Orphan
Hitower, John	8Apr1818	16 yrs 8 mo	Hewit, Nathaniel	Orphan
Brock, J. Vance	8Apr1818	16 yrs	Craighead, Thomas	Orphan. Resc 10Oct1818
Brock, Pierson	8Apr1818	14 yrs	Craighead, Thomas	Orphan. Resc 10Oct1818
Thompson, Zachariah	6July1818	13 yrs 6 mo	Meek, John	
Franklin, Riley	6July1818	17 yrs 8 mo	Hewet, Nathaniel	
Brock, Pierson	10Oct1818		Vance, Samuel	
Brock, John V.	10Oct1818		Vance, Samuel	
Bell, John	6Apr1819	14 yrs	Carmichael, Pumroy	
Withrey, Polly			Campbell, William	Resc 7Apr1819
Eli, John	6Oct1819		Robinson, Willoby	Resc 5Jan1830 (as John Ally), abuse
Cox, Allen	7Oct1819	16 yrs 10 mo	Hewett, Nathaniel	House carpenter. Orphan
Ayles, William P.	8Oct1819		Lindsey, William	Blacksmith
Haynie, Spencer	3Jan1820		Cullen, John M.	Carpenter. Orphan. Resc 1Jan1821
Dennis, Calvin	3Jan1820		Paul, William	
Allen, Andrew	3Apr1820		Lindsey, Moses	
Hamilton, Frederick	4July1820		Haskell, Frederick S.	Printing. Until age 20. Resc 3Jan1825
Blair, Esley	3Oct1820		Little, Christopher	Mulatto girl. Until age 18
Crocket, Alexander	3Oct1820		Lindsey, Robert	
Crocket, Robert	3Oct1820		Meek, John	Tanning & dressing leather. Canc 4Jan1821
Hazlewood, Rachel	4Oct1820		Hazlewood, Benjamin	
Howell,			Lindsey, William	Ind canc 5Oct1820
Crockett, Robert	4Jan1821		Lindsey, Robert	Tanning
McReynolds, Polly	1July1822	12 yrs 5 mo	Formwalt, Eve	
Brown,	5Jan1823		Lindsey, William	Prior ind to J. C. Veale canc
Hope, Samuel	5Jan1823		Backwell, J. W.	

Name	Date	Age	Master	Notes
Childress, Ayres	7July1823		Dew, Carter	
Blair, Ivy	6Oct1823		Bowerman, John	
Nance, Archibald	6Oct1823		Hudaburg, Lewis	
McGhee, James	7Apr1824		Lindsay, Mose	Sadler. Prior ind to Joseph Bartholomew canc
Burnett, Myra	5July1824		McNare, John	Bastard dau of Mabel Burnett
Anthony, John	8Jan1825	16 yrs	Bell, David	Taylor
Presley, John	5Apr1825		Husong, Jacob	
Anthony, George W.	8Apr1825		Bell, David	Taylor
Leech, David J.	9Apr1825		Lind, Moses	Saddler
Carr, Rebecka	3Apr1826	12 yrs	Bell, Samuel	Orphan
Blackwell, Samuel	5Apr1826	17 yrs 4 mo	McReynolds, Robert	Blacksmith
Perry, James	3July1826		Widner, Michael	
Moore, Polly	3July1826		Smith, John	
Comer, Archibald	4July1826		Lindsay, Moses	Sadler
Wiggins, Matthew	2Oct1826	6 yrs on 25Dec last	McLamore, William	
Perkins, Emeline	2Oct1826	10 yrs	McBath, James	Mulatto. Until 18 yrs
Hankins, Hyram	4Apr1827	11 yrs 4 mo	Lindsay, Moses	Orphan
Hankins, Gilbert	4Apr1827	13 yrs 11 mo	Bell, Samuel	Orphan
Carr, Henry	6Apr1827		Crawford, Barnes	
Harris, Isaac	6Apr1827		Crawford, Barnes	
Spears, Mary	7July1828	5 yrs 9 mo	Nance, Peter	Of color
Lewis, Elizabeth	6Oct1828		Tinker, William	
Lyons, John	6Apr1829	4 yrs 6 mo	Knox, Matthew	Orphan
Jack, Ramsey	5July1830		Watson, James	Orphan
Jack, James	5July1830		Watson, James	Orphan
Hopkins, Thomas C.	7Oct1830		Cannon, Zachariah	
Jones, George Houser	7July1831		Houser, George	
Hope, James M.	3Jan1832		Graves, George C.	Copper Smith
Kerr, John	1Apr1833	5 yrs	Timons, Matthew	

Kerr, Calvin	1Apr1833	3 yrs 6 mo	Timons. Matthew	
Hickman, John	7Apr1834		Pratt, James	
Pearson, Henry W.	7Apr1834		Rickets, Reuben	
Eliza	6Oct1834		Burnett, David	Of color
Carlos, Columbus	5Jan1835	10 yrs	Lyons, Daniel	Until 20 years
Conner, Isaac	6Apr1835		Good, Gimeral	
Simpson, Jackson	4Jan1836		Edmonson, Samuel	
Carlos, Lafayett	4Jan1836		Lyon, Daniel	Until age 15
Philips, Hugh D.	4Jan1836		McKinley, Samuel	
McCoy, Isaac	4Apr1836		Cardwell, James H.	
Grady, Carolina Matilda	4Apr1836		Worsham, George J.	
Matthews, Robert L.	6Jun1836	4 yrs	Havely, Isaac B.	Of color
Henderson, Shadrick	5July1836	10 yrs	Baker, William J.	Req of mother, Mary Henderson
Bates, William	5July1836		Nance, Peter	Bound on 6June1836
Graham, Jincy [Jane]	5July1836		Craighead, Jane	Bound on 6June1836*
Boyd, Alfred	3Oct1836	12 yrs on 1May1836	Haris, Elijah	Resc 2Aug1842
Russell, Milly	7Nov1836	15 yrs	Crockett, Mary	Freeborn mulatto. Illegitimate
McCoy, Isaac	Dec1836	13 yrs in May1836	Lindsay, Moses	Saddler
Chavis, Charity	Dec1836	7 yrs in Mar1836	Love, Samuel H.	Of color. Resc 6Jun1840. To mother
Peter	2Jan1837	10 yrs	Clark, Hugh N.	Freeborn mulatto. Illegitimate
Matthews, Matilda	6Feb1837		Landrum, Thomas	Of color
Henderson, Fielding	6Feb1837	9 yrs 10 mo	Baker, William J.	Mulatto. Resc 6Oct1846
Ricketts, Benjamin	5Jun1837	4 yrs	Johnston, James H.	
Quals, Aaron	Oct1837	3 yrs on 20May last	Groves, George	
Chamners, Prior	5Mar1838	16 yrs 9 mo	Lyon, Daniel	Tailoring. Until 18 yrs 7 mo. Cons of mother, Mary Chamners
Smith, George W.	7May1838	5 yrs in June next	Moore, Joshua	Consent of mother, Rebecca Smith
Jett, Polly	7May1838	3 yrs	Tinly, John	Of color. Illegitimate. Feb, 5Mar, 2Apr1838*
Grizzle, John			Britt, Solamon G.	Indenture declared invalid 7May1838, to possession of Susannah Grizzle*

Name	Date	Age	Master	Notes
McAffry, Thomas	1Apr1839	15 yrs 10 mo on 20Apr1839	Champe, Amos K.	Tailor. Consent of mother, Patsy McAffry
Crush, Susan Ann	5Aug1839	4 yrs	Sisk, William	Consent of mother, Sarah Sims
Humphreys, Joseph	4Nov1839	14 yrs	Fraker, George	Mother dead, father abandoned Sept1839*
Carr, Frederick	7Apr1840	14 yrs	Hudaburgh, Alexander	Blacksmith. Consent of mother. Allias Frederick Karns
Karns, Frederick				See Frederick Carr
Taylor, Elizabeth E.	4May1840	7 yrs	Gillaspie, Mark	Orphan of Also Taylor Apr1840*
Taylor, John W.	4May1840	4 yrs	Evrett, Durett	Orphan of Also Taylor Apr1840*
Taylor, Matilda M.	4May1840	9 yrs	Taylor, George	Orphan of Also Taylor Apr1840*
Childress, Mary	4May1840	10 yrs	Smith, Michael	Orphan
Carr, William	3Nov1840	14 yrs 4 mo	Leckie, John W.	Copper & Tiningsmith
Hill, William	7Dec1840	7 yrs	Hopkins, John C.	Chairmaking. Resc 7Feb1842. Neglect
Hill, Edward N.	7Dec1840	18 yrs 4 mo 5 d	Hopkins, John C.	Ornamental painting. Resc 7Feb1842. Neglect
Hill, Carick Crozier	8Dec1840	8 yrs 8 mo	Rose, William	House painting, glazing & paper hanging. Resc 4Oct1841
Childress, Creed Taylor	1Mar1841	14 yrs 7 mo	Tindell, Joshua	
Qualls, Neicy Ann	2Aug1841	12 yrs	Branson, Thomas L.	Illeg dau of Clerissee Qualls. Resc 6Sep1841*
Givens. Nancy Ann	2Aug1841	7 yrs	Knox, John	
Mikles, James Kennedy	2Aug1841	9 yrs 5 mo	Lyon, Daniel	
Harper, Elizabeth Ann	3Jan1842	6 yrs 8 mo	Miller, Jacob	Assent of mother
Davis, Alexander	5Apr1842	9 yrs	Formwalt, Adam R.	Consent of mother, Isabel Davis. Resc 6Aug1849, Davis having left
Boyd, Alfred	1Aug1842	18 yrs 3 mo	Harris, James M.	
Chavis, Alexander	5Dec1842	8 yrs	Smith, James	Of color. Consent of mother
Giddeon, Randal Franklin	5Dec1842	9 yrs 3 mo	McCloud, James M.	Consent of mother
Hill, Edward N.	8Feb1843	20 yrs 6 mo 6 d	Metzger, Frederick	
Hill, William N.	8Feb1843	9 yrs 2 mo	Mitzger, Frederick	
Pin, Marshall	2Apr1844		Rodgers, James	Of color
Pin, Alexander	2Apr1844		Bounds, Francis	Resc 3Mar1851

Pin, Mary	2Apr1844		Crozier, Carrick W.	Until 18 yrs
Pin, Lucinda	2Apr1844		Landrum, Polly	Until 18 yrs
Pin, Wiley	2Apr1844		Morrow, Charrels	Of color
Selvage, Levi	6Nov1844	6 yrs	Morgan, Thomas	Orphan. Assent of Jane Selvage, mother. Resc 6Apr1846
John	5May1845		Rodgers, Thomas	Of color
Johnson, Margaret Isabella	1Sep1845	11 yrs 8 mo	French, Peter	Orphan
Gentry, John L.	2Feb1846	15 yrs 5 mo	Ragsdale, Lewis F.	Consent of mother
Badgett, Sarah Elizabeth	2Mar1846	3 yrs	Johnson, John R.	Orphan
Selvage, Levi	6Apr1846	7 yrs 3 mo	White, Reubin	
Murphy, Joseph M.	6Apr1846	13 yrs	Reynolds, William	
Warnack, William C.	4May1846	15 yrs	Champe, A. K.	
Brewer, Martha	3Aug1846	4 yrs 4 mo	Cloninger, Daniel	Abandoned by parents. 6July1846*
Underwood, Mary	6Feb1837		Baker, William J.	Not entered when bound. Of color. Resc 6Oct1846
Lanning, Richard	2Nov1846	12 yrs 6 mo	Burris, Eliza	Consent of father, John Lanning
Rose, Marian	7Dec1846	16 yrs	Harris, George W.	Male
Graves, Joshua	7Dec1846	11 yrs	Grigsby, N. B.	
Graham, Mary Ann	4Jan1847	8 yrs	Thompson, Loyle B.	
Polly, William	5Apr1847	3 yrs 3 mo	McClanahan, Samuel H.	Of color. Consent of mother, Ann Polly
Aleck	4Jan1848	13 yrs	Timmons, Matthew	Of color
Howell, Thomas	4Sep1848	13 yrs 10 mo	Lea, Samuel	Tin & coppersmith. Resc 1Sep1851
Bayless, James M.	4Dec1848	1 yr 7 mo	Ledgerwood, David	Consent of mother, Eliza Jane Bayless. Father, Stephen Holbert 9Oct1850* Resc 9Oct1850. Ledgerwood leaving county
Roston, James G. B.	2Jan1849	13 yrs 6 mo	Brown, Andrew J.	Consent of mother
Douglass, Lawson D.	5Feb1849	11 yrs 6 mo	Hardin, Robert	
Matthus, Ambrose	2Apr1849	15 yrs on 3Aug1849	Lea, Sam	Tinner & Copper Smith. Request of mother
Hewry, William	7May1849	18 yrs 2 mo	Rodgers, John	
Draper, Samuel	7Jan1850	14 yrs	Bolton, Tandy	Assent of mother

Name	Date	Age	Master	Notes
Draper, Pryor Lea	7Jan1850	10 yrs 4 mo	Gallaher, Jefferson	Assent of mother
Brown, James Cowin	4Feb1850	12 ys	Cunningham, Paul	Canc 6Jan1857, John Brown vs Paul Cunningham settled. 2Feb1857*
Bayless, James M.	9Oct1850	3 yrs 6 mo	Holbert, Stephen	Bastard. Holbert reputed father of James
Pin, William	4Nov1850	8 yrs 2 mo	White, Gideon S.	Of color. Resc 6Dec1852
Mason, James	2Dec1850	5 yrs 4 mo	Webber, Moses A.	
Pin, Alexander	3Mar1851	11 yrs	Nance, Pryor	
McLain, Francis	3May1852	8 yrs	Massey, Sherrod	
Catharine	8June1852		Parker, John	Of color
Hill, Harriet	5July1852	14 yrs	Campbell, James W.	Of color. Mulatto orphan 4Oct1852*
Harmon, Elizabeth	6Sep1852	12 yrs	Jones, John H.	Orphan. Brother, James 2Aug1862*
Davis, Manley	4Oct1852	5 yrs 2 mo	Taylor, Elkanah	Consent of mother
Pinn, William	3Jan1854	11 yrs	Allison, Matthew	Of color
Williams, Harden	6Feb1854	14 yrs	McClellan, William	Cons of mother & child
Garrish, William	3July1854	13 yrs	Plumlee, Joseph	Resc 7Sep1858. William anxious to learn a trede
Austin, John	6Nov1854	13 yrs 6 mo	White, James M. (of Knoxville)	Req of mother, Minerva Austin (of color)
Austin, Jane	6Nov1854	12 yrs	White, James M. (of Knoxville	Req of mother, Minerva Austin (of color)
Austin, Latitia	6Nov1854	9 yrs	White, James M. (of Knoxville	Req of mother, Minerva Austin (of color). Age changed to 11 yrs 3Jan1854*
Austin, Ann	6Nov1854	6 yrs	White, James M. (of Knoxville White, James M. (of Knoxville)	Req of mother, Minerva Austin (of color). Age changed to 9 yrs, as Martha Austin, 3Jan1854*
Austin, Hester	6Nov1854	2 yrs	White, James M. (of Knoxville)	Req of mother, Minerva Austin (of color)
Chandler, John	3Jan1855		Morehouse, Gilbert	Baking & candymaking. Orphan of color
Chandler, Thomas	3Jan1855		Morehouse, Gilbert	Baking & candymaking. Orphan of color
Chandler. James	3Jan1855		Morehouse, Gilbert	Baking & candymaking. Orphan of color
Monday, Abner	5Mar1855	12 yrs	Adair, Alexander	Resc 3Apr1855, as Abner Mundy

Mundy, Abner	3Apr1855		Leak, Richard	Orphan
Williams, John W.	4Jun1855	Born 12May1842	McClellan, William	Orphan
Day, Dorthula	4Jun1855	4 yrs	Bise, William	Until age 21. Dau of Sarah B. Day.
McMahon, William H.	3Sep1855	5 yrs 6 mo	Bise, John	
Chandler, Huldah	1Sep1856	10 yrs	Moorehouse, Gilbert	Until age 18. Of color. Orphan
Epps, Elizabeth Jane	1Sep1856	13 yrs	Crockett, Joseph H.	For 8 yrs. By father, George W. (X) Epps
Epps, William	1Sep1856	8 yrs	Lewis, Josephus	For 12 years. Yearly paym't to father, George W. Epps*
Trent, James Madison	7Apr1857		Smith, James	Of color*. Or James Patterson Trent 6Jan1857*
Trent, Milly Caroline	7Apr1857		Smith, James	Of color. Until age 18*
Trent, John Ryburn	7Apr1857		Bond, George	Of color*
Trent, Margaret Lucinda	7Apr1857		Bond, George	Of color. Until 18 yrs*
Stewart, Jane	2Mar1857		Skaggs, David	Of color. Until age 18
Fetzer, George W.	7Apr1857	11 yrs	Renshaw, James H.	
Stuart, Sarah Ann	7July1857		Rhea, Jane	Of color. Until age 18
Witt, Mary Ann M.	8Sep1857		Moorehouse, Gilbert	Orphan
Patterson, Martha	8Dec1857	11 yrs	Parker, John H.	Of color. Abandoned by mother, father dead 7Dec1857
Betsy	5Jan1858	12 yrs	Hudiburgh, A. S.	Of color
Margaret	5Jan1858	8 yrs	Hudiburgh, A. S.	Of color
McClain, Francis M.	3May1858		Barger, John P.	Req of mother, Martha J. Brown
Ford, Joseph S.	3May1858		Perry, Richard M.	Req of mother, Mandy A. Tarwater
Garrish, William	7Sep1858	17 yrs 10 1/2 mo	Parker, John	Tinner
Nelson, Charles	6Sep1858	14 yrs 5 mo	Burton, Byron	
Isabella	5Apr1859	11 yrs	Scott, Alvis Gettys	Until 19 yrs
Lyons, Jr., John	5Apr1859	8 yrs	Lyons, Clarissa	
Watterford, Charles	6July1859	11 yrs	Brownlow, William G.	Of color. Son of Maria Jane Watterford, dcd., freed by Robinson Ganaway 30Oct1845. Father a slave
Watterford, Orlena Ann	6July1859	6 yrs	Brownlow, William G.	Of color. Son of Maria Jane Watterford, dcd., freed by Robinson Ganaway 30Oct1845. Father a slave
Watterford, Frank	6July1859	4 yrs	Rogers, P. L.	Of color. Son of Maria Jane Watterford, dcd., freed by Robinson Ganaway 30Oct1845. Father a slave

Name	Date	Age	Master	Notes
McClain, Alzira	6July1859	8 yrs 7 mo	McClain, James	Orphan
McClain, Carrick	1Aug1859	12 yrs	Helsley, Henderson	Bench Carpenter
Davis, Hugh	5Sep1859	11 yrs	Knott, Peter R.	Of color
Davis, Milly C.	7Nov1859	10 yrs 3 mo	Harper, James	Of color. Until 18 yrs. Consent of mother. Catherine Davis
Davis, Eliza J.	8Nov1859	8 yrs 11 mo	Harvey, H. C.	Of color. Until 18 yrs. Consent of mother. Catherine Davis
Scott, George	8Nov1859	15 yrs	Coker, Lenard	Of color. Consent of father, Thomas Scott, of color
Scott, Marshall	8Nov1859	14 yrs	Coker, Lenard	Of color. Consent of father, Thomas Scott, of color
McMahon, James	6Dec1859	14 yrs 6 mo	Kelly, C.	Assent of mother, Mrs McMahan
Davis, William	3Jan1860	17 yrs 6 mo	Knott, Andrew	Of color. Consent of mother
Boyd, Thomas	6Feb1860	8 yrs	Carter, James M.	Of color. Consent of mother, Matilda Lyons
Call, Joseph	5Mar1860	10 yrs	Morris, James H.	
Davis, Eliabeth	10Aug1860	11 yrs 3 mo	Knott, William L.	Of color. Until 18 yrs. Mother dead, GM assents
Davis, Russell	10Aug1860	7 yrs 5 mo	Knott, William L.	Of color. Mother dead, GM assents
Davis, Hiram	10Aug1860	5 yrs	Knott, Peter R.	Of color. Mother dead, GM assents
Cobb, Archibald			Adolphus, Samuel	Resc 3Sep1860
Davis, Margaret	3Oct1860	9 yrs	Beard, W. W.	Of color
Davis, Mary	3Oct1860	9 yrs	Beard, W. W.	Of color
Davis, Milton	3Oct1860	7 yrs	Beard, W. W.	Of color
Cunningham, Mary J.	2Oct1860	10 yrs	Pratt, John W.	Abandoned by father, mother dead several years
Davis, Susan	5Nov1860	12 yrs 3 mo	McAffry, James M.	Of color. Mother ill. Abandoned by father
Chandler, Maggie	8Jan1861	10 yrs 6 mo	Moorehouse, G.	Of color
Joy, Hannah	6May1861	13 yrs	Joy, William	Mother, Joana Murphy (or Joy), abandoned*. William is uncle
Harrigan, Michael	5Aug1861	8 yrs	Smith, M. L.	Abandoned by mother, father dead
O'Connor, Mary	2Sep1861	13 yrs	Ricardi, John B.	Parents dead
Lea, Edward	8Jan1862	13 yrs	Marshall, J. C.	Orphan. Canc3Feb1862, Edward taken by relatives
Simpson, Samuel M.	6Oct1862	12 yrs 2 mo	Anderson, M. N.	Request of of John G. Simpson, father

Simpson, John H.	6Oct1862	14 yrs 4 mo	Anderson, Joseph W.	Request of of John G. Simpson, father
Farmer, Franklin	1Aug1864	1 yr 3 mo	Hedgecock, W. E.	Mother dead, abandoned by father
Simpson, Alice	5Dec1864	3 yrs	Quin, James	Abandoned
Howell, Sarah S.	5Nov1866	9 yrs	Hull, C. W.	One of Tabitha Howell's 6 mostly female children, oldest 11 yrs. Husband deserted*
Grizzle, A. J. C.	4Mar1867	8 yrs	Ray, George W., & Edmondson, Peter	Of color. Orphan, of 1st Civil District
Grizzle, George H.	4Mar1867	5 yrs	Ray, George W., & Edmondson, Peter	Of color. Orphan, of 1st Civil District
Elen, Thomas	4Mar1867	3 yrs	Ray, George W., & Edmondson, Peter	Of color. Orphan, of 1st Civil District
Keyhill, Alice R.	6Aug1867	3 yrs 1 mo	Tenwater?, Jacob	Dau of Nancy W. Courtney. Father dead
Chambers, William	2Jun1868	2 yrs	Rogers, John	Of color. Destitute, without any natural protection
Wright, Samuel D.	8Dec1868	6 yrs 6 mo	Griffin, Volney	Consent of mother
Toliver, Hartley	5Jun1871	7 yrs	Smith, M. L.	Farmer. No father or mother
Cagle, Lucinda Ellen	7Aug1871	9 yrs	Johnson, A. B.	Abandoned by father. Mother dead
Maxwell, Joseph C.	4Mar1872	12 yrs	Maxwell, W. N.	Farmer. No father or mother
Bean, Burl	2Sep1872	10 yrs	Scott, W. D. L.	Mother dead. Abandoned by father (left state)
Humphrey, William	3Feb1873	6 yrs	Edmondson, A. C.	No father or mother
Bean, William	3Mar1873	6 yrs 2 mo	Smith, W. S.	No mother. Left by father with E. Hunter, who is unable to support him
Lamb, Isaac	2Jun1873	5 yrs	Smith, M. L.	
Swetman, David	4Aug1873	6 yrs	Gambrill, R. W.	Without a home. Taken from Asylum for the Poor. Mother ?Elizabeth Swetman 6Jan1874*
Bailey, George Washington	4Aug1873	7 yrs	Nipper, W. H.	Without a home
Givens, Andrew J.	3Nov1873	8 yrs 6 mo	Kirby, W. F.	
Kirkpatrick, son of Mary C.			Kirkpatrick, John	Resc 3May1875
Nelson, David Grant	14July1875	6 yrs 4 mo	Lewellen, William	Abandoned by parents, unable to provide

Name	Date	Age	Master	Notes
Woodford, Lettie	24Nov1875	9 yrs	Stratton, R. H.	Until age 21. Mulatto. Consent of mother. Reputed father not supporting. On 6Dec1875 Strattton allowed to remove Lettie from county
Tilson, James S.	6Aug1877	13 yrs	Lord, Claudius B.	Lord a resident of Blount Co. 21Apr1877*

Loudon County

Name	Date	Age	Master	Notes
Jones, Jennie	5Jun1871	3 yrs	Hawkins, York	Until 21 yrs. Orphan
Jones, William	5Jun1871	8 mo	Hawkins, York	Orphan
Lincum, William	2Oct1871	6 yrs 6 mo	Henderson, Thomas	Of color
Brown, William	4Mar1872		Gray, T. A.	Illegitimate child of Elizabeth Brown*
Brown, Harrison	4Mar1872		King, W. H.	Illegitimate child of Elizabeth Brown*
Brown, Hugh Berry	4Mar1872		Blankenship, Peyton	Illegitimate child of Elizabeth Brown*
Low, James	7Feb1876		Keen, G. P.	Abandoned by parents
Boyd, William	7Feb1876		Hammontree, L. H.	Abandoned by parents
Welch, ____	4Apr1876		Box, U. J.	Abandoned. Bond for care until 3 yrs.*
Erwin, Ellahugh Martin	1Oct1877		Billingsley, John	Orphan. Abandoned by parents
Oody, Abner	7Jan1879		Simpson, J. W.	Abandoned by parents. Canc 8Apr1879, returned to father

Marion County

Name	Date	Age	Master	Notes
Thompson, Stephen	3Jan1842	4 yrs on 13Dec1841	Nixon, John	Resc Jan1846
Buckner, Marion?	5Sep1842	10 yrs	Hornbeak, Mary	Child of Elijah Buckner
Buckner, Riley	5Sep1842	8 yrs	Rawlings, D. R.	Child of Elijah Buckner
Buckner, Garrett	5Sep1842	6 yrs	Johnson, Charles M.	Child of Elijah Buckner
Buckner, Mathony	5Sep1842	4 yrs	Searcy, Daniel	Child of Elijah Buckner
Johnson, Harrison W.	2Jan1843	11 yrs	Byrne, Brice	Farming. Orphan

Williams, Margaret	6Mar1843		Gilliam, Hardy	Prob dau of Elizabeth Williams*
Dann, John	5Feb1844		Dann, John	
Dann, Elizabeth	5Feb1844		Dann, John	
Dann, Valentine	5Feb1844		Dann, John	
Dann, Matilda	5Feb1844		Dann, John	
Dann, Andrew	5Feb1844		Ridlin, Elisha	
Dann, Sally	5Feb1844		Ridlin, Elisha	
Ogle, James A.	5Feb1844	13 yrs	Forester, Edward W.	Son of Jane Ogle 1Jan1844*
Wood, Green	7July1845	12 yrs	Webb, Jason	Abandoned 7July1845. Indenture & bond completed 6Oct1845
Smith, William J.	6Oct1845		Deakins, Madison	
Thompson, Stephen	Jan1846		Nixon, Thomas	Prior indenture to John Nixon rescinded
Thompson, Stephen	5Oct1846		Webb, Wiley	
Smith, Alfred	4Jan1847		Condra, James A.	
Wyrick, George W.	4May1846	10 yrs	Burns, Nancy	Farmer. Orphan
Hice, Calvin A.	3May1847	3 yrs	Mead, S. B.(Dr) & Rachel	
Hice, Polly	3May1847	5 yrs	Mead, S. B.(Dr) & Rachel	
Washington, Peter	5July1847		Webb, Berry	Orphan
Pearson, Charles	2Feb1891	8 yrs	Clepper, T. W.	Parents dead. no means of support
Bryant, Homer	3Oct1892	6 yrs	Colston, James	Father dead, mother unable to support
Bryant, Arthur	3Oct1892	8 yrs	Hooper, J. P.	Father dead, mother unable to support

McMinn County

Name	Date	Age	Master	Notes
Geno, David	7Mar1825	2 yrs	Greenway, George	Farming. Orphan
Ragsdale, John	6Sep1825	16 yrs on 11Dec1825	Brown, Joel K.	Tailor. Orphan. For 3 yrs 6 mo
Wylis, Darlin A.	6Sep1825	18 yrs on 16Nov1825	Brown, Joel K.	Tailor. Male
Hood, Brison	6Dec1825	12 yrs on 16Apr1825	Tucker, William R. of Athens	Blacksmith. Orphan

Name	Date	Age	Master	Notes
Ragsdale, Benjamin	6Mar1826	18 yrs on 20Mar1826	Brown, Joel K.	Taylor. Orphan
Edwards, Anderson	6Mar1826	19 yrs on 20May1826	Broyn, Joel K.	Taylor. Orphan
Henigar, Jacob	7Mar1826	7 yrs	Price, Esq, Henry	Farming. Orphan. At age 21 to receive 10 Ac rent free for one year plus 40 Ac as an estate in fee simple
Bond, Henry	5Mar1827		Morrisson, Nathaniel	Orphan. Page X'd out
Withers, John	5Jun1827		Workman, Samuel	Tanning & Currying. Resc 2Jun1834
Hood, Bryson	4Sep1827		Brown, Joel K.	Tanning
Shafer, William	4Sep1827		Lane, Tidence	Orphan 3Sep1827
Newman, Bird	4Sep1827		Lane, Tidence	Resc 1June1829
Duke, George M.	1Dec1828	14 yrs on 6June last	Hayle, Thomas	Farming. Orphan
McCall, Sarah Jane	1Dec1828	2 yrs	Rush, William	Orphan
McDonald, Orleana Jane	1Dec1828	3 yrs	Cunningham, Margarett	Weaving & Spinning. Orphan
Jamison, William	2Dec1828	17 yrs	Turnley, James A.	Potter. Orphan
Melvin, William	2Mar1829	9 yrs on 21May1829	Brown, Joel K.	Taylor. Orphan
Green, Richard	2Mar1829	11 yrs on 20Mar1829	Brown, Joel K.	Taylor. Orphan
Smith, James	1Mar1830		Larrisson, Peter	Assent of mother
Davis, Walter	1Mar1830		Turnley, James A.	Potter
Moore, Jackson	5Mar1830		Tucker, William R.	Blacksmith. Orphan
Martin, Samuel J. B.	6Sep1830		Wilson, John S.	
Senter, John	6Sep1830		May, Sr, John	
Senter, Fortena	6Sep1830		May, Sr, John	
David, Assariah R.	9Mar1831	18 yrs	Brown, Joel K.	Tailor. Orphan
French, Allen	9Mar1831	17 yrs	Brown, Joel K.	Tailor. Orphan. Resc 3June1833. Req of Brown & French
Dilley, Andrew Jackson	6Dec1831	7 yrs	Cunningham, Pleasant T.	Orphan. See J. R. Gilley
Gilley, James Riley	6Dec1831	9 yrs	Hale, Samuel	Orphan. See A. J. Dilley
Collins, Ann	4Jun1832	7 yrs	Patterson, Hardin	Orphan
Webb, Jordon	4Mar1833		Taylor, Larkin	Orphan
Webb, James L.	4Mar1833		Walker?, C. M. D.	Orphan

Mason. Robert	5Mar1833		Ragsdale, Benjamin	Orphan
Mason, Sarah Jone	3Jun1833	4 yrs	Jones, Reese	
Gillis, Francis	4Jun1833	8 yrs	Petty, Joseph S.	
Hill, John C.			Roberts?, Michael	Prior indent resc 2Sep1833. To mother
Hill, Andrew J.			Roberts?, Michael	Prior indent resc 2Sep1833. To mother
Charles	5Sep1833		Brown, Joel	Of color
Smith, William	5Sep1833		Ragdale, Benjamin	
Monroe, James	3Mar1834		Cunningham, John	Resc 7Sep1835. See James Monroe Strong
Dugan, Andrew Jackson	3Jun1834		Ragsdale, Benjamin	
Richards, Elijah L.	5Dec1834		Kelly, Richard	
Richards, John V.	5Dec1834		Ragsdale, Benjamin	Resc 7Dec1835
Hammock, James B.	1Jun1835		R__ley, Hugh	
Hammock, Messor	1Jun1835		Love, Thomas B.	
Airey, Joseph Morgan	1Jun1835		Newman, Bird	
Airey, Rachel Angeline	1Jun1835		Ivey, Hartwell	
Strong, James Monroe	7Sep1835		Lowery, James	
Brown, Lucinda	7Sep1835		Doan, Mary	
Gillial, Andrew Jackson	8Sep1835		McDonnald, Charles W.	
Hulsell, Susanah	6Jun1836		Neal, A. B.	Resc 4July1836
Sulser, Samuel	3Oct1836		Owens, Charles P.	
Casteel, William	5Dec1836	13 yrs	McDonnell, John	Orphan
Hutson, Vincent	6Mar1837		Amos, John F.	
Herrill, Mary	6Mar1837		Stubbs, Claborne W.	Resc 5Nov1837, Mary [Herold] now 7 yrs
Brown, Thomas Elbert	6Mar1837		Baker, Cresley	
Leman, Anderson	6Mar1837		Cowan, James	
Jorden, Benjamin Franklin	3Apr1837		Grisham, Thomas	
Dixon, Onslow Murrell	5Jun1837	4 yrs	Baker, James	
Crawford, John	5Mar1838	4 yrs	Knight, Dennis	
Anderson, Martha	5Mar1838	11 yrs	Neal, A. B.	

Name	Date	Age	Master	Notes
Lankford, Robert	4Jun1838		Seehorne, George	
Lankford, Malinda	4Jun1838		Grayham, John	
Hutson, Peter	5Jun1838		Bogart, Solomon	Orphan
Hutson, Jude	5Jun1838		Bogart, Solomon	Orphan girl
Lankford, William	5Jun1838		Willard, George	Orphan. Consent of father [sic]
George, Calvin	2July1838		Burns, Willliam	Resc 6Jan1840* as John C. George. Returned to father, Isaac George
George, Mary Elizabeth	2July1838		Burns, William	Resc 6Jan1840*. Returned to father, Isaac George
George, William A.	2July1838		Ragsdale, Benjamin	Resc 6Jan1840*. Returned to father, Isaac George
George, Isaac Neuton	3July1838		Attlee, William L.	Assent of Susan George, mother. Resc 6May1839
Lankford, James	3July1838		Casey, Dempsey	Assent of Gibson Lankford, father. 4Mar1839* Resc 5Oct1840
Calhoun, James	6Aug1838		Randolph, Robert	Resc 2Oct1838, then renewed same date. 5Nov1838*
Lankford, John	6Aug1838		McRoy, Allen	Assent of father
Williams, William H.	1Oct1838		Blackwell, Silvester	Blackwell adm of Nancy Williams, dcd
Williams, Arrena	1Oct1838		Blackwell, Silvester	Orphan girl. Blackwell adm of Nancy Williams, dcd
Williams, Zechius L.	1Oct1838		Blackwell, Silvester	Orphan boy. Blackwell adm of Nancy Williams. dcd
Williams, Mary E.	1Oct1838		Grigg, Joel	Orphan*
Burriss, Cornelius	3Dec1838		Ivy, Hartwell	Sibs, Neal, Dolly & Peggy Ann, to remain with mother 5Nov1838
Adams, David	4Feb1839		Ingram, Hiram	Orphan 7Jan1839
George, Isaac Neuton	6May1839		Cunningham, Willam H.	Resc 2Mar1840. Returned to father, Isaac George
Whealer, Peggy	1July1839		Knox, James	Resc 1Dec1839
Robison, James C.	5Aug1839		Ivy, Osly	
Whealer, Peggy	2Dec1839		Dickerson, Thomas I.	
Kennedy, Serena	6Apr1840	12 yrs	Hatton, Henry	Orphan. Until age 21
Adams, Letty	6July1840	10 yrs last May	Julian, Isham	Orphan. Until age 21. Has bro, Stephen, 5Dec1836*
Dixon, Edom	5July1841	6 yrs last June15	Barnett, William O.	Farming. Orphan. Resc 6Sep1852
Robison, William Hutson	4Oct1841		Wallis, George W.	

Robison, Delaney Churchill	4Oct1841		Wallis, George W.	
Martin, William	3Jan1842		Keeton, Benton	
Martin, Elizabeth	3Jan1842		Keeton, Benton	
Anderson, James	7Feb1842	7 yrs	Beck, Absolem	Orphan
Brookshire, Jesse	2May1842	15 yrs	Armstrong, William	Orphan
Dean, James A.	6Jun1842	12 or 13 yrs	Gaston, John	Orphan. Canc 3Mar1845
Dean, Thomas A.	6Jun1842	4 yrs	Gaston, John	Orphan. Resc 4Sep1843
Dean, William Calvin	4July1842	16 yrs on 4July1842	Steed, James	
Lowe, Adison C.	4July1842	18 yrs on 1Sept next	Middleton, Hugh L. & John J.	
Brown, Daniel B.	5Sep1842	10 yrs on 5 March last	Fennell, James B.	
Woods, James R.	3Oct1842	10 yrs	Baker, William	
Pearce, Sarah Ann	7Nov1842	6 yrs last Jan	Johnson, Thomas W.	Until age 21
Lowe, Adison C.	6Feb1843	18 yrs on 1Sept last	Low, Isaac	
Woods, Andrew			Frazier, Lorenzo	Resc 4Sep1843
Woods, Andrew	4Sep1843		Bryant, Elisha	
Morris, William W.	2Oct1843	6 yrs last Christmas	Dobbs, William	
Rector, Sarah Jane	2Oct1843		Boyd, John K.	Resc 6Nov1843
Rector, Sarah Jane	6Nov1843	2 yrs on 6Jan1843	Arnwine, Albartis	
Ruth	5Feb1844	7 yrs	Murrell, Onslow G.	Of color. Until age 18 yrs
Woods, John	6May1844	7 yrs	Barnett, John W.	
Crawford, Thomas	7May1844	11 yrs	McDonold, Charles W.	
Crawford, John	5Aug1844	11 yrs	Burk, R. P.	
Calhoon, James	5Aug1844	11 yrs	Stanfield, James	Resc 2Nov1846
Wilson, George W.	7July1845	7 yrs	Torbert, John	
Cartwright, William	7July1845	11 yrs	Cartwright, Lemuel	Resc 6Oct1845
Marcum, Eli W.	1Sep1845	10 yrs	Sullins, Nathan	
Marcum, Nancy Louisa	1Sep1845	6 yrs	Walker, Henry	
Marcum, Polly S.	1Sep1845	7 yrs	Sherrill, Eli	

Name	Date	Age	Master	Notes
Williams, Henry	6Oct1845	9 yrs last July	Swafford, John	
Williams, George	3Nov1845	14 yrs last July	Atlee, Edwin A.	
John	1Dec1845	8 yrs	Jordan, Samuel H.	Of color
Crawford, John	2Feb1846	13 yrs	Miller, W. F.	
Bonner, Thomas G.	2Mar1846	13 yrs	Bonner, Ezekial	
Cordial, George	4May1846	10 yrs	Ivey, Edwin S.	
Calhoon, James	2Nov1846	12 yrs	Hoyl, John	
Grayson, Joseph	7Dec1846	13 yrs	Dodson, Oliver	
Hoback, George W.	5Jan1847	10 yrs	McCulley, Joseph	
Mabry, William	5July1847	9 yrs next Feb	Thompson, William	Orphan 7June1847
Henderson, James A.	2Aug1847	12 yrs	Braden, James	Orphan
Bigham, Asberry	1Nov1847	14 yrs	Ford, William	Son of Polly Bigham 4Oct1847* See Malinda Caster. Resc Jan1848
Caster, Malinda	1Nov1847	6 yrs	Ford, William	Dau of Polly Bigham 4Oct1847* See Asberry Bigham. 5Feb1849*
Bigham. Asberry	Jan1848	14 yrs	McCallie, William T.	Orphan. 5Feb1849*
Roberson, Henderson	Jan1848	16 yrs	Mayo, James	Orphan, son of Cyntha Roberson Jan1848*
Usom, Tilman	7Feb1848	14 yrs	Wasson, William	Orphan. On 6Mar1848 2 Usom orphans ordered brought to court
Rush, Joseph	7Feb1848	3 yrs	McKinzie, Alexander	Orphan
Pace, Wiley	6Mar1848	13 yrs	Bedford, Seth	Orphan
Shelten, John H.	3Apr1848	10 yrs	Gregory, John	Orphan
Shelton, Samuel	6Jun1848	8 yrs	Gregory, Tapley	Son of Samuel Shelton, dcd. Consent of mother, Mary Shelton. Resc 3Aug1857
Shelton, William C.	6Jun1848	5 yrs on 26Jun1848	Gregory, Tapley	Son of Samuel Shelton, dcd. Consent of mother, Mary Shelton
Dodd, James H.	4Sep1848	14 yrs	Rawles, John A.	Orphan
Dodd, Sarah Jane	2Oct1848	12 yrs	Rowles, John A.	Orphan. Until age 20 yrs
Davis, James R.	5Feb1849	16 yrs	Davis, Isaac	
Acre, Lewis Franklin	5Mar1849		Barrett, William	Son of Mrs Elizabeth Acre

Kelly, Thomas	2Apr1849		Higdon, Noah	Orphan
Ulin, Tillman	2Apr1849		Bedford, Seth	Orphan
Usum, ___ton	7May1849		Crow, John H.	Orphan. 2Mar1848 2 orphans named Usum to be brought to court
Tinney, Eliza Jane	2July1849	7 yrs	Cox, Thomas E.	
Bishop, Elizabeth	6Aug1849		McElrath, H. M. D.	Orphan
Bird, Hiram	3Sep1849		Mayo, George W.	Of color. Son of Matthew Bird, free man of color 6Aug1849*. Assent of mother. Resc 3Nov1851
Bird, Eldred	3Sep1849		Burk, William	Of color. Son of Matthew Bird, free man of color 6Aug1849*. Assent of mother
Bird, Ellen	3Sep1849		Bridges, George W.	Of color. Dau of Matthew Bird, free man of color 6Aug1849*. Assent of mother
Bird, Ivory	3Sep1849		Bridges, George W.	Of color. Son of Matthew Bird, free man of color 6Aug1849*. Assent of mother
Wilson, George W.	4Aug1851	13 yrs on 22Dec next	Mesimer, William	
[Bird], Hiram	3Nov1851		Wilson, Hugh P.	Of color
Hackler, William B.	1Mar1852		Jameson, Benjamin C.	
Hackler, Charles F.	1Mar1852		Harden, Joseph	Resc 7Apr1853
Washam, Hiram	6Sep1852		Everton, Thomas	
Dixon, Edom	6Sep1852		Dixon, Eli	
Henderson, James	7Feb1853	17 yrs	Braden, R. F.	
Finney, James W.	7Feb1853	8 yrs	Sweeny, Moses	
Finney, Thomas D. J.	7Feb1853	4 yrs	Sweeny, Moses	
Hackler, Charles H.	4Apr1853	9 yrs	Jameson, Benjamin C.	
Dickson, Charles	2May1853	4 yrs	Worthy, Thomas	
Hambrick, Harrison	2May1853	12 yrs	Culton, James	6Jun1853* 2Jan1854*
Hambrick, Malissa	2May1853	14 yrs	Culton, James	6Jun1853* 2Jan1854* On 6Feb1854 age changed to 7 yrs
Hambrick, Emaline J.	2May1853	20 yrs	Johnston, E. R.	6Jun1853* 2Jan1854*
Night, Lewis	6Jun1853	15 yrs	Moon, William	Resc 4July1853. Lewis returned to parents
Barlow, Leander	6Jun1853	11 yrs	Hutsell, George M.	

Name	Date	Age	Master	Notes
Henry	3Oct1853	15 mo	Thomas, Jonathan	Mulatto
Pike, James	6Nov1854	5 yrs in May last	Erickson, Williamson	Resc 6Oct1857
Knight, Lewis	5Mar1855	17 yrs	Porter, William B.	
Finney, Mary Ann	5Jun1855		Burke, William	Dau of Matilda Finney 7May1855
Johnson, William B.	1Oct1855		Barnet, J. M.	
Johnson, Charles D.	1Oct1855		Barnet, J. M.	
Johnson, Milton M.	1Oct1855		Barnet, J. M.	
Underwood, James	1Oct1855	12 yrs	Small. G.	
Hambrick, Harrison	3Dec1855	14 yrs	Cutton, A.	
Hambrick, Melissa	3Dec1855	10 yrs	Rudd, William	
Philio, James	5Jan1857	8 or 9 yrs	Hales, Thomas	
Shelton, Isaac N.	5Jan1857	3 yrs	Wilson, William	
Underwood, William	Apr1857	10 yrs	Carter, James	
Philio, Maranda	Apr1857	7 yrs	Walker, John	
Robertson, James	3Aug1857	13 yrs	Foster, William	Orphan
Shelton, Samuel	3Aug1857	17 yrs on 6Jun1857	Gregory, James	Orphan
Robertson, John	4Aug1857	11 yrs	Foster, John R.	Orphan
Pike, James R.	6Oct1857	6 yrs on 8May1857	Maxwell, Martha	Orphan
Pike, John	7Dec1857	8 yrs	Burk, A.	Orphan
Shelton, Thomas	1Feb1858	4 yrs	Edwards, John B.	Of color. Orphan. Ordered to court 4Apr1859, Edwards to leave county
Hackler, Morgan	6Sep1858	7 yrs	Newman, John	Orphan
Frasier, John	4Oct1858	11 yrs	Rogers, A. R. T.	Orphan
Ivory	2May1859		Burk, William	Son of Bird, of color
Shelton, Thomas	2May1859	5 yrs	Jenkins, R. F.	Of color
Underwood, Robert	3Oct1859		Carter, Henderson	
Hackler, Hustin	2July1860	5 yrs	Newman, Bird	Son of Clarissa Hackler 2Apr1860. Canc 7July1873
Hackler, George	2July1860	10 yrs	McPhail, William	Son of Clarissa Hackler 2Apr1860
Youngblood, Mary A.	6Aug1860	5 yrs	Cash, Bagan	

Pike, John	3Sep1860		Gregory, Benjamin	
Richards, William H.	4Sep1860	5 yrs	Allen?, John L.	Of color. To care of Hannah Richards, GM, on 3Dec1860
Grisham, Thomas	1Oct1860	15 yrs	Porter, William W.	Illeg son of Ursula Pearce. John Grisham dcd, the reputed father. 2July1860*
Malone?, William	4Mar1861	13 yrs	Zollard?, M. B.	
Shelton, Frank	3Jun1861	3 yrs	Rogers, Thomas	
Shelton, Tipton	3Jun1861	4 yrs	Rogers, Thomas	
Youngblood, Mary Ann	2Sep1861		Eakin, Andrew J.	
Hammontree, Daniel	3Feb1862		Moon, Jr., William	Cons of mother, Martha Hammontree
Gann, Lucinda	3Feb1862		Witson, H. P.	Of color. Until age 18 yrs
Coot, Howard S.	8Apr1862		Rogers, Esq, William	Of color. Request of Coot. Bound for life of Rogers
Tidwell, William C.	5Jan1863	8 yrs	Sivils?, Jeptha	
Hackler, Huston	2Mar1863	9 yrs	Newman, Rebeca	
Robinson, John	6Apr1863	17 yrs	Rinds?, Rotinson?	
Hackler, Morgan	6Apr1863	13 yrs	Cate, O. L.	
Hackler, George W.	4May1863	13 yrs	Wattenbarger, Peter	
Rayburn, Newton M.	4Jan1869	8 yrs next March	Lewis, Z.	Farmer. Orphan
Foster, Charles	4Jan1869	16 yrs in Nov1868	Foster, William	Farmer. Of color. Orphan. Resc 2July1872, Charles having left
Erwin, Calvin	3May1869	11 yrs in Nov1869	Erwin, John R.	Farmer. Orphan
Ballew, Harriet	6Sep1869	13 yrs on 25Dec1868	Briant, W. H.	Housekeeping. Of color. Orphan
Orick, John	4Apr1870	6 yrs on 17April last	Buttram, William	Farming. On petition of Martha Orick
Stuart, Adeline	6Feb1871	12 yrs on 6Feb1871	Moss, E. T.	Housekeeping. Of color
Henry, Sarah R.	6Mar1871	3 yrs on 6Feb1871	Henry, Lerah (fe)	Housekeeping
Martin, Leroy	3July1871		Bishop, J. M.	Farming. Cons of mother, Rebecka Jane Woods
Rentfroe, James	4July1871		Helm, John J.	Of color
Hurst, Laura	2Oct1871	10 yrs	Hurst, John L.	Of color. Until 21 yrs
Hurst, Frank	2Oct1871	7 yrs	Hurst, John L.	Of color
Floyd, James M.	2Oct1871	4 yrs	Shell, C.	White

Name	Date	Age	Master	Notes
Taylor, Bell	6Nov1871	8 yrs	Briant, W. H.	Housekeeping. Of color
Brannum, J. G.	5Aug1872		Hutsell, C. L.	Farming
Brannum, Martha	5Aug1872		Hutsell, C. L.	Housekeeping
Head, Marilda J.	7July1873	12 yrs	Helm, M. A.	
Epperson, W. J.	Jan1868		Epperson, Thomas N.	Orphan. Canc 6Apr1874. To care of mother, Mrs Kitty Buffington, who has reformed her character and now lives in Georgia
Hocker, Jones S.	1Nov1875	9 yrs	Deathrege, George M.	Farmer
McCroy, John M.	3Apr1876			Orphan
Smith, Emma	2Oct1876		Smith, Simon	Illegitimate
Brown, Elizabeth	1Apr1878	12 yrs	McKinsey, Alexander	White

Meigs County

Name	Date	Age	Master	Notes
Jeno, David	5Sep1836		Shaver, Esq, Mathias	Cabinet maker & carpenter. Son of Patsey Jenoe
Jeno, Calvin	5Sep1836		Shaver, Esq, Mathias	Cabinet maker & carpenter. Son of Patsey Jenoe
Cole, James Madison	6Nov1836	8 yrs on 18Oct1836	Hanah, Ivory	Cons of mother, Sarah Cole
Lawson, Jacob	2Jan1837		Smith, John W.	Orphan. Son of Nancy Lawson 7Nov1836. Sibs Anass & Rachal Lawson
Danell, Ezkiel Melvin Obediah Jackson John Gusty Delamey	2Oct1837	8 yrs on 7Dec next	Robertson, Benjamin	Orphan. Bound at request of Robertson & Ann Danell
Mayes, Calvin	5Feb1838		Haners, Avery	
Lawson, Anness Elveney	5Mar1838		Putman, Benjamin	Dau of Nancy Lawson 7Nov1836. Resc 3Sep1838
Cantwell, Joseph H.	6Aug1838	6 yrs	Vernon, James H.	Req of Comrad Cantwell
Lawson, Elveria Ann	3Sep1838	7 yrs 6 mo	Brown?, Alexander	
Eakin, Alexander	6Apr1840	5 yrs	Simpson, Richard	Agriculture. Req of mother, Katherine Akin (Eakin)
Carell, James Wesly	1Jun1840		Fine, Peter	Orphan

Warrack, Eliza	7Sep1840	3 yrs	Eaves, Violet	Orphan. Of color. On 2Aug1858 Eaves released from schooling Eliza, as no school available for her in the county
Thompkins, William	4Jan1841		Griffith, James	Tanning & currying. Orphan
Thorp, Calvin	1Mar1841		Atkinson, John	Orphan
Snider, James	1Mar1841		Atkinson, John	Orphan
Snider, Sarah Ann	1Mar1841		Buckner, Burrow	Orphan
Crow, Henry	7Jun1841		Mizer, Hartwell	Orphan
Crow, William	7Jun1841		Mizer, Hartwell	Orphan
Crow, John	7Jun1841		Mizer, Michael	Orphan
Crow, Isaac	7Jun1841		Mizer, Michael	Orphan
Click, Jane	3Apr1843	4 yrs on 12Feb last	Cate, Joseph H.	Orphan
Rhineheart, Jesse	7July1845	13 yrs 6 mo	Pierce, William	Resc 7Jan1850, consent of guardian
Bennet, William	4Aug1845	13 yrs	Pierce, James P.	
Bennet, John	4Aug1845	11 yrs	Huie?, James F.	
Wells, Constant	7Sep1846	10 yrs 9 mo	Wood, Samuel	Husbandry. Orphan. 5July1847 Wood reported Constance died on 25Apr1847
Moore, Thomas	5Jan1847	16 yrs	Martin, Jesse	Husbandry. Orphan. Until age 20. On 1Feb1847 Jesse Martin appt'd guardian to James & Thomas Moore, minor orphans of John Moore, dcd., late of Pickens Co, AL, who was son of Thomas & Elizabeth Moore, dcd., late of Clarke Co, MS
Lawson, William	1Mar1847	16 yrs	Stokes, Edward S.	Husbandry. Orphan
Mayfield, Abraham	1Mar1847	14 yrs	Kincannon, Thomas H.	Husbandry. Orphan
Newberry, John	5Apr1847	11 yrs	Martin, Wilie O.	Husbandry. Orphan
Gallen, Abraham	5Apr1847	14 yrs	Davis, Thomas P.	Agriculture. Orphan
Hatfield, Martin	5Apr1847	5 yrs	Busten, David	Agriculture. Orphan. Son of Ally Hatfield. Stolen by mother 6Nov1848
Knight, Alexander	6Mar1848	15 yrs in Mar1848	Eldridge, John B.	Orphan. Resc 1Nov1852
Hatfield, James C.	6Mar1848	12 yrs	Peak, Newton	Orphan. Son of Ally Hatfield 7Feb1848. 4Sep1848* Stolen by mother 6Nov1848

Name	Date	Age	Master	Notes
Tharp, Winey	4Apr1848	10 yrs	Adams, William L.	Servant. Mulatto. Dau of Sally Tharp 7Feb1848
Briant, Wiley	3July1848	14 yrs	Norman, Mathew	Orphan
Price, Lee	4Dec1848	7 yrs on 1June next	Hail, George W.	Req of mother, Sarah Sweatman, formerly Sarah Price. Resc 4Jan1853. Hail dcd.
Ussum, Tie	1Apr1850	8 yrs	Cate, William	Husbandry. Orphan. Resc 7Oct1850
Tharp, Michael	3Jun1850	11 yrs on 15March	Miller, Pleasant M.	Tanning business. Son of Sally Tharp 7Feb1848, 6May1850
Ussum, Tie	7Oct1850	8 yrs	Collins, William D.	Husbandry
Rhinehart, James	3May1852	6 yrs in Oct next	Ingle, Sr., William	
Rhinehart, Caswell	3May1852	10 yrs on 19Dec1852	Conell, Christian	Orphan
Lawson, Mary	3May1852	9 yrs in May1852	Atchley, Joseph	Dau of Catherine Lawson, dcd. 6Apr1852
Lawson, Eliza	7Jun1852	4 yrs	Lockmiller, James	Housekeeping. Dau of Catherine Lawson, dcd. 6Apr1852
Whaley, Martha A.	4Feb1856	11 yrs	Shaver, Mathias	Orphan
Whaley, Sarah T.	4Feb1856	6 yrs 6 mo	Cate, Noah	Orphan. Resc 6June1859
Whaley, Joseph Lea	4Feb1856	4 yrs	Miller, P. M.	Orphan
Lawson, Jackson	2Feb1857	12 yrs next May	Shaver, Mathias	Orphan
Tillery, Polly	4Apr1859	7 yrs	Bolin, Henderson	Dau of Jacob Tillery 7Oct1861* To Coffield Tillery 2Dec1861
Tillery, Letty Ann	4Apr1859	9 yrs	Knight, Levi H.	Dau of Jacob Tillery 7Oct1861* To Coffield Tillery 2Dec1861
Tillery, Sarah	4Apr1859	5 yrs	Knight, James H.	Dau of Jacob Tillery 7Oct1861* To Coffield Tillery 2Dec1861
Tillery, Samuel H.	5Apr1859	11 yrs	Ingle, William	Son of Jacob Tillery 7Oct1861* To Coffield Tillery 2Dec1861
Whaley, Sarah T.	6Jun1859	9 yrs 11 mo	Cooley, Jessee	Resc 5May1862
Civils, William	4Mar1861	13 yrs on 28Mar1861	Smith, John W.	Illeg son of Martha Brown. SF Hutson Brown 6Aug1860*
Whaley, Sarah	5May1862	12 yrs on this day	Cate, Robert E.	
Evaline	3Nov1862	6 yrs	Morrison, William H.	Of color. Dau of a free woman raised by Mrs Craighead
John	3Nov1862	4 yrs	Morrison, William H.	Of color. Son of a free woman raised by Mrs Craighead

Harriet	3Nov1862	3 mo	Morrison, William H.	Of color. Dau of a free woman raised by Mrs Craighead
George	6Feb1866	16 yrs	Hutchison, W. C.	Of color. No father or mother
Stewart, Adaline	2Apr1867	9 yrs	Cecil, Thomas	Orphan. Of color. Resc 6May1867
Stewart, Samuel	2Apr1867	7 yrs	Knight, J. H.	Orphan. Of color
Stewart, Adeline	6May1867	9 yrs	Davis, T. A.	Orphan. Of color
Stegall, Nero	2Dec1867	8 yrs	Knight, J. S.	Of color
Smith, Ally	4May1868	7 yrs	Cecill, Joseph M.	Of color. Resc 1Jun1868, returned to M Smith, mother
Smith, Julia	7Sep1868	6 yrs	Smith, B. W.	Of color
Locke, Joseph M.	2Nov1868	8 yrs	McNabb, N. P.	
Locke, Thomas L. G.	7Dec1868	6 yrs	Gamble, W. A.	
Locke, Mary Ann	4Jan1869	11 yrs	Solomon, W. P.	Until age 21.
Adams, Jefferson	4Jan1869	9 yrs	Lentz, W. R.	Of color. Alias Tharp
Tharp, Jefferson				See Jefferson Adams
Turk, H. L. M.	1Aug1870	4? years	Wasson, John J.	Farm life. Mother dead. Abandoned by father
Turk, Mandy H.	1Aug1870	8 yrs	Wasson, John J.	Farm life. Mother dead. Abandoned by father
Price, Jefferson D.	4Mar1872	12 yrs	Harris, Thomas C.	Farm hand. Abandoned
Thomas, Martha	6Oct1873	8 yrs	Johnson, Sally	Housework. Orphan. Resc 1May1876, Johnson dead. Martha not rebound
Higdon, Sarah Jane	7Sep1874	8 yrs on 6Dec1874	Davis, W. R.	Housekeeping. Of color. Abandoned by mother
Francisco, Emma	7Aug1876	12 yrs	Hutcheson, W. C.	Housework. Orphan

Monroe County

Name	Date	Age	Master	Notes
Simms, Samuel D.	6Dec1858		Axly, S. D.	Orphan
Shield, John O.	3Jan1859	15 yrs	Gibson, John	
Shields, Thomas O.	3Jan1859	12 yrs	Stakely, John	Resc 7Oct1861
Shields, John O.			Watson, William	Resc 3Jan1859, Watson deceased*
Shields, Thomas O.			Watson, William	Resc 3Jan1859, Watson deceased*
Arnge	2May1859		Johnson, F. M.	Of color

Name	Date	Age	Master	Notes
Hicks, John	4July1859		Webb, Jasper	Orphan. Canc 5Mar1860, returned to father, James Hix
Williams, James			Shaffer, Daniel T. (or Samuel)	Canc 5Sep1859. Custody to mother, Peggy Jane Williams
Malone, Louisa	5Dec1859		Walker, Mordecai	Orphan. Resc 6May1861
Hampton, John P.	6Feb1860		Vaughn, John C.	Orphan, living with David Rogers 2Jan1860
Halcomb, John	4May1860		Ramsey, John	Orphan
Smith, David	3Sep1860	Abt 7 or 8 yrs	Robinson, Isaac	Orphan of James Smith, 10th Dist. Sibs Clark, Joseph 5Aug1860
Thompson, John W.	3Sep1860		Keller, Phillip	Mulatto. Child of Elizabeth Thompson 5Aug1860
Kizer, Martha	3Sep1860		Johnston, J. H.	Mulatto. Dau of Mary Kiser 5Aug11860
Smith, David	1Oct1860	Abt 7 or 8 yrs	Atkins, William	Orphan of James Smith, 10th Dist. Sibs Clark, Joseph 5Aug1860
Emory, Mary	3Dec1860		Clayton, T. D.	Orphan
Hardin, Wiley	7Jan1861		Taylor, William H.	Of color
Serrat, Mary	7Jan1861		McKeehan, William H.	Orphan
Serat, John William	7Jan1861		Caltharp, G. H.	Orphan. Resc 4Feb1867. Willis taken by his mother in 1864
Lankford, Miller	7Jan1861		Bricknell, W. N.	Of color
Lankford, Miller			McCord, H. J.	Of color. Resc 7Jan1861
Broun, Eliza	4Feb1861		McCallie, Samuel	Orphan. Resc 2Feb1863 as "McCauly"
Horn, Leonidas	4Feb1861		Heiskell, E. D.	Cabinet maker. Orphan
McConkey, Joseph	4Feb1861		Lane, G. W.	Orphan
Cockram, Mary B.	4Mar1861	8 yrs	Wilson, John	Orphan. Dau of Anna Cockram 4Feb1861*
McConkey, Elizabeth	4Mar1861		Lea, G. W.	Orphan
McConkey, Rachel	4Mar1861		Lea, G. W.	Orphan
Patterson, Lazarus	4Mar1861		Lane, George	Orphan. Revoked 2July1866, Lazarus Patterson vs George W. Lane
Serat, Mary	4Mar1861		Kirkland, Benjamin	Orphan
Simms, Joseph	1Apr1861		Duncan, William	Orphan
Millsaps, Mary E.	1Apr1861		Cunningham, D. B.	Orphan of Jonathan Milsaps 4Feb1861*

Hicks, Jonathan	6May1861		Houston, J. E.	Orphan. Resc 2Dec1861
Sitzler, William			Daily, Daniel	Resc 7Oct1861
Shields, Thomas O.	7Oct1861		Cathcart, Joseph	Orphan
Esther	4Nov1861	1 yr	Carson, A. L	Of color. Until 18 yrs
Richeson, Peter	2Dec1861		Cole, Isaac	Of color. To be paid $25 annually
Richeson, Harrison	2Dec1861		Cole, Isaac	Of color. To be paid $12.50 annually
Richeson, Cass	2Dec1861		Cole, Isaac	Of color. To be paid $12.50 annually
Harris, Madison	7July1862		Wright, Josiah	Capias issued
McKenzie, Margaret P.	6Oct1862	13 yrs	Smith, Dennis S.	Orphan
Bales, G. W.	5Jan1863	2 yrs	Sharp, Samuel T.	Orphan
Broun, Eliza	2Feb1863		Thomas, Jonathan	Orphan
Samuel	3Apr1865	13 yrs	Cooke, Robert F.	Of color. Former slave of Cook
Jerry	3Apr1865	10 yrs	Cooke, Robert F.	Of color. Former slave of Cook
Thomas	3Apr1865		Cooke, Robert F.	Of color. Former slave of Cook
Broun, Elizabeth A.	7Aug1865	12 yrs	Swanner, J. J.	Orphan
McDonald, William	5Feb1866		Joins, D. H.	Orphan
McDonald, Martha J.	5Feb1866		Joins, D. H.	Orphan
Broun, Elizabeth A.	5Mar1866		Henderson, Samuel J.	Orphan. Resc 2Nov1868. To stepfather, Edward Smithwick
Bell, Clarance	3Sep1866	8 yrs 10 mo	Carr, Samual	Resc 5Aug1867. Bell decoyed away by mother
Wyric, Samuel			Cunningham, James R.	Resc 7Jan1867, Wyric having left by persuasion of his mother
Cleveland, Ann	6July1868		Berry, Frank K.	Of color
Lillard, Francis J.	7Sep1868		Cleninger, John W.	Orphan
Phillips, James J.	5Oct1868		Phillips, Isaac	Orphan
Smith, David	3Jun1869		Minis, John	Orphan
Boyd, Joakum	5July1869		Etter, Jefferson	Orphan. Jeremiah Boyd, surety. Resc 7Feb1870, as Joe Akum Boyd
Morriss, George	3Jan1870		Johnson, Lewis	Orphan
Morriss, John	3Jan1870		Johnson, Lewis	Orphan

Name	Date	Age	Master	Notes
Isbell, Susan	4Apr1870		Hall, Edwin	Orphan. Consent by Nelson Isbell, father. Resc 6Feb1871
Waller, John	1Apr1872		Stiles, Aurelius	Orphan
Richeson, Moriah	1July1872		Hicks, A. T.	Of color. Orphan
Coon, John A.	2Dec1872	5 yrs	Cluck, P. B.	Orphan
Young, John B.	5May1873		Hall, Edwin	
Young, James H.	5May1873		Hall, Edwin	
Trotter, Jasper	6Oct1873	13 yrs	Ramsay, J. E.	Orphan
Gunn, William	1Dec1873		Kinser, Jacob	Orphan
Newcomb, Moses E.	6July1874		Lerned, George E.	On petition of mother, Elizabeth Newcomb
White, Amanda J.	3May1875		Breeden, F. M.	

Morgan County

Name	Date	Age	Master	Notes
Anderson, Alfred J.	6Jan1851	11 yrs in Feb next	Hurst, Anderson & Martin	Farming. Orphan
Barns, John	7Jun1852	3 yrs	Crenshaw, John W.	Saddling. Mulatto. Orphan
Baans, John	3Oct1853	5 yrs	Cross, Elijah	House carpenter. Mulatto. Orphan
Bailey, Benjamin	6Nov1854	8 yrs	Schooler, William L.	Orphan. Farming
Henry, Samuel	5Feb1855	7 yrs	Frances, C. S.	Farming. Orphan
Beneke, Irvin	8Dec1857	7 yrs	Krisch, Dederick	House carpenter. Orphan*
Beneke, Anna Aurelea	8Dec1857	3 yrs	Needle, Elizabeth	Weaving, sewing, housewifery. Orphan*
Beneke, Joseph L.	1Feb1858	5 yrs	Duper, William	Farming. Orphan*. Brother, Frederick, 2 y/o 8Dec1857*
Benneke, Anna	7Mar1859	5 yrs	Engert, Frederick	Orphan
George	7Mar1859	13 yrs	Laymance, John W.	Farmer. Free baseborn child of Elizabeth Campbell
Benneke, Frederick	4Apr1859	4 yrs	Henderson, Thomas	Orphan
Laymance, Reuben	3Oct1859	4 yrs	White, John	Orphan. $4 for coffin of M. J. Laymance paid by County
Brient, ______			Duncan, Enoch R.	Male heir of James M. Brient. Canc July1874, child delivered to GF, Russell Scott, Sr.

Carrol, Walter	7Dec1874	3 yrs	Everett, Orville	Farming. Orphan
Medlock, Jesse	5July1875	8 or 9 yrs	Guffee, Alvin	Farming. Of color. Abandoned by parents
Barnes, Katie	3Apr1876	5 mo	McGill, William	Until age 21. Abandoned by father
Barnes, Lucinda	3Apr1876	6 yrs	Mehlhorn, Frederick	Until age 21. Abandoned by father
Barnes, Lavina Matilda	1May1876	11 yrs	Henderson, Rufus	Until age 21. Abandoned by father. Canc 4Feb1878, returned to father
Dillion, Nancy Caroline	5Nov1877	8 yrs	Hannah, John H.	Until age 21. Orphan of Christopher & Hopey Dillion, dcd
Shoemaker, Henry L.	4Feb1878	11 yrs on 28July1877	Sanders, William T.	Consent of mother. Abandoned by father
Jones, Preston	7July1879	11 yrs	Petitt, John B.	Parents dead. Consent of relatives. 2Feb1880*
Jones, Dora	7July1879	6 yrs	Blake, Columbus C.	Until age 21. Parents dead. Consent of relatives. 2Feb1880*

Polk County

Name	Date	Age	Master	Notes
Owens, Sarah Katharine	6July1840	10 yrs	Parris, Moses	
Owens, Martha Ann	6July1840	8 yrs	Parris, Moses	Receipt for share from Parris on 5Dec1853
Yancy, John	5July1841	4 yrs	Shields, Banner	Orphan
Davis, Allen	2May1842	7 yrs	Dickey, Samuel H.	Resc 3Nov1845, in possession of father
Davis, George W.	4Sep1843	14 yrs	Bradford, Michael	Orphan of Robert Davis, dcd
Davis, John H.	4Sep1843	13 yrs on 5Dec next	Williams, John	Orphan of Robert Davis, dcd
Davis, Elizabeth Matilday	4Sep1843	8 yrs on 5Feb1843	Williams, John	Orphan of Robert Davis, dcd
Davis, Robert B.	4Sep1843	7 yrs on 8May last	Kaneaster, Reuben	Orphan of Robert Davis, dcd. Terms comp 5Jan1857
Davis, James R.	6Feb1844	11 yrs	Stephenson, Andrew R.	?Orphan of Robert Davis, dcd 4Sep1843*
Russel, James Riley	2Dec1844	11 yrs on 31July last	Zigler, Jacob C.	Orphan of Major Russell, dcd
Russel, Sarah Ann Elizabeth	2Dec1844	9 yrs on 8July last	Horton, Hiram	Orphan of Major Russell, dcd. Resc 7Sep1846
Russel, Mary Hood	2Dec1844	5 yrs in March next	Kline, William R.	Orphan of Major Russell, dcd
Russell, William Anderson VanBuren	6Jan1845	7 yrs on 11Mar next	Blankenship, John	Prob orphan of Major Russell, dcd 2Dec1844
McLemore, John	7Apr1845	12 yrs	McMahon, Sevier	Orphan

Name	Date	Age	Master	Notes
Poplin, George	6July1846	8 yrs	Copeland, James T.	Orphan
Poplin, Jonathan	6July1846	11 yrs	Copeland, John R.	Orphan
Russel, Sarah Ann Elizabeth	7Sep1846	9 yrs on 8 July last	Zigler, Jacob C.	Orphan
Collins, Delpha Jane	2Aug1847	3 yrs 2 mo	Witt, Burgess	Orphan. Until age 21
Rite, Isaac	3July1848	7 yrs this month	Witt, Polly	Orphan
Annie	3July1848	14 yrs	Witt, James H.	Indian. Has absconded. Witt allowed to recapture her
Carruth, Russell Reno	2July1849	3 yrs 4 mo	Burk, Tilmon A.	Orphan
Prince, Celia Malinda	1Apr1850	12 yrs	Rymer, William	Orphan
Rice, Milly	7Apr1851	7 yrs	Higdon, Michael	Orphan. Until age 21
Collins, Jesse	4Aug1851	5 yrs	Ladd, Amos	Orphan
Russell, William A. V. B.	1Nov1852	7 yrs on 11Mar1845	Blankenship, Stephen	Orphan
Graham, Rebecca	3Oct1853	10 yrs 6 mo	Huckabay, Arthur	Housekeeping. Orphan
Musselwhite, Joseph F.	3July1854	8 yrs on 10May1854	Harvel, Joel	Farming. Orphan
Rollins, Nathan	6Aug1855	10 yrs	Greenlee, Lewis	Farming. Orphan
Rollins, Louisa	8Oct1855	9 yrs	Ferguson, Robert C.	Orphan
Rollins, George	8Oct1855	5 yrs	Loughly, J. Y.	Farming. Orphan
Carroll, James Taylor	5Nov1855	6 yrs on 4Mar1855	Davis, William C.	Farming. Orphan
Buchanan, Thomas	2Jun1856	14 yrs	Douglass, H. D.	Farming. Orphan. Resc 4Aug1856 at req of bro, Wm. R. Buchanan
Miller, Isabella Twombs	6Oct1856	11 yrs on 1Nov1856	Kimbrough, John H.	Orphan. Resc 6Apr1857* for abuse
Rollins, Nathan	6Oct1856	11 yrs 6 mo	Gatewood, Benjamin D.	Orphan
Miller, Isabella	6Apr1857		Mills, Sarah	Orphan
Carroll, James Taylor	6July1857	8 yrs on 4Mar1857	Stephenson, Elijah	Tanin. Orphan
Rockhole, Tolbert	4Nov1861	7 yrs on 4Nov1861	Kelley, Payten	Blacksmith. Mulatto, without living parents
Rochold, Tolbert	5Jan1863	9 yrs 2 mo	Denton, James	Blacksmith. Mulatto
Runnion, Reuben	2Apr1866	7 yrs 10 mo 1 day	Rymer, J. W.	
Roggers, Roda	4May1868	14 yrs on 4May1868	Bible, P. L.	Of color
Pearson, James C.	7Jun1869	12 yrs 4mo 10 d	Kaneaster, Ruben	Farming

Clark, Elizabeth	4Apr1871	10 yrs	Garner, J. C. C. (Dr)	Orphan. Dau of Sarah Clark 6Feb1871*
Clark, William	4Apr1871	12 yrs	Kimbrough, William S.	Orphan. Son of Sarah Clark 6Feb1871* Resc 6Oct1872
Clark, Mary Tennessee	4Apr1871	6 yrs	Moline, Cressein	Housekeeping. Orphan. Dau of Sarah Clark 6Feb1871* Resc 6Jun1871
Clark, John	7Aug1871	14 yrs	Dunn, N. B.	Orphan. Son of Sarah Clark 6Feb1871*
Nix, Francis Barto	4Sep1871	10 yrs	Taylor, John F.	Orphan
Nix, Daniel Jones	4Sep1871	7 yrs	Taylor, John F.	Orphan
McAlister, Elijah Monroe	2Oct1871	9 yrs	Carver, W. R.	Farming
Bates, Dan	5Feb1872	8 yrs	Fouts, M. F.	Of color. Orphan
Bates, Jack	5Feb1872		Ladd, Amos	Of color. Orphan. Resc 2Dec1872
Bates, Mariah	5Feb1872		Ladd. Amos	Of color. Orphan. Resc 2Sep1872
Bates, Mariah	7Oct1872	13 yrs	Peck, W. O.	Of color. Orphan. Resc 2Aug1875
Clark, William	6Oct1873		Kimbrough, W. P.	Orphan. Resc 3Apr1876. Clark absconded
Green, Addaline	6May1874	2 1/2 yrs	Clemmer, W. M.	Dau of Mary Ann Green* Resc 1Jun1874. 6July1874*
Green, Jacob	6May1874	6 yrs	Clemmer, W. M.	Son of Mary Ann Green* Resc 1Jun1874. 6July1874
Green, Mary	6May1874	4 yrs	Sweeny, Moses	Dau of Mary Ann Green* Resc 1Jun1874. 6July1874*
Green, John	6May1874	8 yrs	Clemmer, John F.	Son of Mary Ann Green* Resc 1Jun1874. 6July1874
Bates, Mariah	2Aug1875	13 yrs	Prince, William A.	Of color
Cunningham, George	6Mar1876	10 yrs	Wimberly, William H.	

Rhea County

Name	Date	Age	Master	Notes
Dickson, Joshua	28Jan1811	12 yrs	McMeans, Isaac S.	Orphan
Smith, Lotty	27July1813		Jack, Thomas	Orphan
Crow, Isaac	25Apr1814	14 yrs	Hubbard, Nathan	Orphan. Named as son in will of Patience Crow, prob 27Apr1814*
Parker, Elisha	25July1814	3 yrs	Parker, Elisha	Orphan. Resc 24Apr1815
Myers, Jane	27July1814	4 yrs	David, Azariah	Orphan. 26Jan1814* Resc 6Feb1826
Parker, Elisha	24Apr1815	4 yrs	Evans, Evan	Orphan

Name	Date	Age	Master	Notes
Eaton, Patsy	27July1815	5 yrs	Barcley, William	Orphan
Jinkins, Charlotte	27July1815		Harwood, Turner	Prior indent to Thomas Jack rescinded
Harrison, John	5Nov1821	15 yrs on 19Jun1821	Berry, James	Saddlery. Orphan
Sheffy, Fanny	6Nov1821		Bolding, John	
Jones, Polly	4Feb1822	4 yrs	Stuart, Murray	Orphan
Peppers, Repen? D.	4Feb1822	1 yr in Apr1821	Williams, Joseph	Male orphan
Burden, Hezekiah	6May1822		Benson, Spenser	Boot & shoe making. Orphan
Piper, Eliza	5May1823		McCanse, James	For 11 yrs
Carter, Wright	4Aug1823		Stewart, James	For 4 yrs from 12June last. Orphan
Chapman, Leroy Pope	2Aug1824		Howerton, Micajah	Orphan
Chapman, George	2Aug1824		Robinson, John	Orphan. Resc 7Feb1827
Chapman, James Madison	2Aug1824		Darwin, James A.	Orphan. Resc 7Nov1825
Davis, George	2Aug1824		Thompson, John	Orphan
Johnson, Polly	2Aug1824		Witt, Abner	Orphan. Revoked 1Nov1824
Johnson, Colombus	2Aug1824		Wit, Abner	Cabinet Making. Orphan. Revoked 1Nov1824
Ledford, Delila	1Nov1824	8 yrs	Pharis, James	For 10 yrs. Orphan
Chapman, James Madison	7Nov1825		Woodward, William	
Chester, Benjamin			Howerton, Jeremiah	Resc 7Nov1825
Coats, Charles	8Nov1825		Day, John	Blacksmith. For 5 yrs 2 mo. Orphan
Braselton, Harmon W.	7Aug1826		Braselton, Sr, Isaac	For 16 yrs
Chapman, Wellington	4Aug1828		Chastain, John	For 13 yrs. Orphan
Daniel, William I.	3Nov1834		Rush, Isaac	For 10 yrs. Orphan
Daniel, Mary Ann	3Nov1834		Rush, Isaac	For 10 yrs. Orphan
Cole, Charles	2Feb1835	9 yrs	Hannars, Avary	Farming. For 11 yrs. Orphan
Minnick, Samuel	3Aug1835	11 yrs 1 mo	Riggle, George W.	Orphan. 1Aug1836*
Minnic, Isaac			Barnett, James R.	Resc 6Jun1836. To care of Harrison Barnett
Mainas, Susan			Frazier, Samuel	Resc 4July1836

Minach, Isaac	1Aug1836		Howerton, Micahah	James A. Darwin app'd Guardian of Martha, Samuel, Isaac & William Minach, heirs of Samuel Minach, dcd
Edgin, Matilda	6Feb1837		Holland, John	For 10 yrs
Edgin, John C.	6Feb1837		Godbehire?, John B.	For 18 yrs
McDonell, Luticia	1May1837	11 yrs 3 mo	Griffitt, Henry	
McDonell, William	1May1837	7 yrs 3 mo	Griffitt, Henry	
Edgin, Eli Corrathers	1May1837	5 yrs	West, Mary	
Mineck, Samuel	5Mar1838		Smith, Mumferd	Orphan. 1Aug1836*
Minich, William M.	5Mar1838		Smith, Hewlett W.	Orphan. 1Aug1836*
Stacy, Jefferson Monroe	4Feb1839		Britten, Andrew	Tanner
Johns, John	1July1839		Howard, Albert	
Guerin, Howard	2Dec1839		Guerin, Jacob C.	Consent of Nathan Guinn, father. 6Jan1840*
Johns, Henry	6Apr1840		Hicks, Joseph	Farming. Orphan. Resc 4Jan1847. Johns abandoned Hicks
Geron, Evalinda	7Apr1840		Dunn, Elizabeth	Until age 18. Orphan. Of color*
McDaniel, Crawford	7Apr1840	8 yrs	Bell, William H.	Farming. Orphan
McDaniel, Rody	7Apr1840		Worth, William	Orphan girl
Huddleston, William W.	2Nov1840	Born 20Nov1832	Roddy, Jesse	Orphan
Dean, Houston	4Apr1842		Thompson, Jesse	Farming. Orphan
Gearin, Rebecca Ann	6Jun1842	Born 6Mar1838	Garrison, Jacob	Housewifery. Until age 21. Orphan
Gearin, Elizabeth Jane	6Jun1842	Born 6Mar1838	Garrison, Jacob	Housewifery. Until age 21. Orphan
Minnick, William	4Sep1843	13 yrs	Minnick, Peter	Farmer. Orphan
McDaniel, Rhoda	2Oct1843	10 yrs	Boling, John	Household affairs. Orphan
Braddly, Benjamin	1May1854	12 yrs on 29Sep1853	Smith, Nathaniel H.	Farming. Orphan
Bell, John	3July1854	Born 14Aug1848	Knox, Daniel W.	Farming. Orphan. Bond renewed 2July1860
Sanders, Abraham	2Mar1857	14 yrs	Robinson, James	Orphan
McGee, William	5July1858	3 yrs	Ferguson, Lewis C.	Farming. Orphan
Jones, Columbus	5July1858	6 yrs	Pritchett, John	Farming. Orphan of Edward Jones 5May1858
Jones, Richard	5July1858	16 yrs	Snider, A. R.	Wool carding. Orphan of Edward Jones 5May1858. Bond renewed 2July1860, Snyder removing from county

Name	Date	Age	Master	Notes
Jones, Henry	5July1858	13 yrs	Wyatt, John	House carpenter. Orphan of Edward Jones 5May1858
Frasley, Hiram	3Apr1860	10 yrs	Howard, John	Blacksmith. Orphan. Son of Nancy Frasley
Frasley, John	3Apr1860	13 yrs	Howell, Samuel H.	Farming. Orphan. Son of Nancy Frasley
Frusley, Mary E.	4Apr1860	6 yrs in June next	McDonald, John	Housekeeping. Orphan. Dau of Nancy Frusley. Resc 7July1862
Lowry, Elizabeth	7May1860	11 yrs	Keith, John H.	Housekeeping. Orphan. Dau of Mrs Lowry
Talbert, William E. T.			Thompson, John W.	Resc 6Aug1860. Talbert abandoned Thompson's service
Trusley, Mary E.	7July1862	8 yrs in June last	Rigg, W. B.	Housekeeping. Orphan. Formerly bound to John McDonald. See Frusley
Wright, William S.	1Sep1862	15 yrs	Henry, W. R.	Farming. Orphan of Calvin Wright 4Aug1862*
Wright, Joseph	6Oct1862	14 yrs	Shook, John M.	Farming. Orphan of Calvin Wright 4Aug1862*
Davis, Reuben	1Apr1844	16 yrs	Long, Joel	Farming. Orphan
Davis, Andrew	1Apr1844	12 yrs	Orr, John	Farming. Orphan
Condley, John V.	4Nov1844	4 yrs	Guinn, William	Cabinett maker. Orphan
ScottWilliam	7July1845	12 yrs	Brock, Josiah	Farming. Orphan
Scott, George	7July1845	9 yrs	Brock, William	Farming. Orphan
Davis, William	4Aug1845	3 yrs	Timmons, Matthew	Farming. Orphan, son of Susanah Davis July1845. 3Nov1846*
Stone, John S.	2Feb1846	2 yrs 2 mo	Knight, Thomas	Farming. Orphan
Clark, Adaline	2Nov1846	10 yrs	Whaley, John	Housekeeping. Until age 21. Orphan
Clark, Alexander	2Nov1846	7 yrs	Whaley, John	Farming. Orphan
Clark, Anderson	2Nov1846	5 yrs	Whaley, John	Farming. Orphan
Clark, Lucindy	7Dec1846	3 yrs	Britten, Andrew	Housekeeping. Until age 21. Orphan
Trusley, John	7Dec1846	7 yrs	Bryson, Abraham	Farming. Orphan
Trusley, Tilmon	7Dec1846	13 yrs	Bryson, Abraham	Farming. Orphan
Reace, Clark	2Mar1847	16 yrs	Cruse, Rufus M.	Farming. Orphan
Woodly, Nancy	5Apr1847	7 yrs	Wyatt, John	Until age 21. Orphan*
Woodly, Elizabeth	6July1847	6 yrs	Wollard, Charles A.	Until age 21. Orphan. 5Apr1847* Resc 2Jan1849. Eliz to poor house

Sam [Bell]	7Aug1848	18 yrs 11 mo	Day, John	Blacksmith. Of color. Son of Sophie Bell, manumitted in will of Robert Bell, dcd. 6Jun1840*
Granville [Bell]	7Aug1848	18 yrs	Morgan, Washington	Blacksmith. Of color. Son of Sophie Bell, manumitted in will of Robert Bell, dcd. 6Jun1840*
Claibourne [Bell]	7Aug1848	16 yrs	Faust, Joab	Blacksmith. Of color. Son of Sophie Bell, manumitted in will of Robert Bell, dcd. 6Jun1840*
Dearing, Sarah M.	2Oct1848	21 yrs [sic]	Broyles, Cornelius	Housekeeping. Until age 21. Orphan
Dearin, John T.	7May1849	9 yrs	Darnin, Thomas C.	Farming. Orphan
Pickard, Mary J.	7May1849	10 yrs	Buttram, Elsey	Spintress. Until age 21. Orphan
Dyer, Frederick P.	1Oct1849	7 yrs 3 mo	Thompson, Moses C. R.	Farming. Orphan
Dyer, Amanda	5Nov1849	3 yrs	Scroggins, D. G.	Housekeeping. Until age 21. Orphan
Dyer, Margaret V.	5Nov1849	6 yrs	Boyd, John	Housewifery. Orphan
Dean, Thomas	7Jan1850	13 yrs	Wright, A. G.	Farming. Orphan
Milton	7Jan1868	12 yrs	Henry, Cyrus W.	Farming. Of color. Orphan. 2Dec1867*
Pierce, General G.	1Feb1869	5 yrs	Dungan, James L.	Orphan. Consent of mother, Margaret P. Pierce, of Hamilton Co. On 6Sep1869 to care of John Pearce
Woods, Susan	1Mar1869	6 yrs	Allen, W. G.	Mother dead. Abandoned by father
Woods, Susan	7Mar1870	6 yrs	Spence, James	Mother dead. Abandoned by father
Darwin, Alexander	7Aug1871	9 yrs	Gass, W. T.	Farming. Of color. Req of Susan Darwin, mother. Abandoned by father
Darwin, Andrew	7Aug1871	7 yrs	Darwin, William P.	Farming. Of color. Req of Susan Darwin, mother. Abandoned by father
Darwin, Polly	7Aug1871	9 yrs	Darwin, William P.	Housewife. Req of Susan Darwin, mother. Abandoned by father
Locke, John	3Oct1871	8 yrs	Colville, R. W.	Orphan. Abandoned*. Collville an Adm of estate of Newton Locke 6Sep1875
Munsey, Mollie Jane	6Sep1875	Born 24May1864	Cash, Jesse W.	Housewifery. Request of mother, Harriet Munsey
Munsey, James Albert	6Sep1875	Born 9Jan1869	Cash, Jesse W.	Farming. Request of mother, Harriet Munsey

Roane County

Name	Date	Age	Master	Notes
Buchanan, Elijah	25Mar1808	8 yrs	Archer, Moses	Hatter
McNutt, William	19Dec1808	15 yrs	Dixon, John	Orphan
Buchanan, John	19Dec1808		Adair, William	Orphan
Donelson, Betsy	24Mar1809	10 yrs	Trimble, James	Dau of Rhoda Donelson, free mulatto. Resc 23Apr1813
Donelson, Cresse	24Mar1809	7 yrs	Trimble, James	Dau of Rhoda Donelson, free mulatto. Resc 23Apr1813
Hagewood, Thomas	18Sep1809	7 yrs 2 mo	McClellan, David	Orphan
Hagewood, Ruth	18Sep1809	10 yrs	McClellan, Barbara	Orphan
Burk, Robert	21Dec1809		Adair, William	Orphan. Of color. Resc 22Dec1809, returned to Mrs Cooper, widow of John Cooper
Burk, Robert	18Apr1810	14 yrs	Robinson, James	Of color
McNutt, William	18July1810	16 yrs 7 mo	Clark, Thomas C.	Orphan
Pippins, Francis	21Apr1812	16 yrs	Mansfield, Nicholas	For 3 yrs 6 mo
Drake?, Sally	21Apr1812	18 mo	Dunlap, Hugh	Mulatto
Drake, Francis	21Apr1812	3 mo	Dunlap, Hugh	Mulatto
Margrave, Drury	20Oct1812	6 yrs	McCamy, John	?Son of John Margrave 16July1810*. Resc 19Oct1815
Donelson, Betsey	23Apr1813		Williams, Nancy	Dau of Rhoda Donelson, of color
Donelson, Cressy	23Apr1813		Williams, Nancy	Dau of Rhoda Donelson, of color
Margrave, Drury	19Oct1815	9 yrs	Aout?, Samuel	
Clinch, Thomas J.	15Jan1816	11 yrs	Jones, Edward	
Smith, William	15Apr1816	5 yrs	Foshee, John	
Benton, Peter	15July1816	6 yrs	Pickle, George	
McPherson, James Alexander	15July1816	8 yrs	McPherson, James	
Tutle, Absalom	21Oct1816	7 yrs	McMullin, Thomas	
Sappington, Joseph	22Oct1816	3 yrs	Dickson, William	
Sappington, Nancy	22Oct1816	7 yrs	Dickson, William	

Cletcher, Stokes	23Apr1817	6 yrs	Lacy, Joseph	Son of Cletcher Stokes [sic] 22Apr1817. Resc 26July1819
Seat, Mary Ann	21July1817	8 yrs on 27Apr last	Osburn, Isaac	Orphan
Seat, Betsy	22July1817	3 yrs on 2May last	McPherson, Joseph	Orphan. Resc 27July1818
Small, George W.	27July1818	6 yrs on 14Dec last	McKamey, William	Orphan. Canc 28July1828 as Washington Small
Scott, Peggy	26Oct1818		Pride, Allen	Bound by Daniel & Mary Scott, parents
Wilkinson, Celia	25Jan1819	7 yrs	Gideon, Roger	
Wilkinson, William	25Jan1819	6 yrs	Gideon, Roger	
Wilkinson, Roger	25Jan1819	4 yrs	Gideon, Roger	
Wilkinson, Samuel	25Jan1819	2 yrs	Gideon, Roger	
Wilkinson, Martin R.	25Jan1819	1 yr	Gideon, Roger	
Sappington, John	25Jan1819	10 yrs	Galbreath, William	
Allen, William	25Oct1819	13 yrs	Burnet, John	
Bell, George	25Oct1819	7 yrs	Best, Jeremiah	Orphan. Resc 22Oct1827
Allen, David	25Oct1819	11 yrs	Oliver, William	
Dennet, Fleming C.	25Oct1819	11 yrs	Ladd, John C.	
Cletcher, Stokes	25Oct1819	8 yrs on 23Aug last	Hacker, Julius	Canc 25July1825*, Hacker dcd.
Sweany, Susan	25Oct1819	11 yrs	Smith, John	Orphan 29July1819
Howell, Gabriel	24Jan1820		McDougald, Malcome	
Waren, Thompson	24Apr1820	9 yrs last June	Waren, Jacob	
Donolson, Shepherd	25Apr1820	3 yrs in Dec1818	Brown, Thomas	
Donolson, Jesse	25Apr1820	1 yr in Nov1818	Brown, Thomas	
Miles, John	24July1820	8 yrs	Thompson, Charles	
Eaton, John	23Apr1821		Bogel, Samuel	Resc 29Jan1822
Wiggins, Benjamin	23Apr1821	14 yrs	Hewit, Nathaniel	
Ragsdale, John	28Jan1822	12 yrs	Lollar, John S.	
Ragsdale, William	28Jan1822	10 yrs last July	Ligget, Henry	
Eaton, John	29Jan1822	10 yrs last June	Crow, William	
Abbott, Levi	22Apr1822	9 yrs	Harvey, Jonathan	Orphan
McCormack, Samuel	22july1822	18 yrs next March	Stephens, George	Orphan

Name	Date	Age	Master	Notes
Musgrove, Elijah	23July1822	16 yrs	Ligget, Henry	
Wilson, James	27Jan1823	17 yrs on 4May next	Margrove, Samuel	
Pryor, Skipyou	28Apr1823	12 yrs	Nail, Andrew	
Harper, Nathaniel M.	28Apr1823	17 yrs	Liggett, Henry	
Morris, Jesse E.	28July1823	9 yrs on 14Feb last	Eldredge, Jesse	Resc 25Oct1830, Morris having left
Conner, Thomas J.	27Oct1823		Danel, Thompson	Orphan
Howard, Mary Jane	26Jan1824		Howard, Finly	Until age 16
Calhoun, John Clay	28Jan1824	7 yrs	Hewit, Nathaniel	Orphan 26Jan1824. Or Coal C. Houn. Resc 28July1828. See John Colehouse
Allison, Elizabeth	26Apr1824	7 yrs	Preston, James	Until 16 yrs. Dau of Letitia Allison
Brown, Rachel	26July1824		Nassy, Henry	Orphan
Morris, James M.	24Jan1825		Toliafero, Charles	
Smith, Stephen	24Jan1825		Deever, John	
Tucker, Jackson	22Jan1827		Hatcket?, James	
Fletcher, Findley?	22Jan1827		Hatcket?, James	Child of Luvinia Fletcher 24July1826* 25July1827*
Cofer, Baty	25Jan1827		Underwood, Jonathan	Orphan. A prior binding to Ba___ Underwood resc
Conner, Isaac	23Apr1827		Danel, Thompson	Orphan
Derick, George	23Apr1827		Derick, Andrew	Orphan
Lewis?, Coty (Caty?)	23Apr1827		Scroggans, Jacob	Orphan
Swinney, Julian	23July1827		Liles, Robert	Female
Liles, Alexander	24Oct1827		Harvy, Jonathan	Orphan
Vaughn, James Vance A.	24Oct1827		Craighead, Thomas	Orphan
Williams, Peter	24Oct1827		Mahan, Robert L.	Orphan
Allen, Isaac	28Apr1828	11 yrs	Allen, William	
Allen, Catharine	28Apr1828	8 yrs	Allen, William	
Paget, Nancy	28Apr1828	5 yrs	Allen, William	
McNutt, Francis	28Apr1828	6 yrs	Marney, Robert	
Small, Washington	28July1828		Wroe, Hiram S.	
Colehouse, John	27Oct1828	11 yrs 6 mo	Buckhannon, James	See John C. Calhoun

Allen, Sophia	27July1829	3 yrs 4 mo	Allen, Sr, William	
Wormsley, Betsy	26Apr1830	12 to 13 yrs	Good, Gimerl	
Wormsley, Catharine	26Apr1830	7 yrs 5 mo	Cox, Samuel	
Wormsley, William	27Apr1830	13 yrs	Ligget, William	Orphan
Austin, Lethe	26July1830	7 or 8 yrs	Hankins, Ruth	Dau of Ann Austin, dcd 26Apr1830
Casey, Barnett	26July1830	2 yrs	White, George	25Oct1830* On 2Sep1844 alleged abuse not sustained
Casey, Scina	26July1830	3 to 4 yrs	White, George	Female. 25Oct1830*
Lea, William	25Oct1830	7 yrs	Sylar, Peter H.	
Liles, Jasper	25Apr1831	7 yrs on 27th this mo	Liles, Robert	
Liles, Francis Marian	25Apr1831	6 yrs next Sept	Liles, Robert	
Ashhurst, Martin	22Oct1832	18 yrs on 7Feb next	Ferguson, John L.	Orphan
Fletcher, James			Stow, Robert	Taken from Stow 28Jan1833*
Kelly, John	28Apr1834	16 yrs on 10Sep next	Hood, Bryson	
Bench, Albin	28July1834	6 yrs	White, Bloomer	On 5Dec1836 mother, Polly Binge, alleged abuse. Now called Almond Binge. Indenture cancelled 6Feb1837
Ashley, Joel	27Apr1835	15 yrs on 14Dec next	Hood, Bryson	
McDaniel, George M.	27July1835	14 yrs on 4May1835	Hood, Bryson	Resc 5Mar1838. Maltreatment. Diseased in body
Collins, Daniel	27July1835	14 yrs	Lutrell, Caswell	
Love, Joseph N.			Hood, Bryson	Resc 28July1835. Love free to leave
Thomas, William	25Jan1836	17 yrs 6 mo	Crawford, John H.	
Thomas, George	5Sep1836	13 yrs	Underwood, William	$20 yearly to Underwood for George's support*
Lyon, Jeremiah	7Nov1836	12 yrs 10 mo	Hood, Bryson	Taylor. Alias Jeremiah Swain. Resc3Jun1839
Swain, Jeremiah				See Jeremiah Lyon
Walker, Jacob	7Nov1836	16 yrs on 16May next	Driskell, William Y.	
Binge, Almond				See Albin Bench
Hatton, William	1Jan1838	8 yrs	Billingsly, John	Canc 6Apr1846, Helton having run away
Cole, Wesley	5Feb1838	3 yrs	Sutherland, Alvis	Resc 4Nov1839. Sutherland dead
Thomas, Alexander	8Jan1839	8 yrs	Felts, Archibald	Resc 1Apr1839. Thomas unable to render service
Lavender, Solomon	1July1839	15 yrs	Biddo, Philip	
Haley, Mary	7Oct1839	8 yrs	West, John J.	Until age 21

Name	Date	Age	Master	Notes
Haley, Martin	7Oct1839	6 yrs	Johnston, Esq, James	
Cole, Wesley	4Nov1839		Francis, Charles	
Hankins, Jefferson	4Nov1839	14 yrs	Stegall, Richard	
Mayfield, Isaiah	6Jan1840	12 yrs	Bacon, Hezekiah J.	Ordered taken from Bacon 7Jun1841, as Josiah. Abuse alleged. Req of Elizabeth Mayfield* Removed 4Sep1843
Mayfield, Martha Jane	6Jan1840	11 yrs	Bacon, Hezekiah J.	Until age 21.Ordered taken from Bacon 7Jun1841. Abuse alleged. Req of Elizabeth Mayfield* Removed 4Sep1843
Mansfield, Elizabeth	3Feb1840		Hurt, Gillington	Until age 21. Dau of Maryann Mansfield 2July1838
Lawson, Leroy	2Mar1840	15 yrs	Johnston, James	
Carpenter, Jesse	7Sep1840	14 yrs on 14Aug last	Bacon, Drury A.	
Thomas, David	2Nov1840	17 yrs on 2Feb last	Mathis, Ancel	Orphan, Has sister, Polly 5Sep1840
Swain, James M. [Maddison]	7Dec1840	12 yrs	Dugger, John	2Nov1840* Resc 5Apr1841
Walker, West	1Feb1841	13 yrs	Wells, Jr, Moses	Of color 1Mar1841
Dennis	5Apr1841	8 yrs	Jordan, Lewis W.	Of color
Eliza Jane	5Apr1841	5 yrs	Jordan, Lewis W.	Of color. Resc 3Jan1848
Solmon, Washington	2Aug1841	16 yrs next April	Wilson, Samuel	
Voiles, John	6Sep1841	15 yrs last Jan	Jones, Thomas	
Solomon, Jesse	6Sep1841	13 yrs last April	Fisher, Noah	Orphan. On 7July1845 indent modified, Jesse sickly
Hatten, Orrington	4Oct1841	18 yrs	Ballard, Washington	
Burton, Thomas	3Jan1842	6 yrs	Reynolds, William	
Burton, Martha	3Jan1842	4 yrs	Reynolds, William	Until age 21
Edmonds, David	5Dec1842	3 yrs on 10Sep1842	Fouts, Solomon	Canc 5July1852, David having run off
Pollard, Elizabeth	6Mar1843	6 yrs	Smith, Ralph E.	Until age 21. Dau of Ann Pollard 6Jun1842. Resc 4Dec1843
Mayfield, Isaiah	4Sep1843		Turner, Nathaniel	
Mayfield, Martha Jane	4Sep1843		Turner, Nathaniel	
Pollard, Elizabeth	4Dec1843	7 yrs	Pyott, Samuel	Until age 18. Resc 5Aug1844. Returned to mother

Martin, George Washington	4Mar1844	12 yrs	Bailey, Elizabeth	Resc 5Apr1852, Martin having left
Martin, Delila	4Mar1844	13 yrs 6 mo	Philips, Leon	Resc7Oct1844. To E. C. Scarbrough of Anderson Co
Martin, James	4Mar1844	7 yrs	Underwood, William	
Martin, Caroline	4Mar1844	9 yrs	Williams, Powel	
Clark, Lewis	4Nov1844	15 yrs 6 mo	Montgomery, John W.	
Carter, Francess	6Jan1845	10 yrs	Hotchkiss, Clabourn M.	
Christian, Nancy Ann	6Oct1845	13 yrs	Clark, Nancy Ann	Brothers Lewis Z. & John M. 1Sep1845
Christian, Elizabeth Jane	6Oct1845	6 yrs	Clark, Nancy Ann	Brothers Lewis Z. & John M. 1Sep1845
Thompson, Ezekial T.	5Jan1846	11 yrs	Minton, Calvin	On 5Jan1846 $20 to Minton for next years support of Polly Ann Thompson
Christian, Lewis Z.	6Apr1846	12 yrs	Taliaferro, Charles	1Sep1845* Canc 3May1852. Lewis now with father
Bryant, George W.	3May1847	14 yrs on 13Mar1847	West, John J.	
Burns, John G.	5July1847	7 yrs last January	Robinson, Joseph	Son of William H. Burns, dcd
Burns, Henry W.	5July1847	7 yrs last January	Robinson, Joseph	Son of William H. Burns, dcd
Goodman, Abraham	4Oct1847	12 yrs	Eblen, John	Orphan
Branham, Lindsey	6July1846		Purselley, James	
Bowers, John	6July1846		Wright, John	Of 6th district
Bowers, Elizabeth	6July1846		Masan, Thomas J.	Of 6th district. Resc 4Oct1847, ret to mother, Catharine Scott
Powell, Jr, Rhoads	6Dec1847	15 yrs 3May1848	Warren, Felix J.	Canc 3Apr1854. Powell a runaway 2 or 3 yrs ago
Eliza Jane	3Jan1848	12 yrs next April	Duncan, Esq, Robert D.	Of color
Powell, Maria	6Mar1848	8 yrs	Bacon, Isiah J.	Resc 5Aug1850. To friend, Rhodes Powell
Powell, Margaret	3Apr1848	12 yrs	Ellis, William M.	
Burns, Nancy Jane	3July1848	6 yrs	Walker, John	
Dorren, James L.	2Oct1848	8 yrs on 24Aug1848	Moore, George W.	Until age 20. Orphan. Lived with mother @ John Spencer's in 2nd Dist. 2June1848. On 2July1849 ordered to court, abuse alleged.
Thompson, Malinda Jane	3Jun1850	10 yrs on 21May1850	Arnold, Michael	Consent of mother. Resc 3Oct1853
Thompson, Zerelda M.	5Aug1850	8 yrs on 12Aug inst	Salmon, John B.	Orphan. On 4Sep1853 Salmon ordered to answer charge he is about to leave county

Name	Date	Age	Master	Notes
Taylor, James	3Mar1851	9 yrs	Martin, James R.	Of color
Benge, Martha	2Jun1851	11 yrs	McNutt, James W. (Dr)	Mulatto. Canc 5Apr1858, Martha having married Timothy Martin, of color.
Benge, William H.	2Jun1851	9 yrs	Martin, James R.	Mulatto. Has sister, Martha 2May1851
Pelphow, Sarah E.	7July1851	3 yrs last February	Surrett, William T.	
Williamson, Jerman	7July1851	14 yrs	Cooper, Azariah	Of color. 2Sep1850*
Parks, Samuel H.	1Mar1852	11 yrs	Moore, Andrew J.	Resc 1Dec1856. Moore's wife deceased
Bradberry, William	1Mar1852	11 yrs last August	Taylor, Esq, Samuel	No father or mother. Taylor also app't guardian. Canc 5Apr1858, William having run off
Christian, George	5Apr1852	10 yrs	Patty, Josiah	Middle initial "W"? 1Apr1850
Mullins, William R.	5Apr1852	11 yrs on 29Apr1852	Culvahouse, Edward	
Sanly, Nicholas	5Apr1852	16 yrs	Stegall, Richard A.	
Branson, Robert W.	6Dec1852	4 yrs on 4Mar next	Hambree, George W.	Consent of mother, ____ Branson
Phifer, George	2May1853	4 yrs on 15Sep1852	Phifer, Barton	
Moore, Maria Elizabeth	2May1853	3 yrs	Felts, Archibald	Resc 6Jun1853. Returned to mother
Thompson, Malinda J.	3Oct1853	13 yrs	Headrick, William L.	
Chandler, James	2July1855	9 yrs	Doss, John L.	Of color
Chandler, Thomas	2July1855	11 yrs	Cox, Rufus	Of color. Terms completed 5Feb1866. Released
Christian, John			Huffine, Benjamin	Resc 7Apr1856
Harris, Columbus	1Sep1856	19 yrs on 27th this mo	Suddath, Alexander	Canc 5Apr1858, Colombus having run off
Vinson, George M.	3Nov1856	5 yrs on 4Mar next	Billingsley, B. F.	Consent of parents
Parks, Samuel H.	1Dec1856	15 yrs last October	Boyd, John P.	
Dunkum, William J.	6Dec1858	13 ys on 19Feb next	Smith, William of Post Oak Spring	Orphan
Dunkard, James K.	3Jan1859	6 yrs in Feb next	Boyd, Robert W.	
Rayle, George W.	4Jan1859	11 yrs on 5th instant	Byrd, Robert K.	Son of Mary A. Rayle. Sister not bound. Father Samuel Short? 1Sep1851* 5Dec1853* 6Sep1858*
Doren, Samuel	4Jan1859	10 yrs on 11Nov1858	Turner, Sterling T.	Orphan
Doren, Rufus	4Jan1859	7 yrs on 21Dec1858	Turner, Sterling T.	Orphan

Doren, John	4Jan1859	12 yrs on 21Sep1858	Wright, George D.	
Colier, John	7Feb1859	16 yrs on 10Mar next	Cox, Rufus	Orphan. Terms completed 5Feb1866. Released
Branson, Mary Ann	7Mar1859	5 yrs next April	Hambree, George W.	
Columbus	7Jan1856		Johnston, Francis M.	Of color. Resc 2May1859. Johnston leaving county
Columbus	2May1859	6 yrs on 7Jan1859	Johnston, John H.	Of color. Johnstons were brothers. Canc 6July1868*, req of Johnson [sic]
Griffith, John Williams	3Apr1860		Graves, J. M.	Bastard
Ladd, Charles	6Aug1860	13 yrs on 10Aug1860	Ladd, William J.	"Orphan" X'd out of entry
Wright, Adaline	6Aug1860	9 yrs	Ingram, Sanford	Orphan
Gowens, Obediah S.	8Jan1861	8Jan1861	Robinson, Esq, Joseph	Son of Obediah (dcd) & Cynthia Gowens 8Nov1859. 5July1858*. Consent of mother. Canc 5Oct1868
Jackson, Tennessee	2Apr1861	6 yrs	Scott, Israel	Canc 6Jan1862, Tennessee sent to Poor House
Jackson, Rhoda	6May1861		Campbell, Alexander W.	
Dorran, Sarah	4Nov1861	6 yrs on 25Dec1860	Swabe, Charles A.	
Lynn, Asberry	6Oct1862	13 yrs	Kincaid, Clingon McDonald	Orphan
Rail, William	3Nov1862	6 yrs on 26Jan1862	Odem, Eldredge	Son of Mary Ann Rail of 10th Dist 6Oct1862
Lawson, David	3Sep1866	16 yrs	Houston, R. F. P.	Canc 4Feb1867. David having left Houston
Armstead	5Nov1866	13 yrs	McElwee, William E.	Of color. Until age 14. Orphan
Hamilton, Alexander	3Apr1867	13 yrs	Doughty, George W.	One of three children. 6May1867*
Hamilton, Andrew J.	6May1867	10 yrs	Soward, Henry W.	One of three children. 6May1867*
Byrd, Mary	3July1867	8 yrs	Byrd, R. K. (Col.)	Of color
Orange	7Jan1856		Johnson, F. M.	Of color. Resc 7Oct1867
Armstead	2Dec1867	14 yrs	McElwee, William E.	Of color. Until age 15. Orphan
Hudson, William H.	5Oct1868	15 yrs	Weatherford, William T.	Of color. Until age 16. Orphan
Delozier, Abe	2Nov1868	12 yrs	Billingsly, John	Of color. Orphan. Resc 6Feb1871
Blair, James	7Dec1868	13 yrs	Bacon, W. A. & A. S.	Of color. Orphan
Carter, Dennis	1Feb1869	6 yrs	Cox, Rufus	Of color. Orphan
Thomas, Benjamin F.	1Mar1869	12 yrs	Johnston, F. M.	Orphan

Name	Date	Age	Master	Notes
Blair, James	7Jun1869	14 yrs	Bacon, W. A. & A. S.	Orphan. Prior bond challenged by Lowdon Taliaferro, of color, GF of Blair
Scales, Mary Ann	1Nov1869	13 yrs	Martin, Joseph B.	Orphan. Until age 21
Ned	3Oct1870	9 yrs	Browder, W. D.	Of color. Orphan
Ebben, Celia	4Oct1870	7 yrs	Denning, R. M.	Of color. Until age 21. Orphan
Hogwood, Madison	4Oct1870	14 yrs	Branson, John A.	Orphan
Crow, Samuel	4Oct1870	18 yrs	Suddeth, F. K.	Of color. Orphan
Alfred	7Aug1871	13 yrs	Watson, A. G.	Of color. Orphan. Resc 4Sep1871. Unable to locate
Mary	7Aug1871	10 yrs	Watson, A. G.	Of color. Orphan. Resc 4Sep1871. Unable to locate
Senter, Lewis	7Aug1871	12 yrs	Sturges, Thomas H.	Of color. Orphan. Resc 4Sep1871
Oaten, Susan	7Aug1871	8 yrs	Watson, William J.	Of color. Orphan. Resc 4Sep1871. Unable to locate
Wilson, Joseph	7Oct1872	11 yrs	Billingsley, James H.	Of color. Orphan
Center, Lewis	10Apr1873		Crumbliss, H.	Of color. Living with A. J. Cofer
Reed, William Franklin	2Mar1874	3 yrs on 29Jan1874	Browder, William D.	Orphan
McCarroll, Sarah L.	6Oct1874	13 yrs 6 mo	Miller, J. D.	Until age 21. Orphan. Canc 1Nov1875. Refractory & disobedient
McCarroll, James T.	6Oct1874	8 yrs 5 mo	Miller, J. D.	Mechanic. Orphan
Taliaferro, Charles	1Mar1875	11 yrs	Billingsley, James A.	Of color. Orphan
Tipton, Joseph	2Aug1875	8 yrs 3 mo	Weatherford, T. W.	Orphan
Tipton, Mary	2Aug1875	12 yrs 2 mo 18 d	Eskridge, Carpenter	Of color. Orphan

Scott County

Name	Date	Age	Master	Notes
Wallis, Visey	5Oct1857	4 yrs	Hatfield, Esq., Ale	Orphan 6Oct1857
Tramwell, James	5Oct1858	8 yrs	Putteet, John	Orphan, son of Patsy Tramwell
Tramwell, Nancy Jane	5Oct1858	6 yrs	Putteet, John	Orphan, dau of Patsy Tramwell
Daugherty, John Franklin	5Jan1859	8 yrs	Hughett, John	Illeg son of Sarah Clay Daugherty. Also adopted and name changed to Hughett. Appealed by Elisha Dorty 5Apr1859.

Dohority, Levina Mary	5Jan1859		Dohority, Levina	Housekeeping. For 10 yrs 8 mo
Phillips, Joseph	4July1859	5 yrs last April	Brown, John B.	Illegitimate. 4Apr1859*
Silcox, John Marrion	4Oct1859	6 yrs on 13Oct1859	Smith, Sterling C.	Illeg son of Elizabeth Silcox
Wallace, Thomas	2Jan1860	17 yrs	Looper, Joel	Illegitimate
Adkins, Lacy	3July1860	5 yrs on 6Apr last	Risden, Isaac	Until 20 years. Son of Lemuel Adkins. Assent of mother, Sarah Adkins
Adkins, Andrew	3July1860	3 yrs on 8Feb last	Risden, Isaac	Until 20 years. Son of Lemuel Adkins. Assent of mother, Sarah Adkins

Sequatchie County

Name	Date	Age	Master	Notes
Hatfield, Martha Patience	5Apr1858	8 or 9 yrs	Hatfield, Granville	Child of Martha Hatfield
Hatfield, James	5Apr1858	5 or 6 yrs	Hatfield, Granville	Child of Martha Hatfield
Hatfield, John	5Apr1858	3 or 4 yrs	Hatfield, Granville	Child of Martha Hatfield
Haney, William	3Oct1859	15 yrs	Henson, W. R.	Manual labor. Orphan. Resc 1Oct1860
Samples, Charlotte	2Apr1860	14 yrs	Hatfield, Oliver M.	Orphan
Porter, Mary Elizabeth	2Apr1860	6 yrs	Brimer, Aaron	Orphan. Resc 2Oct1865
Bryant, Preston	7Jan1861		Savage, Jesse	Resc 7May1866
Porter, Mary	2Oct1865		Henson, W. R.	Orphan
Samples, Elizabeth	4May1868	3 yrs on 1Jan1868	Hatfield, Eli	
Dill, James William	2Aug1869	11 yrs	Price, E. H.	Farmer. Baseborn, mother [Eliza] unable to support. In April 1880 Dill adopted by Price.
Presley, John Wesley	2Aug1869	7 yrs	Mansfield, John W.	Farmer. Mother dead, abandoned by father. Permitted to take from the county 4July1870
Jackson, William Henry	7Feb1870	12 yrs	Farmer, B. L.	Farmer. Resc 1Sep1873
Jackson, Nancy	6Jun1870	7 yrs	Hatfield, William H.	Dau of Mandy Jackson 2May1870* Resc 6July1874. Absconded
Jackson, Luticia	4July1870	8 yrs	Price, E. H.	Domestic affairs. Dau of Mandy Jackson 2May1870*
Jackson, Margaret	1Aug1870	5 yrs	Clemmons, S. E. (Mrs)	Dau of Mandy Jackson 2May1870*
Cron?, James	June1871		Cron?, Caleb	Blacksmith

Name	Date	Age	Master	Notes
Hudson, John	1May1876	8 yrs	Mansfield, Norman	Farmer. Son of Sarah Hudson, alias Teaters. Sister, Hattie, not bound 2Apr1877
Narramore, William F.	6Jan1879	11 yrs	Pankey, William G.	
Narramore, Thomas	6Jan1879	9 yrs	Pankey, William G.	
Narramore, Vesta	6Jan1879	7 yrs	Pankey, William G.	
Hill, James W.	7Apr1879	14 yrs	Price, E. H.	
Murray, Huston	3Oct1881		Jones, L. B.	Sureties released 3July1882
Teeters, Luther	3Oct1881		McGlothlin, William	1May1882*
Leuke?, John	3Apr1882		Smith, M. G.	
Teeters, Hattie	3July1882		Layne, Madison	Until 21 yrs. 1May1882*
Teeters, Wiley	3July1882		Smith, M. G.	1May1882*

Sevier County

Name	Date	Age	Master	Notes
Stephens, Lorenzo	7Apr1856	5 yrs	McMahan, Wilson	
Nichols, Richard N.	5Nov1856	5 yrs	McMahan, Sanders	Of color. Resc 5Sept1859
Nichols, Alfred	5Nov1856	7 yrs	McMahan, Sanders	Of color
Rebecca	6Jan1857	8 yrs	Burns, L. W.	Of color
Stephens, Noah	7Apr1857	14 yrs	Atchley, P. M.	
Stephens, Solomon	4May1857	9 yrs	Jones, William	
Thompson, Samuel	4May1857	14 yrs	Atchley, Benjamin	
Williams, Perry	3Aug1857		McMahan, James P.	
Manis, Fanny C.	1Feb1858	9 yrs	Hank, Henry	
Myers, Jane	7Jun1857	2 yrs	Richards, Isaac	
Breden, Nancy Jane	6Sep1858	11 yrs	Breden, William	
Branom, Martha Jane	4Jan1859	10 yrs	Baxter, William A.	
Thomas, Rachel	4Apr1859	11 yrs	Rafter, Charles	Resc 1Apr1861 for abuse. 7Jan1861*
Nichols, Richard A.	5Sep1859	8 yrs	Rowlan, Joab	Of color

Nichols, Alfred	5Sep1859	9 yrs	Rowlan, Joab (?)	Of color
Hancock, Perry	3Oct1859	10 yrs		
Beck, Elihu	5Dec1859	3 yrs	Covington, John	To possession of Covington 3Oct1859*
Hancock, Benton B.	3Jan1860	13 yrs		
Justice, Mary	7May1860	5 yrs		Roberts given temp possession 2Apr1860*
Merritt, George Washington	5Nov1860	8 1/2 yrs	Underwood, John	Orphan
Bailey, Mary A.	8Oct1861	10 yrs	Murphy, John	Until 21 yrs
Breeden, Andrew	3Mar1862		Bird, Adam	Son of John Breeden, dcd. & Eliz. 3Feb & 22May1862* Resc 7July1862
Breeden, Nancy	3Mar1862		Frame, John H.	Dau of John Breeden, dcd. & Eliz. 3Feb & 22May1862* Resc 7July1862
Breeden, Harriet	3Mar1862		Breeden, Nancy	Dau of John Breeden, dcd. & Eliz. 3Feb & 22May1862* Resc 7July1862
Breeden, John A.	3Mar1862		Thomas, Anderson	Son of John Breeden, dcd. & Eliz. 3Feb & 22May1862* Resc 7July1862
James, William P.	6Apr1863		Atchley, William	Orphan
Girl	1June1863	14 yrs	Wayland, Lewis	Of color
Nueman, James	6Mar1865	4 yrs	Dikes, Mary	
Down, John	5June1865		Blazer, Jacob	
Down, William H.	5June1865		Forgason, John	
Roberts, William	3Aug1865		Bird, John	Son of William Roberts, Jr., dcd. 4Apr1865
Roberts, Harriet	3Aug1865		Bird, John	Dau of Wiliam Roberts, Jr., dcd. 4Apr1865
Downs, Joseph M. Filmore	7Aug1865		Stafford, John	
Roberts, Samuel	7Aug1865		Reneau, Marcus	Son of William Roberts, Jr., dcd. 4Apr1865. Resc 6Oct1873
Jenkins, James	2Oct1865	15 yrs	Walker, James C.	
McCarter, John	1Jan1866		Fox, Tilman	? Son of Mary McCarter 1Oct1860* 4July1865*
Hurst, Isaac	5Feb1866		Thomas, John A.	
Hurst, Westley	5Feb1866		Hurst, Andrew	

Name	Date	Age	Master	Notes
Covington, Elizabeth	1Oct1866	8 yrs	Underwood, Thomas	
Covington, William	1Oct1866	6 yrs	Underwood, Thomas	
Covington, Polly	1Oct1866	4 yrs	Underwood, Thomas	
Justus, Mary Ann			Lewis, B. S.	Resc 3Oct1866, cruelty. To cust of bro, J. A. Justus
Webb, George Washington	8Jan1867	5 yrs	Smith, Marian [J. M.]	2Apr1867 motion by mother, Rebecca Webb, to have child returned to her dismissed. Resc 7Jan1868. On 1June1868 indent reinstated. On 6July1868 upheld
Lackings, James G.	1Apr1867	7 yrs	Roberts, Levi I.	Resc 6July1868, as James P. Lackey
Reed, Charles N.	5Aug1867		Gibson, James K.	
Willis, Emma	8Oct1867		Murphy, James M.	Of color
Willis, Jane	8Oct1867		Snapp, Joseph	Of color
King, Riley	7Jan1868	5 yrs	McCarter, A. W.	Age from poor farm report 7Jan1868. 1Mar1869*
Breeden, Aaron	3Feb1868	13 yrs	Thomas, J. A.	
Lackey, James G.	6July1868	10 yrs	Runyan, John K.	Resc 3Jan1871, "Yachy" having left
Jinkins, Buster	1Feb1869		Tuder, J. W.	
Jinkins, Abraham	1Feb1869		Tuder, J. W.	
Ellis, Alise	1Feb1869		Maples, Redman	Male
Dykes, James			Dykes, Mary	Taken from Samuel Boles & wife 5Apr1869, having been bound. Resc 6Nov1876, boy having left home
Cunningham, George	2Aug1869		Cunningham, J. W.	Son of Sarah Cunningham 7June1869*
McMahan, John	2June1870		Duggan, Wilson	Resc 2Feb1874
Partin, Cornelius	3Oct1870	2 yrs 3 mo	Smith, J. M.	
Spurgen, James	3Feb1873	12 yrs	Shults, William H.	Orphan
Roberts, Samuel	Oct1873	15 yrs	Fox, George	Farming. Orphan. Consent of Fox
Quilliams, Leander			Hardin, James	Indenture rescinded 5Oct1874. To poor farm
Alfred, James M.	4Oct1875	6 yrs 1 mo	Widener, Jacob	
Ownly, James W.	4Jan1876	3 yrs 1 mo	Ownly, Aaron	
Ellege, Samuel	1May1876		Parker, R. E.	
Quilliams, George			Garner, John	Indent resc 3Apr1877, Quilliams having left Garner

Sullivan County

Name	Date	Age	Master	Notes
Yonas, J. J. B.	3June1861		Himes, John	Approval of mother, Rachel Yonas
Terry, Lawrence			Morrall, John R.	Indenture canc 7Oct1861. Morrall in Confed. Army
Nathaniel			Narkleroad, William N.	Of color. Canc 18Dec1865. Ret.to father, Tennessee
Steele, Burton	5Mar1866		Holt, Ambrose	Orphan
Girtman, Daniel			Booher, Jesse B.	Indenture canc 6Aug1866, Girtman having left
Gossett, John			Rhea, Robert B.	Indenture canc 6Aug1866, Gossett having left Rhea
Erwin, Elen	2Sept1867	9 yrs	Miller, David M.	Orphan
Hudson, Emeline	6July1868		Snapp, L. N.	
Hudson, Julia	6July1868	7 yrs	Johnson, David F.	Resc 1Nov1869, returned to mother
Hudson, John	8July1868		Carden, James	
Davis, Joseph	5Apr1869		Spahr, A. M.	
Smallwood, George W.	6Sept1869	8 yrs	Bowen, Charles H.	Husbandry. Orphan
Smallwood, George W.	7Nov1870	9 yrs	Rader, Calvin M.	Husbandry. Orphan
Boling, Sarah E.	8Oct1872	9 yrs	Cox, Samuel E.	Housekeeping. Orphan
Hill, James N.	2Jan1873	15 yrs	Keller, William N.	Tinner. Also spelled Hull, Hills
Thomas, Joseph	2June1873	11 yrs	Thomas, Rebecca	Farmer. Orphan. Of color. J. S. & Jacob Thomas on bond
Jones, Jeanette	6Oct1873	3 yrs	Buner(Bumer?), A. A.	Housekeeper. Orphan.

Union County

Name	Date	Age	Master	Notes
Owens, George	8Apr1856		Sharp, John	Of color*
Weaver, Sarah E.	8Apr1856		Sharp, John	
Owens, General T.	5May1856		Bayless, Isaac	Agriculture. 5Apr1856*
Owens, James A.	5May1856		Ousley, William	Agriculture. 5Apr1856*
Owens, Alvis	5May1856		Pike, Isaac	Agriculture. 5Apr1856* Resc 4Oct1858

Name	Date	Age	Master	Notes
Wyrick, Susan	4Aug1856		Graves, Plesant	Dau of Josiah Wyrick. 2June, 7July1856*
Wyrick, Jane	1Sept1856		Cowen, Joseph H.	Dau of Josiah Wyrick. 2June, 7July1856* 1Sept1856* Resc 7 Apr1857
Branson, Thomas	3Feb1857	13 yrs	Salling, James	
Garrott, Stephen	2Mar1857	16 yrs in July1856	Warwick, Haden	Agriculture. Consent of Rubin Garrott, father
Kitts, Rubitha	2Mar1857	11 yrs in July last	Sharp, James	
Taylor, Polly	June1857		Hamilton, Alexander	Dau of George Taylor, lunatic
Taylor, Sebra	June1857		Owens, C. J.	Dau of George Taylor, lunatic
Taylor, William	June1857		McBee, John	Son of George Taylor, lunatic
Weaver, William Willey Halfacre	June1857		Brogan, John	Son of Lida Weaver. 4May1857* Resc 4July1859
Furry, Sterling	3May1858		Monroe, Pryor L.	Farmer
Cloniger, John	4Oct1858	13 yrs	Hurst, Allen	
Cloniger, Burton C.	4Oct1858	8 yrs	Hurst, Allen	
Cloniger, George W.	4Oct1858	11 yrs	Sharp, John	Farmer
Taylor, Patsey	4Oct1858	7 yrs	Braden James	
Tharp, Roda	7Mar1859	10 yrs	Hamilton, William	Orphan
Mullins, George W.	7Mar1859	8 yrs	Dunahoe, William	Farmer. Orphan
Norris, William	4Apr1859	5 yrs	Irick, Solomon	Illigitimate child. Resc 1Aug1859
Owens, Taylor	4Apr1859	10 yrs	Robertson, John	Illigitimate child. 8Apr1856* 7Mar1859*
Owens, Alvis	4Apr1859	14 yrs	Ledgerwood, Samuel	8Apr1856* 7Mar1859*
Carter, Jackson	5Apr1859	9 yrs	Carter, J. G.	Illegitimate child. 4Apr1859*
Lovel, Samuel	4July1859	12 yrs	Hickle, Druary A.	1Aug1859*
Norris, William	1Aug1859	5 yrs	Ailon, John & Samuel	
Lovel, Drucilla	1Aug1859	5 yrs	Ousley, Mathew	
Weaver, William Wiley	5Sep1859	10 yrs	Kincade, William	Permitted to take boy out of county on 5Dec1859
Colvin, Mark A.	3Oct1859	12 yrs	Lambdin, W. W.	
Kitts, Samuel E.	7Nov1859	4 yrs	Kitts, George	
Shelton, William	5Dec1859	14 yrs	Dinwiddie, J. M.	
Coonce, Harvy A. N.	5Dec1859	10 yrs	Ledgerwood, A. P.	

Moore, Caswell	6Feb1860	10 yrs	Gibbs, William W.	2Jan1860*
Moore, Squire	6Feb1860	15 yrs	Russell, Alexander	2Jan1860*
Satterfield, Emly	2Apr1860	1 yr	Plaster, M. M.	
Chatt, Allen	2Apr1860	18 yrs	Hamelton, William	Of color
Collins, George W.	2July1860	10 yrs abt Christmas 1859	Hubbs, Howell M.	
Groves, Eliza	1Oct1860	3 yrs	Groves, Sophia	
Carter, Saunders	1Oct1860	14 yrs	Murry, John	
Norris, Isaac	5Nov1860	12 yrs	Groves, Henry	
Daniel, George W.	5Nov1860	14 yrs	Lett, James D.	Sibs Ruth, Wesley, Nicholas 1Oct1860*
Taylor, Henderson	3Dec1860	8 yrs	Braden, James	Parents dead. Poor health. 3Sept1860*
Daniel, Rutha Jane	3Dec1860	16 yrs	Monroe, Mark	Sibs George, Wesley, Nicholas 1Oct1860*
Garrett, John	7Jan1861	14 yrs	Clapp, Calvin	
Romines, Jerry	5Aug1861	16 yrs	Whited, Alvis	Illegitimate 1July1861*
Romines, Asa	5Aug1861	14 yrs	Monroe, W. G.	Illegitimate 1July1861*
Brewer, Jesse	2Dec1861	11 yrs	Walters, Thomas S.	
Garrett, William Anderson	7Apr1862	11 yrs	Warwick, Orange	Resc 1Sept1862, consent of Rueben Garrett
Tharp, Richard	6May1862	12 1/2 yrs	Cleaveland, John A.	Tanner. Illegitimate. Sibs Polley, Lety, Louisa 7Apr1862*
Lovell, Drucilla	2June1862	8 yrs	Ousley, Susanah	
Warwick, Clemantine	1Dec1862	13 yrs	Leinart, A. L.	
Warwick, William	5Jan1863	10 yrs	Monroe, W. G.	
Carter, John	6Apr1863	12 yrs	Hubbs, William	
Warwick, James M.	6Nov1865	12 yrs	Lane, John	
Warwick, Sterling L.	6Nov1865	7 yrs	Lane, John	
Lovell, Marilda	5Mar1866	4 yrs	Chesney, Oliver	
Hubbs, Anna	4June1866	13 yrs	Hubbs, Sr, John	Of color
Hubbs, Lewis	4June1866	10 yrs 5 mo	Hubbs, Sr., John	Of color
Evans, Isaac	6May1867	14 yrs	Albright, John	
Evans, Elizabeth	6May1867	10 yrs	Davis, James	

Name	Date	Age	Master	Notes
Evans, William	3June1867	12 yrs	Albright, William	
Carter, Mary M.	1June1868	10 yrs	Cox, Narcissus	
Cricy	6Feb1871	12 yrs	Ledgewood, W. L.	Of color
Maples, Marion	7Oct1872		Huddleston, William C.	Son of Nancy Maples, bro of Rebecca 3June1872*
Norris, Parelell L. D.	6Jan1874	10 yrs	Miller, Alfred S.	
Cooper, Isaac	6Apr1874	6 yrs	Cox, James P.	Abandoned by father, Nicholas Cooper. On 5Aug1878 control transfered to Winnie Cooper, sister of Isaac. Cox (alias Brooks Cox) in jail*
Washam, Frankie B.	3Aug1874	3 yrs	Ridenour, David	Ind ex 6July1874. Dau of Robert Washam, abandoned
Olla	2Nov1874	4 yrs	Graves, Akilen	
Cofman, Joseph	4Jan1875	14 yrs	Hamilton, Ezra A.	Of color
Baker, John F.	6Aug1876	3 yrs	Pike, Benjamin	
Smith, William M.	1Oct1877	11 yrs	Hammock, Joshua	Farming. Abandoned by mother
Smith, Sarah	1Oct1877	8 yrs on 21March last	Hammock, Joshua	Housekeeping. Abandoned by mother
Hubbs, Josiah	7July1879	7 yrs in Sept1878	Smith, Josiah	

Washington County

Name	Date	Age	Master	Notes
White, Marguret	26Aug1778		McNabb, Baptist	Orphan girl
Newman, Ann	26Aug1778		Tate, Samuel	Tate asks confirmation of indenture from Washington Co. Court in Va. Denied. Ann set free. Appealed
Still?, Charles	Feb1779	6 yrs	Bacon, Michael	Orphan boy. Put in custody. Bound?
Craft, Olif	Feb1779	9 yrs	Bacon, Michael	Orphan girl. Put in custody. Bound?
Craft, Archillis	Feb1779		Bacon, Michael	Orphan boy. Put in custody. Bound?
Bundy, George	29May1781		Walls, William	Orphan of Sevier Bundy, dcd.
Bundy, Reuben	29May1781		Walls, William	Orphan of Sevier Bundy, dcd.
Williams, Betsy	25Feb1782		Higgons, Edward	Orphan. Dau of Mary Williams, now Mary Newbery

Maccashlin, Robert	25Feb1782		All___, James	Orphan. Bound by George King and Margaret.
Bond, Georgia	28May1782	13 yrs	Clark, John	Blacksmith. Orphan boy. Clark appt'd Bond's guardian
Mcguff, Ed.	28May1782	7 yrs	Morris, Gideon	Orphan
Handly, Mary			White, William	On 28May1782 indent declared fradulent. Cancelled
Cross, Absolom	4Nov1782	13 yrs	Kenedy, Esq, Daniel	Orphan of Ben Cross, dcd.
Bundy, Nathaniel	4Nov1782		Turbott, James	Orphan of Simon Bundy, dcd.
Bundy, Reuben	4Nov1782		Turbott, James	Orphan of Simon Bundy, dcd.
Robertson, John	5Nov1782	5 yrs	Robertson, Elijah	Orphan
Carlin, Isaiah	3Feb1783	4 yrs on 15Aug last	Willson, Esq, Joseph	Bastard son of Margaret Carr
Dye, William	3Feb1783	4 yrs	McMahon, Joseph	Orphan
Mosely, William	6May1783	16 yrs	Newman, Esq, John	Orphan
Corland, Joshua	2Feb1784	5 yrs	Willson, Esq, Joseph	Weaving. Orphan
Long, James	3Aug1784	14 yrs	Green, Alexander	Orphan
Shanks, Miche	4Aug1784	7 yrs 4 mo	Strain, John	Orphan
McGlohlin, Sary	7Nov1785		English, Jane	Weaving.
Postle, John	13May1788		Oldham, Henry	
Postle, Abel	13May1788		Oldham, Henry	
Dedman, Edith	Nov1788	4 yrs	Carson, William	Baseborn child
Hooper, Philip	Feb1789	12 yrs	Stephenson, William	Baseborn child
Grissam, John	Feb1789	9 or 10 yrs	Lincoln, Isaac	Orphan
Garner, Sarah	Feb1789	5 yrs	Hammer, Esq, John	
Grimes, Emanuel	Feb1789	3 yrs	Lemmon, John	Baseborn
Brown, John	Aug1789	6 yrs 9 mo	Pigg, Richard	Weaver. Baseborn
Brown, Jesse	Aug1789	3 yrs 11 mo	Pigg, Richard	Taylor. Baseborn
Wilson, Robert	Nov1789	6 yrs	Taylor, Leeroy	Silversmith
Cooper, William	10May1790	10 yrs	Abell, Ezekiel	Blacksmith. Orphan
Tipton, Samuel	10Aug1790	13 yrs	Hedrick, Joseph	Blacksmith
Tipton, John	10Aug1790	10 yrs 2 mo	Jones, Henry	Fuller
Cooper, James	Feb1794?		Gorden, James	Hatter
Hampson, James	27Feb1794		McKie, Allexander	Shoemaker

Name	Date	Age	Master	Notes
Hampson,	27Feb1794		McKie, Allexander	Female
Goodpasture, Margaret			McNitt, Anthony	Indenture cancelled on 27Feb1794
Norton, Sally	26May1794		Hunter, John	Sew, spin & nitt
Roberts,Ann	27May1794		Hunter, Abraham	
Stout, Magdalin	28May1794		Broyles, Nicholas	Female
Stout, Aron	28May1794		Broyles, Nicholas	
Stout, Moses	28May1794		McAllister, John	
Straton, Absalom	27Aug1794		Evans, John	Carpenter. For three years. Dated 15July1794
Stillmant, Thomas Hants	27Aug1794		Caldwell, William, of Jonesborough	For four yrs. By Father, John Hants Stillmant, Sr*
Stout, Daniel	18Nov1794		Blackburn, Thomas	
Stout, David	18Nov1794		Bkackburn, Thomas	
Stout, George	18Nov1794		Carson, Andrew	Cancelled 20Nov1795
Hamelton, Nancy	May1795		Begart, Henry	
Stout, George	20Nov1795		____, John	Shoemaking
Roberts, Sarah	18Feb1796		Chester, William Patterson	
Roberts, James	18Feb1796		Chester, William Patterson	
Roberts, Roda	18Feb1796		Harrison, Micheal	
Payton, John Whilson	Nov1788	17 yrs last April	Abell, Ezekial	Blacksmith
McFarland, William	May1798		Blair, William	Blacksmith
Palson, Israal	May1798		Hail, Sr., George	Shoemaking
Randolf, James	8May1799		Gyer, Jacob	
Murrey, Ann	8Feb1809		Elsey, Thomas	
Whitaker, Julian	8Feb1809		Wiley, Abel	Until age 18
Elroy, David M.	8Feb1809		Broyles, Thomas	
Cofman, Conrod	1May1809		Patton, Thomas C.	
Cofman, Jacob	1May1809		Lineberger, Nicholas	

Cofman, Mathias	1May1809		Keyes, Conrod	
Cofman, John	1May1809		Adams, John	
Cofman, Sarah	1May1809		Keyes, Conrod	
Goforth, Nancy	10May1810		Bayles, Daniel	
Bayles, Abraham	6Aug1810		Bayles, Samuel	
Johnston, William	10May1811		Vance, William K.	
Jemimar	7Aug1811		Kubler, Jacob	Girl of color
Betsey	7Aug1811		Kubler, Jacob	Girl of color
Johnston, Elem	5Nov1811		Cloyd, James	
Polly	4May1812		Hunt, Sr., Jesse	Free girl of color
Hall, Daniel	4May1812		McCeahen?, John	Of color. Resc 17Apr1820
Carrell, Catharine	5Aug1812		Brown, Mary	
Carrel, Sally Hensley	5Aug1812		Achen, Mathew	
Kelley, Margaret	2Nov1812		Fanesher, Frederick	
Carder, Thomas	2Nov1812		White, David	
Lasley, George	2Feb1813		Baker, Robert	
Whitaker, William	2Feb1813		Wiley, Able	
Ward, Alfred	4Feb1813		Boren, John	
Goforth, Absolem	3May1813		McGinnis, John	
Gilmore, Elizabeth	4May1813		Payne, William	
Mitchell, Sally	5May1813		Million, Robert	Resc 18Apr1816. Thos. Mitchell to pay Million $45.
Mitchell, Thomas	5May1813		Million, Robert	Resc 18Apr1816. Thos. Mitchell to pay Million $45.
Parker, Alfred	2Aug1813		Achen, Mathew	
Kelly, Polly Kilsey	2Aug1813		Grist, Robert	Resc 18Apr1816.
Carder, Samuel	3Aug1813		Grimsley, John	
Brown, James	3Aug1813		Baker, Robert	
Chittister, Alexander	3Aug1813		Gates, John	
Collins, Ambrous	8Feb1814		Millen, William	
Allen, Samuel	Aug1814		Garner, Griffin G.	
Chittyles, John	2Aug1814		Gyre?, Henry	

Name	Date	Age	Master	Notes
Brown, James	5Aug1814		Kennedy, John	
Sands, John	8Nov1814		Guinn, Thomas	
Collins, Henry	8Nov1814		Parsel, George	Resc 16July1821
McGinnis, Abraham	4May1815		McGinnis, John	
Sands, Henry	6Nov1815		Howell, Henry	Hatting
Kenord, Thomas	19Jan1816		Willet, Nimrod	
Varnam, Sidney	19Jan1816		Kortz, John	Female
Patterson, James	16Apr1816	11 yrs on 14May next	Church, Robert	Resc 22Oct1819*
Patterson, Sarah	16Apr1816	Born 7Oct1807	Starnes, Jacob	
White, Samuel	18Apr1816		Howel, Charles	
Kelly, Mary K.	18Apr1816		Chester, William P.	
Large?, Solomon	19Apr1816		Faubush, Hugh	
Gillespie, George	18July1816	17 yrs on 2Oct next	Church, Robert	Saddler?
Powel, Joseph	21Jan1817		McCade, John	
Patterson, Elizabeth	21Jan1817		Brown, Abraham	
Betsy Ann	21Jan1817		Boyles, Hezekiah	Taken from John Clark. Alias Betsy Ann Coffman
McGinnis, Abraham	19Apr1819		Leukin, Rus	Until age 15
Stephen	19Apr1819		Hicks, Joseph	Mulatto. Bound for 14 yrs
Caskey, Elizabeth	19Apr1819	11 yrs	Bell, Ann	
Hilton, James	23Apr1819		Lewis, Samuel	Resc 16July1821
Weat, John	21July1819		Mouler, Henty	
Hart, James E.	18Oct1819		Estes, John M.	Resc 17Apr1820
Hart, Andrew Jackson	18Oct1819		Estes, John M.	
Chisney, Moris?	18Oct1819		Willet, Zadoch	
Ford, Thomas?	18Oct1819		Thompson, Jesse M.	
Patterson, James	22Oct1819		Guinn, James	
Helton, Joseph	22Oct1819		Patton, John	
Helton, Jesse	22Oct1819		Chester, Samuel G.	
Kennedy, Robert	22Oct1819		Charleton, Pointon	

Cashidy, Elizabeth	17Apr1820		Walker, Elias	
Hall, Daniel	17Apr1820		Guinn, James	
Hart, Jonah	17Apr1820		Estes, John B.	
Helton, Pheane?	17July1820		Hoss, Henry	Female
Agee, James	17July1820		Grisham, Prior	
Nelson, Margaret	18July1820		Nelson, Agnes	
Coffman, Lucinda	20July1820		Bottles, Henry	
Patterson, Thomas	21July1820		Guin, James	
Brown, Hiram	16Oct1820		Wilson, Alexander	
Draughtan, Louisa	15Jan1821	Born 15March1816	Ingle, Adam	
Rose, Jeremiah	15Jan1821	6 yrs	Biddle, Samuel	Resc 12Jan1824
Norton, Epharim	18Jan1821		Huston, John	
Kelly, Mary	18Jan1821		Thompson, Jesse M.	Resc 15Oct1821
Polly	16Apr1821		Hartsell, Jacob	Spin & weave. Of color
Daniel	16July1821		Gibson, Spencer E. (Doctor)	Of color
Right, William	16July1821		Davis, Charley	
Right, Betsy	16July1821		Davis, Charley	
Hilton, James	16July1821		Wilson, Alexander	
Brown?, John	15Oct1821		Hale, Walter	
Collins, Charles	9Apr1822		McAdams, Robert	
Gaines, Wilkerson	12July1822		Beane, Baxter	
Burris, ___ B.	16Oct1822		Clem?, Michael	14Oct1822*
Bowers, David	14Apr1823		Ferguson, Nelly	Weaver
Scott, Shepherd	14July1823		Bean, Baxter	Resc 21Oct1833
McAdams, Thomas M.	14July1823		Salter, James	
Stephens, Samuel	12Jan1824		Conley, Samuel	Waggon making. Until 27Feb1827
Kennedy, James	12Jan1824		Barns, Nathan	
Rose, Jeremiah	12Jan1824		Marsh, Jr, Henry	Resc 12Oct1829
Tyler, Irah	12Apr1824		West, Jr, Edward	Taylor. Of color

Name	Date	Age	Master	Notes
Shepherd, Linville	12Apr1824		McCracken?, John	Farming
Norris, William	11Oct1824		Lilburn, Andrew	
Moser, James	11Oct1824		Kitsmiller, David	
Rosodey?, Roderick	11Oct1824		Dameron, John & Lyle, Samuel	
Shields, Joseph	10Jan1825		Ellis, Ezikiel	Son of Zachariah Shields
Wright, Thomas	11Apr1825		Wright, Samuel	
Hinkle, Caroline	11July1825		Cary, Joseph	Orphan
Alford	10Oct1825	7 yrs	Nelson, David	Of color
Julia	9Jan1826	8 yrs	Bovill, John V.	Of color. Emancipated by Bovill same day
Burris, Elijah	10July1826		May, John	Resc 13Oct1829
Joseph	9Oct1826		Harris, William	Son of a free woman of color
Grimsley, James	9Oct1826	12 yrs	White, David	Son of William Grimsley, Esq, dcd
Joseph	8Oct1827		Gyre, Jonas	Of color. Resc 15Oct1832
Helms, William	11Oct1827		Robison, John	Orphan
Helms, Permelia	11Oct1827		Robison, John	Orphan
Deed, Eleanor	14Jan1828		Harris, John C.	Orphan
Deeds, Vina	14Jan1828		Templin, Jacob	Orphan
Deeds, Hickman	14Jan1828		Harris, William A.	Orphan
Mahoney, Everett	14Apr1828		Cochran, George	
McGinnis, Abraham	17Apr1828		Tucker, Reese	
Garns, Josephine	17Apr1828		Garns, Adam	Dau of Adam Garns & Eliza Sheen. 14Apr1828*
Childers, William	13Oct1828		Estes, John B.	
Brannum, Isaac	12Jan1829		Clem, Michael	
Norton, Ephraim	13July1829		Belcher, George	
Headerick, Rolan	13July1829		Headerick, Samuel	
Rose, Jeremiah	12Oct1829		Marsh, Abell	
William	12Oct1829		West, Mark	Of color
Burris, Elijah	13Oct1929		_____, George	

Norton, Landon	13Oct1829		Garnes, Adam	
Bowman [Brannon], Isaac	11Jan1830		Ryland, John	Released 5Oct1846* as Isaac Cassady, term expired. Mother, Polly Brannon, white.
Wright, William	12Apr1830	16 yrs	Smith, John	
Witty, Francis	12Apr1830		Scott, Joseph	
Boren, Isaac P.	12Apr1830		Longmires, John	
Bell, John R.	11Oct1830		Jobe, Abraham	
Bell, Julia A.	11Oct1830		Jobe, Abraham	
Christie, John	11Oct1830		Howard, Jacob	Printing 16July1832. Resc 16July1832
Gains, Joseph	12Jan1831		Lyle, Samuel	
Patterson, William	11Apr1831		Brown, James	
McClure, Thomas	12Apr1831		Clemm, Michael	
Norton, Ephraem	13Apr1831		McCorkle, John	
Dulaney, Jonah	11July1831		Harvey, James	
Huffine, Daniel	11Oct1831		Chester, William P.	
Kelly, Jackson	11Oct1831		Young, Thomas	Resc 18Jan1836
Harris, George L.	9Jan1832		Harris, Jonathan G.	
Harris, Lucinda	9Jan1832		Harris, Jonathan G.	
Christy, John	16July1832		Lucky, Seth W., Emmerson, Thomas & Giffort, Lawson	Printing
Stuart, Martha	15Oct1832		Zetty, Christian	
Joseph	15Oct1832		Templin, John	Of color. Resc 19Jan1835
Hail, George	15Oct1832		Eles, Elijah	Of color
Gilton, Mauher	15Apr1833	13 yrs on 11Jun next	Shipley, Asa	Male
Ruble, W.	15Apr1833	3 yrs	Johnston, Elam	Male
Johnston, David	16July1833		Hale, Joseph	
Woods, Mernerva	16July1833		Bradley, Joseph	
Jackson, A. [Andrew]	21Apr1834		Cox, James	Resc 20Oct1831
Simmerman, Margarett	21Apr1834		Bradley, James	

Name	Date	Age	Master	Notes
Gain, Crampton H.	19Jan1835		Bean, Robert	
Henkle, Lemuel G.	19Jan1835		Shipley, James T.	Resc 19Oct1835
Joseph	19Jan1835		Clum, Michael	Of color
Waggoner, William	22Apr1835		West, R. J.	
Barns, David	19Oct1835		Naff, Jacob	
Flinn, John	21Oct1835	6 yrs	Thompson, Jessee M.	Son of James Flinn. 19Oct1835* Resc 7Oct1839
Flinn, William	21Oct1835	9 yrs	Green, Samuel	Son of James Flinn. 19Oct1835*
Flinn, Nancy	21Oct1835		Hunter, Clark	Dau of James Flinn. 19Oct1835* Resc 5Nov1837
Smith, William	1Aug1836		Devin___, Alfred	
Moody, John	1Aug1836	13 yrs	Markwood, Lewis A.	Hatter. ? alias John Geroin. 7Nov1836*
Geroin, John			Markwood, Lewis A.	Resc 7Nov1836. ? alias John Moody.
Rebecca	7Nov1836		Harris, John C.	Of color
Freeman, Hiram	3Apr1837		Hoss, Calvin	
Bean, Crampton H.	3Apr1837		Gifford, Lawson	
Bayles?, _ynund	1May1837		Lyle, Samuel	
Bayles, James	1May1837		Lyle, Samuel	Of color. Canc 1Sept1845, Lyle dead.
Betsy	1May1837		Emmerson, Thomas	Resc 4Sept1837. Emmerson dead
Betsy	4Sep1837		Emmerson, Catharine	Catharine was widow of Thomas Emmerson
Freeman, Levi	4Sep1837		Hartsell, Jacob	
Drauen(?), Wesley	5Nov1837		Edwards, Able	
Flinn, Nancy Emeline	5Nov1837		Hartsell, Jacob	
Thomas, Malinda	5Nov1837		Bowers, Levi	Canc 5Feb1838
Garvin, John	1Jan1838		Boyd, Jeremiah	Cabinetmaker
Johnston, John			Boyd, Jeremiah	Cabinetmaker. Resc 1Jan1838. To William Dosser on trial
Johnston, John	5Feb1838		Dosser, William	Farming
Evans, Samuel	5Feb1838		Barkley, John	
Thomas, Malinda	5Feb1838		Risler, John	Resc 2Mar1840
Leach, Susan	5Mar1838		Vance, D. G.	

Coppinger, E. [Elihu]	7May1838		Early, William	Resc 6Mar1854
Wright, Jonathan P.	6Aug1838		Brown, James	
Wright, Thomas C.	5Nov1838		Shirfey, Sol Q.	
Rose, Ery Jane	3Dec1838		Horn, John	Ordered taken from Elizabeth Rose. Resc 7Jan1839*
Davis, Lena	1Apr1839		Bayles, Young	
Stuart, George	6May1839		Gifford, Lawson	Of color. Father consenting
Jones, James	1July1839		Mason, A. G.	Son of Benjamin Jones. 3June1839* Resc 3Mar1840
William	1July1839		Hunter, Joseph	Of color
Flinn, John	7Oct1839		Bawman, Samuel D.	
Jones, William	7Oct1839	14 yrs	Reed, William	Son of Benjamin Jones. 3June1839*
Jones, David	7Oct1839	15 yrs	Thacker, Thomas	Son of Benjamin Jones. 3June1839*
Mona	7Oct1839		Nelson, Orvelle P.	Of color*
Cummons, Mary	4Nov1839		Moon, Moses	Resc 6Apr1840
Bugles, M. M.	6Jan1840		Carder, G. W.	
Waller, George	3Feb1840		Whitlock, George	Resc 7Dec1840
Waller, John	3Feb1840		Waller, John [sic]	
Eildridge	2Mar1840		Stuart, Thomas	Girl of color
Caly	1Jun1840		West, Sr, Edward	Of color. With mother, Ara, emancipated by West this date
Syntha	1Jun1840		West, Sr, Edward	Of color. With mother, Ara, emancipated by West this date
Jane	1Jun1840		West, Sr, Edward	Of color. With mother, Ara, emancipated by West this date
Rebecca	1Jun1840		West, Sr, Edward	Of color. With mother, Ara, emancipated by West this date
Mumford	1Jun1840		West, Sr, Edward	Of color. With mother, Ara, emancipated by West this date
Scott, Baxter	7Sep1840		Mason, A. G.	Blacksmith. Resc 4Oct1847, as Baxter Bean
Barnett, William	5Oct1840		Shirfey, Sol Q.	
Campbell, John	5Oct1840		Bradley, James	Resc 4Apr1840. To father, Galloway Campbell
Cloyd, Joseph G.	5Oct1840		Jenning, James L.	For 4 yrs from 1Oct1840

Name	Date	Age	Master	Notes
Bise, Patton	5Oct1840		Jenning, James L.	For 4 yrs from 1Oct1840
Spears, John	1Mar1841	11 yrs on 15April next	Biddle, Thomas	Resc 6Mar1848
Lilburn, Polly Ann	5Apr1841		Kennedy, Thomas R.	Until age 21. Resc 7Mar1842
Russell, Zaney	6Dec1841		Cunningham, Samuel B.	Of color. Resc 1Oct1849
Landon	7Feb1842		Armstong, E.	Of color
Scalf, Elizabeth	7Feb1842		Gwenn, John	Dau of Elizabeth Scalf. 3Jan1842*
Scalf, Amanda	7Feb1842		Biddle, Thomas	Dau of Elizaberh Scalf. 3Jan1842*
Dunnehoe, Jack	7Feb1842		Thomas, D.	Of color
Lilburn, Polly Ann	7Mar1842	18 yrs in Oct1851	Gillilan, William	Age corrected 6Jan1851*
May, John			Boyd, Jack	Previously bound to Boyd. Resc 4Apr1842
May, Jessee			Naff, Jacob	Previously bound to Naff. Resc 4Apr1842
May, Marlin			Naff, Jacob	Previously bound to Naff. Resc 4Apr1842
Gilles, _____			Kitzmiller, John	Previously bound to Kitzmiller. Resc 4Apr1842
Marks, Jacob	6Jun1842		Walters, George	At request of mother, Patsy Marks
Vena, Thompson	5Sep1842		Drain, John	To serve 5 yrs
Rebecca	3Oct1842		Harris, Sarah	Of color. Sarah, widow of J. C. Harris
Irwin, Jessee	3Apr1843		Haws, James	
Flinn, Emeline	5Jun1843		Hartsell, Nancy	Widow of Jacob Hartsell
Hair, Julia	7Aug1843		Beard, James	Resc 5July1847, as Nancy Hare
Martin, Joseph	6Nov1843		Davison, Samuel	
Cofman, Robert	3Jun1844		Brown, Stephen	Req of mother, Lucinda Cofman, alias Moore. Of color
Cofman, William	3Jun1844		Brown, Stephen	Req of mother, Lucinda Cofman, alias Moore. Of color
Cofman, Sophia	3June1844		Brown, Stephen	Req of mother, Lucinda Cofman, alias Moore. Of color
Gowers, Julia C.	7Oct1844		Bolton, David	With assent of mother
Harrison, Sarah E.	2Dec1844		Morey, Ira	Resc 6Mar1848
Bayles, Biddy L.	3Feb1845		Bayles, Ruben	Of color
Bayles, Matilda J.	3Feb1845		Bayles, Ruben	Of color
Helms, William			Lyle, Samuel A.	Of color. Indenture date?. Canc 5May1845*. Lyle dead

Finch, Ann E.	6Oct1845		Emmerson, Catharine	Of color. Until 18 yrs. Resc 4Apr1853
Price, James	1Dec1845		Wyley, Samuel G.	
Mosely, Enoch	5Jan1846		Crouch, William H.	Of color. With consent of Mosely
Margaret	5Jan1846		Kennedy, Thomas R.	Of color
John	2Feb1846		Ragan, Mrs.	Of color
Green, Martin V. B.	6Apr1846		Smith, William H.	
Green, William Thompson	6Apr1846		Smith, William H.	
Harrison, Henry C.	4May1846		Entsler, John	Orphan. Resc 3June1861
Jane	1Jun1846		Wilds, John A.	Of color. Until 18 yrs.
Frost, George	7Sep1846		Bayles, Reese	Of color
Cassady, Isaac				See Isaac Bowman 11Jan1830
Martin, Hannah	11Jun1847		Pickson, Isaac	Orphan
Lilburn, Maria	1Nov1847		White, Joseph	Orphan
Allen, Daniel W.	6Dec1847		Clark, Daniel	Orphan. Resc 5Dec1853
Hayes, Janes K. P.	3Jan1848		Staton, James	Blacksmith
Allen, Martha Jane	7Feb1848		Barkly, William S.	
Allen, Elizabeth	7Feb1848		Klepper, Madison	
Spears, John	6Mar1848		Lane, Francis	Brickmason
Allen, James P.	6Mar1848		Bayles, Reese	
Adamson, Lucinda	5Jun1848		Smith, W. H.	
Harrison, James	7Aug1848		Hartman, Isaac	
Darcus	2Oct1848		Taylor, Henry	Of color
Abel	2Oct1848		Simpson, Joseph R.	Of color
Roberts, Isaac	6Nov1848		Hoss, Calvin & Henry	At request of father, William Roberts
Kelsey, John	5Feb1849		Arrington, John	Cabinetmaker
Kelsey, William	5Feb1849		Arrington, John	Cabinetmaker
Willis, Thomas Reed	1Oct1849		Sams, Jacob C.	Farming
Willis, Samuel P.	1Oct1849		Sams, Jacob C.	Farming
Willis, William M.	1Oct1849		James, Mary	Farming
Drawn, Mary Jane	7Jan1850		Ferguson, William	

Name	Date	Age	Master	Notes
Adams, Cynthia Ann	7Jan1850		Slemens, William C.	Orphan
Russell, Cary M.	4Feb1850		Emmerson, Catharine	Until age 18 yrs. Girl of color
Denney, Francis	4Feb1850		Simpson, James	Resc 3Feb1851
Allen, Margaret	1Apr1850		Oliver, Josiah	Orphan
Griffith, George	7Oct1850		Ford, James	
Denney, Francis	3Feb1851		Hartsell, Isaac W.	
Hays, Rebecca	3Feb1851		Williams, Isaac	
Thompson, Amanda A.	7Apr1851		Taylor, A. D.	
Mathis, John	2Jun1851		Ellis, Daniel	By consent of mother. Resc 6Mar1854
Mathis, Rebecca J.	2Jun1851		Shipley, Silas C.	By consent of mother. Resc 2Feb1853
Bowers, Van Buren	7July1851		Jeremiah	For term of 5 yrs. By consent of his mother
Thomas, Elberst S.	7July 1851		Maxwell, Samuel G.	Resc 2Feb1852
Frazier, Jacob M.V. B.	1Sep1851		Taylor, Abraham D.	Of color
Johnson, William	6Oct1851		Philips, John	Orphan
Andes, Hiram	3Nov1851		Greer & Sparks	Printing. Consent of mother. Resc 4Aug1856, weak eyes
Johnson, Joshua	3Nov1851		McClary, William	Orphan
Sarahphiner, Nancy	3Nov1851		Bolton, David	Until 18 yrs. Of color.
Johnson, Lyddia	5Jan1852		May, William	
Cofman, Robert	2Feb1852		Brown, Elizabeth	Widow of Stephen Brown, Dcd.
Cofman, Sophia	2Feb1852		Brown, Elizabeth	Widow of Stephen Brown, Dcd.
Cofman, William	2Feb1852		Brown, Elizabeth	Widow of Stephen Brown, Dcd.
Brooks, Elizah	1Mar1852		Leonard, Joseph	Of color. Until age 18. Resc 2Mar1863
Brooks, Keziah	1Mar1852		Leonard, Joseph	Of color. Until age 18. Resc 2Mar1863
Bayless, Cassandra	7Jun1852		Mathes, E. L.	Of color
Moss, Sary Jane	7Jun1852		Burton, Thomas	Dau of Jack Moss. 7Nov1853*. Resc 7Nov1853
Allison, Thomas F.	5July1852		Allison, Beard	Beard the father of Thomas. Of color
Loggins, Alexander	2Aug1852		Tucker, N. B.	Orphan. Resc 4Apr1853
Garst, William	6Sep1852		Bashore, Jr, Michael	

Geeslon, Alexander	6Sep1852		Ferguson, Henry	
James Edward	4Oct1852		Stuart, Phoebe (Mrs)	Of color
Minerva Jane	4Oct1852		Stuart, Phoebe (Mrs)	Of color
Hannah Eliza	4Oct1852		Ferguson, Henry	Of color
Moss, George	6Dec1852	5 yrs	Northington, David	
Loggins, Alexander	4Apr1853		Arrington, John	Cabinetmaker, carpenter
Finch, Ann	4Apr1853		Dosser, Thomas E.	Of color. Until age 18
Butler, John	4July1853		Broyles, Adam A.	Of color
Adalaide	4July1853		Broyles, Adam A.	Of color
Fellers, Elizabeth	5Sep1853	9 yrs	Broyles, Ephraim	Dau of Elizabeth Fellers, Dcd. 1Aug1853* 5Dec1853*
Fellers, David	5Sep1853		Harmon, Phillip	Son of Elizabeth Fellers, Dcd. 1Aug1853* 5Dec1853*
Fellars, Salina	5Sep1853	3 yrs	Johnson, Sparling	Dau of Elizabeth Fellers, Dcd. 1Aug1853* 5Dec1853*
William	7Nov1853	7 yrs	Telford, George W.	Of color
Anderson	7Nov1853		Mitchell, Samuel D.	Of color
Allen, Daniel W.	5Dec1853		Clark, Jacob	Resc 3Apr1854
Presnell, Charlotte L.	7Aug1854		Given, William.	
Stanton, Samuel Montgomery	4Sep1854		Walter, Peter	
Green, Martin Van Buren	2Oct1854		Smith, Mary Ann	
Green, Wiliam T.	2Oct1854		Smith, Turner	
Green, Levi	4Dec1854		Smith, John R.	Resc 7June1858 at req of Levi, his mother & Smith
Sliger, David	1Jan1855		Harris, J. E. T.	Req of mother, Rebecca. Of color. Resc Aug1866* Indenture reinstated 3Sept1866*
Adams, Elizabeth	5Feb1855		Armstrong, Eduard	Dau of Joshua Adams
Bayless, John	2Apr1855		McKorkle, John	Of color
Grimsley, Caroline G.	2Apr1855		Houser, David	
Pope, G. W.	7May1855		Bearde, R. D.	
White, David	7May1855		Harris, A. N.	
Hatcher, Thomas Robert	4Jun1855		Henly, Joshua	
Lanney, Andrew J.	6Aug1855		Aiken, Robert L.	Of color
Ford, Benjamin Lawson	Sep1855		Sell, John	

Name	Date	Age	Master	Notes
George	3Mar1855		Hoss, Calvin	Of color
Alexander	3Mar1855		Nelson, O. P.	Of color
Emaline	3Mar1855		Harris, J. E.	Of color. Until 18 yrs
Hampton, Dulaney	7Apr1855		Hampton, Thomas	Male. Resc 5May1856 at req of mother, June Moore
Mayfield, Elizabeth	3May1856		Entsler, Noah	
Mayfield, Martha	3May1856		Templin, Samuel	Resc 6Oct1856. Templin about to leave the county
Mayfield, Martha	6Oct1856		Deakins, James	
Henson, Franklin	5Jan1857		Beard, R. D.	Assent of mother. Resc 6July1857 at req of mother
Henson, Richard [Richmond] P.	5Jan1857		Grey, Matilda	Assent of mother. Resc 6Sept1858*, req of mother, Mrs Sampson
Henson, William T.	5Jan1857		Grey, Matilda	Assent of mother. Resc 6Sept1858*, req of mother, Mrs Sampson
Miller, William	6Apr1857		May, Samuel	Son of Nance Miller, free, of color. Resc 1Feb1858
Miller, Joseph	6Oct1857		Miller, James D.	
Vaughn, Um	6Oct1857		McCathren, James	
Sam	3Nov1857		Deaderick, J. T.	
Grimsly, Lofton	4May1858		Peoples, A. J.	
Grimsley, Nathan	4May1858		Phink, Samuel	Resc 7May1860
Cassady, William	7Jun1858		Haus, James	Of color
Payne, Dicy	5July1858		Squibb, George F.	Of color, Until 18 yrs
Britt, Sophrina Ellen	2Aug1858		Bell, William A.	Assent of mother. Resc 4June1860
William	2Aug1858		Nelson, O. P.	
Derry, Aquilla	1Nov1858		Derry, Marion	
Hale, Fletcher	1Nov1858		Kincheloe, Enos	Of color
Babb, Henry	6Dec1858		Naff & Coffman	Tinner. For 5 yrs from 17Nov1858. Assent of mother [Sarah F. Babb?]. Resc 7Oct1861*
Lucy	6Nov1858		Coffman, William	Of color. Assent of mother. Resc 7Nov1859
Willis, N. T. [Lafay]	7Feb1859		Coggen, Owen	Male. Resc 3Dec1860*
Miller, George	7Feb1859		Hoss, Henry	Of color

Goforth, N. S. J. [Sarah Ann]	7Feb1859		Ford, James	Female. Resc 4Nov1861
McKenzie, E. M.	7Feb1859		Dove, Alpheus	Resc 7May1860
Moore, William	2May1859		Telford, G. W. (Col)	Of color
Moore, Robert	2May1859		Cowan, William	Of color
Moore, Sophia	2May1859		Cowan, William	Of color. Until 18 yrs
Morris, John	2May1859		Peregry, D. N. M.	
Hale, Mark	6Jun1859		Crouch, Alfred	Of color. Resc 5Dec1859
Oliver, John	1Aug1859		Oliver, J. M.	Assent of mother. Resc 2Sept1861
Atkinson, Henry Cate	6Nov1859		Naff & Coffman	Tinner. For 4 yrs from 1June last. Assent of father, William Atkinson. Resc 7Oct1861*
Parker, Charles Henry	6Feb1860		Murray, Isaac	Son of J. G. Parker, Dcd.*
Bunton, E. J.	5Mar1860		Miller, Henry	
Miller, Hester			Nichols, Dock	Of color. Indenture rescinded 7May1860
Miller, Hester	7May1860		Chester, Elizabeth C.	Of color. Baseborn. Apprenticed 4June1860*. Resc 2July1860
Tompkins, William	2July1860		Carter, Joshua	
Scott, Martha	1Apr1861		Jones, C. R.	Of color
Harrison, Henry C.	3Jun1861		Entsler, Noah	Resc 5Aug1861
Mosely, Dimman	4Nov1861	16yrs on 13Feb1861	Allison, Mary M. C.	
Brooks, Elizah	2Mar1863		Leonard, F.	Of color
Brooks, Keziah	2Mar1863		Leonard, F.	Of color
Bayless, Nancy	6Apr1863	5 yrs last Dec	Pearse, William	Of color. Until 18 yrs
Bayless, John	6Apr1863	4 yrs Feb last	Pearse, William	Of color
Henson, Archibald H.	5Mar1866		Earnest, Josiah W.	
Perkins, William Jasper	2July1866		Kelly, Esq, Jonathan	
Tullock, Zachariah	5Nov1866		Grisham, George E.	Printer
Brown, W. T. Sherman	7Jan1867		Brown, Alfred	Infant abandoned by its parents
Unnamed	2Sep1867	10 yrs	Grimes, Allen	
Henson, Rebecca W. E. C.	6Nov1865		Henson, James	Resc 6Jan1868. Mother able to keep her
Ross, Ellen	3Feb1868		St John, G. W.	Of color

Name	Date	Age	Master	Notes
Harris[on], Sarah Ann	3Feb1868		Klepper, H. C.	Minor sibs Levi, Andrew N., & Jerriah Isabella. Dau of Solomon Harrison Alexander Kirk app'td guardian 7Sep1868. Resc 7Dec1868*
Edwards, James	6Oct1868	5 yrs	Edwards, Jerry	Son of Mary. All of color
Cousins, George	6Oct1868	6 yrs	Cousins, James C.	Alias George McAllister. Of color.
Hays, Henry	1Mar1869	5 yrs on 25Apr next	Stephenson, Thomas	Brickmason. Orphan. Both of color
Maxwell, Jacob	1Mar1869	15 yrs	Maxwell, Ferdinand	Farmer. Orphan
Chapman, James	1Mar1869	17 yrs	Bayless, John W.	Orphan. Resc 4Oct1869
Charlton, Ann Eliza	3May1869	7 yrs in Oct next	Helton, Melvina	Orphan. Abandoned by mother
Brown, George W.	7Mar1870	13 yrs	Grisham, George E.	Until 17Mar1875. By mother, Margaret Brown, widow of James Brown. Resc 2Feb1874*
Gaddess, John	1Aug1870		Brown, James M.	
Chase, Milly Frances	5Sep1870	7 yrs	Chase, Milly	Spinster
Chase, William Henry	5Sep1870	9 yrs	Chase, Milly	Farmer
Norris, Isaac	5Sep1870		Stephens, John H.	
Harrison, Isabella J.	7Nov1870		Garber, Isaac	
Spears, James	5Dec1870		Dove, Aaron	Nathan, Margaret, Joseph & Samuel Spears also ordered brought to court
West, Mary Alice	3July1871	11 yrs on 14April	West, Edward	Orphan
West, Benjamin A. A.	3July1871	7 yrs 11 mo 20 days	West, Edward	Orphan
Shaw, Gibson M[anerva]	7Aug1871	16 yrs on 20Oct1871	Goff, James	Resc & reinstated 7Oct1872.
Perkins, T. J.	7Jan1873	11 yrs on 4July last	May, Isaac	
Click, Henry Clay	7Apr1873	12 yrs on 8Dec1872	Whillock, W. S.	
Kinchelow, Samuel	3Nov1873	5 yrs on 3May last	Mathis, William E.	Orphan
Armstrong, Adolphus P.	1Jun1874	2 yrs 2 mo on 1Jun1874	Payne, W. G.	Farming. Abandoned by mother

INDEX

Note: Names may appear more than once on a page

John F , 20
Willis V., 20
Arwood
John Madison, 11
Asberry, 86
Asher
Larkin, 92
Ashhurst
Martin, 133
Ashley
Joel, 133
John, 66
Ashlock
Obediah, 2
Ashurst
Elijah, 2
J. M , 2
Atchley
Benjamin, 140
Joseph, 118
P. M , 140
William, 141
Atkins
James, 40
Malinda, 36
Nancy, 36
William, 40, 120
Atkinson
Henry Cate, 161
John, 117
William, 161
William L , 35
Atlee
Edwin A., 112
Attlee
William L., 110
Augustus, 74
Ausbum
Mahlon, 58
Austin
Ann, 102, 133
Hester, 102
Jane, 102
John, 102
Latitia, 102
Lethe, 133
Martha, 102
Minerva, 102
Auston
James, 83
Jane, 82
Minerva, 82
Rachel, 82
Ayles
William P., 97
William Preston, 96
Ayres
John, 81
Baans
John, 122
Babb
David, 47
Henry, 160
Sarah F., 160
Backwell
J. W., 97
Bacon
A S., 137, 138
Drury A , 134
Hezekiah J., 134
Isiah J., 135
Michael, 146
W. A , 137, 138
Badgett
Sarah Elizabeth, 101
Bagley
John, 73
Bailey
Benjamin, 122
Carr, 84
Christopher, 1
David, 69
Elizabeth, 135
George Washington, 105
John, 75
John B , 75
John M., 92
Joseph M., 84
Mary A., 141
Bails
A. W., 75
Carter M , 75
Baily
Nelly, 78
Baines
John M , 78
Baker
Andrew J., 66, 75
Cresley, 109
Gideon, 90
Henry B , 63
James, 109
John, 87
John B., 66
John F , 146
Lucy, 43
Mathias B., 24
Nathan D., 37
Robert, 149
Thomas, 18
William, 85, 111
William J., 99, 101
William R., 90
Baker, Jr
Isaac, 49
Bakins Creek, 15
Balch
James P., 85, 89
John, 54
Kezekiah, 56
Bales
G. W., 121
William, 86
Baley
William, 49
Ball
Lewis, 54
Lewis B., 66
Margaret Jane, 12
Mary Jane, 84
Peter, 84
Wiley M., 77
Ballard
Eleanor H., 90
George, 72
Lucinda Catharine, 72
Richard, 22, 72
Washington, 134
Ballenger
Dempsey, 15
Ballew
Harriet, 115
Baltrip
Elizabeth, 27
Frederick, 27
Bandy
Malinda, 3
Manervy, 3
Manervy Catherine, 3
Barclay
William, 95
Barcley
William, 126
Barger
John P., 103
Barkley
Barkley, 56
John, 154
John T., 54
William, 52, 55
Barkly
William S., 157
Barlow
Leander, 113
Barnard
P. W., 29
Sturlin J., 29
Barnes
Cornelius, 54
David H., 91
James, 15
John Macksy, 46
Katie, 123
Lavinia Matilda, 123
Leander, 67
Lucinda, 123
Polly, 54
Teressa D. D., 91
Barnet
J. M., 114
Barnett
Harrison, 126
James R., 126
John W., 111
Willam, 155
William O., 110
William R., 87
Barns
____, 20
David, 154
Elizabeth, 20
John, 122
Nathan, 151
Barrett
S S., 21
Thomas, 76
William, 112
Barris
Abililah, 46
Barry
Charles, 93
Bartholomew
Joseph, 96, 98
Bascom
Reuben J., 90
Bashore, Jr
Michael, 158
Basinger
Catherine, 56
Eliza Jane, 56
Michael H., 54
William, 56
Bates
Calib, 79
Dan, 125
Henrietta Elizabeth, 73
Jack, 125
Mariah, 125
Thomas, 18
William, 99
Batey
Edward, 75
Battrip
Elizabeth, 27
Batty
Edwin W., 7
Bauldwin
Wiley, 28
Bawman
Samuel D., 155
Baxley
Sally, 54
Zephariah, 53
Zephimah, 51
Baxter
James, 22
William A., 140
Bayles

Samuel, 98
Silvester, 110
Blair
Esley, 97
G. J., 21
Ivy, 98
James, 137, 138
William, 20, 148
Blake
Colombus C., 123
Blakley
Lewis, 33
Blanchard
Thomas J., 86
Blanchord
T. J., 15
Thomas J., 15
Blankenship
John, 123
Peyton, 106
Stephen, 124
Blaylock
Allen, 7
Benjamin Franklin, 7
Margaret, 7
Blazer
Jacob, 141
Josiah, 68
William, 68
Blevens
William M., 91
Blevins
Dills, 16
Henry Clay, 76
Isaac, 16, 17
John, 16, 75, 76
Luny, 16
Ncholas, 16
William, 75
Bloomer
Isaac, 76
William, 77
Blount
James F., 16
Boatman
Henry, 31, 32, 35
Nathan A., 14
Rebecca J., 14
Sarah, 14
Bogard
Benjamin, 46
Bogart
Solomon, 110
Bogel
Samuel, 131
Bogert
Jeremiah, 24
Samuel, 24
Bok
Betsy, 81
Bolden
Wiley, 28
Bolding
John, 126
Bolen
John, 11
Mitchell, 11
Boles
Samuel, 142
Bolin
Henderson, 118
James A., 18
Boling
Benjamin, 13
Caroline, 13
John, 127
John A., 14
Sarah E , 143
Bolinger
Frederick, 26
Bolton
David, 156, 158
Tandy, 101
Bond
Benjamin, 93
Elizabeth, 94
George, 103
Georgia, 147
Henry, 108
Isaac, 94
Joel, 94
Joseph, 93
William, 94
Bonham
James S., 3
John, 10
Bonine
Jacob, 80
Smith, 80
Bonizer
David, 96
Bonner
Ezekial, 112
Thomas G., 112
Boo
Rudolph, 45
Booher
Jesse B , 143
Booth
David J., 11
Edwin E., 95
Jackson, 11
Matilda, 11
Boothe
Jackon, 13
Boran
Abraham, 33
Bord
John, 26
Borden
Lea, 43
William, 43
Boren
Isaac P., 153
John, 149
Boshears
Isaac, 22
Botten
Thomas G, 1
Bottles
Henry, 151
Bouman
Ellen, 76
Bounds
Francis, 100
Bovill
John V , 152
Bowan
William, 95
Bowen
Charles H., 143
James, 32
Bowerman
John, 98
Bowers
Chresley, 52
David, 151
Davis, 69
Elizabeth, 135
John, 135
Levi, 154
Van Buren, 158
Bowers, Jr
Jacob, 69
Leonard, 25
Bowes
Abraham J., 25
Bowling
H. B., 5
Bowman
Daniel, 72
Isaac, 153, 157
James, 72
Jeremiah, 37
Josiah, 10
Madison, 75
Sparling, 67
Box
Hessiah, 94
U. J., 106
Boyce
William, 61
Boyd
Alfred, 99, 100
Jack, 156
Jeremiah, 121, 154
Joakum, 121
Joe Akum, 121
John, 129
John K., 111
John P., 136
John W., 82
Lavidgo, 77
Robert, 9
Robert W., 136
Thomas, 104
William, 11, 13, 106
William D., 14
Boyette
Jonathan, 22
Samuel, 22
Boyle
George, 53
Boyles
Hezekiah, 150
Brabson
John, 44
Robert, 50
William, 44
Bradberry
William, 136
Braddly
Benjamin, 127
Braden
Charles, 4
Hiram, 5
James, 4, 112, 144, 145
Mary A., 4
R. F., 113
Wesley, 4
Wilie, 4
Bradford
Anthony, 91
James, 82
Michael, 123
Samantha C., 20
Bradfute
Archibald, 93
Bradley
George Curtis, 34
James, 153, 155
Joseph, 153
Bradshaw
George, 76
John P., 82
Richard, 79
William, 78
Bradwell
James N., 55
Brady
Jesse, 94
Marion, 62
Bragg
John, 80, 81
Brakebill
Sally, 10
Branham
Lindsey, 135
Branner
Benjamin, 84
Casper, 79
George, 83
John, 87
Michael T., 86
Samuel, 91
Branner, Jr

Michael, 79, 82, 83
Brannon
Henry, 63
Isaac, 153
John, 55, 62
Polly, 153
Brannum
Isaac, 152
J G., 116
Martha, 116
S. E., 17
Branom
Martha Jane, 140
Bransen
Nathaniel, 41
Branson
John, 28
John A., 138
Levi, 89
Mary Ann, 137
Obed, 82
Rebecca, 82
Robert W., 136
Thomas, 82, 144
Thomas L , 100
Tilman, 38
Branston
Harriet, 82
Braselton
Harmon W., 126
Braselton, Sr
Isaac, 126
Braswell
John, 71
W. A., 93
Bratcher
Charles, 22
John, 22
Brazelton
William, 80
Breakbill
Sally, 12
Breden
Nancy Jane, 140
William, 140
Breeden
Aaron, 142
Andrew, 141
Eliz., 141
F. M., 122
Harriet, 141
John, 72, 141
John A., 141
Nancy, 141
Brender
Shedereck, 33
Brewer
Jesse, 145
Martha, 101
Briant
W. H., 115, 116
Wiley, 118
Bricknell
W. N., 120
Bridewell
Margaret, 56
Martin, 57
Bridges
George W., 113
Brient
____, 122
James M., 122
Bright
Charly, 51
David, 13
Brimer
Aaron, 139
Britt
Solamon G , 99
Sophrina Ellen, 160
Britten
Andrew, 127, 128
Daniel, 57
George G., 64
Margarit, 61
William H., 64
Britten, Jr
James, 50
Britten, Sr
James, 64
Britton
Daniel, 60
James, 59
Britton, Sr
James, 58, 61
Brizendine
James, 87
John, 87
Thomas, 87
Broaden
Lewis, 21
Brobeck
Philip, 56
Brock
Allen, 96
Byror, 27
J. Vance, 97
John V , 97
Josiah, 128
Pierson, 97
William, 128
Brogan
John, 144
Brooks
Armstead, 28
Auston G., 30
Elizah, 158, 161
Hiram, 14
Jesse, 27
Joseph, 94
Keziah, 158, 161
Levi, 28
Marian W., 68
Nancy J., 14
Nathaniel, 28
Polly, 14
William P., 82
Brookshire
Jesse, 111
Broun
Eliza, 120, 121
Elizabeth A., 121
Browder
W. D , 138
William D., 138
Brown
Abraham, 150
Alexander, 116
Alfred, 161
Andrew J., 101
Catharine, 34, 60
Charles F., 61
Christina, 22
D. A., 6
Daniel B., 111
David, 96
Elisha, 15
Eliza, 62
Elizabeth, 6, 61, 106, 116, 158
Ephram, 5
Gabriel, 96
George, 23, 24, 51, 68
George M., 57
George W., 162
Harrison, 6, 106
Hiram, 151
Hugh Berry, 106
Hutson, 118
Isaac, 70
J. C , 75
J. D., 70
James, 31, 149, 150, 153, 155, 162
James Cowin, 102
James M., 20, 162
Jesse, 147
Joel, 109
Joel K , 107, 108
John, 14, 17, 33, 57, 79, 102, 147, 151
John B , 139
Joseph H., 66
Levaney, 5
Lucinda, 109
Lucy A., 29
Lydia, 34
Margaret, 162
Martha, 5, 6, 118
Martha Letecia, 61
Martha Leticia, 61
Martha P., 103
Mary, 149
Mary E., 5
Moses, 2
O. M., 73
Polly, 95
Rachel, 132
Richard W., 63
Robert, 96
Solomon, 15, 47
Sparling, 68
Stephen, 156, 158
Thomas, 10, 131
Thomas Elbert, 109
W. J., 5
W. T. Sherman, 161
William, 6, 22, 69, 106
William A., 66
William Alexander, 65
William F., 66
Zerelda, 5, 6
Brown,, 97
Brownlow
William G., 103
Broyle
Jeremiah, 46
Broyles
Adam A., 159
Cornelius, 129
Elizabeth, 46
Ephraim, 159
Jacob, 45
James A., 63
Nicholas, 148
Thomas, 148
Broyn
Joel K , 108
Brubaker
Henry, 66
Bruckner
Charles F., 81
Brumley
Alfred, 62, 64
David, 66
J. C., 64, 65, 67
Brummet

Elizabeth, 1
Bruner
Samul, 66
Brunner
Joseph, 61
Bryan
Eunice, 46
Bryant
A. J., 77
Arthur, 107
Braxton, 11
Elisha, 111
George W., 135
Homer, 107
Preston, 139
William, 32
Bryson, 108
Abraham, 128
James Momar, 7
Sarah Ann, 7
Buch
Charles, 33
Buchanan
Elijah, 130
Isaac S., 30
John, 130
Thomas, 124
Wm. R., 124
Buck
Isaac, 24
Buckhannon
James, 132
Buckner
Burrow, 117
Elijah, 106
Garrett, 106
Marion, 106
Mathony, 106
Riley, 106
Buffington
Kitty (Mrs), 116
Bugles
M. M., 155
Buice
Sterling, 26
William, 26
Bulcher
Isaac B., 37
Bull
John, 34
Bullington
Laura, 69
W. M., 69
Bumpas
Elizabeth, 45
James, 45
Job, 45, 46
Lettia, 45, 46
Sarah, 46
Bunch
David E., 23
Hamilton, 39
Henry H., 40
James, 28, 39
John, 33, 34
Josiah C., 34
Mahala, 37
Thomas, 32, 33, 34
William, 37
Bundren
Green, 41, 42
Bundy
George, 146
Nathaniel, 147
Reuben, 146, 147
Sevier, 146
Simon, 147
Buner
A. A , 143
Bunton
E J., 161
Burchan
Isaac S G., 72
Burchfield
Jeramiah, 30
Josiah H., 29
Martin, 30
Robert, 91
Samuel, 77
Burden
Hezekiah, 126
James, 39
Katherine, 39
Lemuel, 39
Mary Ann, 39
Richard, 39
Burgess
Charlott T., 22
Thomas, 22
William, 22
Burk
A , 114
R P , 111
Robert, 130
Tilmon A , 124
William, 113, 114
Burke
William, 114
Burket
Christley, 79
Christopher, 79
George, 37
Burkey
Polly, 54
Burnet
John, 131
Burnett
David, 99
Edward P , 81
Mabel, 98
Myra, 98
Burns
Henry W., 135
John G., 135
L. W., 140
Nancy, 107
Nancy Jane, 135
William, 110
William H., 135
Burrell
B. L., 72
Burris
___ B., 151
Abelilah, 46
Eiljah, 152
Elijah, 152
Eliza, 101
John, 46
Burriss
Cornelius, 110
Dolly, 110
Neal, 110
Peggy Ann, 110
Burrus
Julia Ann, 59
Burton
Byron, 103
John, 31
Martha, 134
Thomas, 134, 158
Burts
M L (Mrs), 70
Bush
Nancy, 94
Busky
John, 63
Bussile
B___ W., 72
Busten
David, 117
Buster
Isabella, 59
Thomas, 59
Butcher
Hasten, 2
Butler
Davis, 56
John, 1, 159
Tallufarro, 22
W. A. T J., 67
Buttram
Elsey, 129
William, 115
Byerly
Isaac, 18
Byran
Margaret Ann, 22
Byrd
Mary, 137
R. K. (Col), 137
Robert K., 136
Byrne
Brice, 106
Byrum
Samuel Henry, 89
Cable
Casper T., 92
Cagle
Lucinda Ellen, 105
Cagley
William D., 78
Cain
Thomas, 95
Cain, Jr
Hugh, 71
Caits
Lewis, 36
Caldwell
Anthony, 80
George, 15
J. M., 17
James, 17
Malvina Jane, 17
N. D., 17
Reuben, 68
Robert, 85, 88
Sarah, 17
Thomas, 47
William A., 85
William, of Jonesborough, 148
Willis, 94
Caldwell, Jr
Anthony, 81
Calhoon
James, 111, 112
Calhoun
James, 110
John C., 132
John Clay, 132
Call
Joseph, 104
Caltharp
G. H., 120
Calvert
Jane, 45
Caly, 155
Calyer
Pharoah C., 85
Cameron
Jacob, 24
William O., 21
Campbel
James, 28
Campbell
Adam P., 65
Alexander W., 137
Charles, 28, 36
Eli, 81
Elizabeth, 122
Galloway, 155
George, 28
Jackson, 60
James M., 19
James W., 102
Joel H., 76

John, 155
Margarett Matilda Catherine, 22
William, 97
William C., 66
Canary
James, 87
Cannon
Isaac, 64
Mark M., 7
Stephen, 56
Wesley, 64
William, 64
Zachariah, 98
Canter
Allen, 92
Ezekiel, 23
Henry, 22
Jesse, 22
William A. A., 92
Cantwell
Cornrad, 116
Joseph H., 116
Carback
Eliza, 44
Carbough
George, 50
Carden
James, 143
Carder
G. W., 155
George, 49
John, 48
Jonathan, 48
Samuel, 149
Thomas, 149
Cardwell
James H., 99
Carell
James Wesley, 116
Carleton
William, 68
Carlin
Isaiah, 147
Carlisle
Elisha, 92
Robert, 46
Carlos
Columbus, 99
Lafayett, 99
Carlton
Caroline, 25
Carmichael
Lemuel, 88
Pumroy, 97
Richard, 70
Thomas J., 88
Carmon
Calib, 81
Carnutte
Madison, 4
Carpenter
Jesse, 134
Samuel, 17
Carr
Frederick, 100
Henry, 98
John H., *30*, *31*
Margaret, 147
Rebecka, 98
Samual, 121
Whelem Lilburn, 83
William, 100
Carrel
Sally Hensley, 149
Carrell
Catharine, 149
Elizabeth, 25
Carrick
Samuel (Reverend), 94
Carrigan
Hugh, 31
Carrol
Patsey, 33
Walter, 123
Carroll
James Taylor, 124
Carruth
Russell Reno, 124
Carson
A. L , 121
Andrew, 148
David, 78
John, 45
John L., 79
William, 147
Carter
Abraham, 63
Benjamin, 9
Dennis, 137
Elizabeth, 23
Francess, 135
Henderson, 114
Hugh, 64
J G , 144
Jackson, 144
James, 67, 114
James M., 104
James W , 66
Jessee, 51
John, 145
John A., 59
Joshua, 161
Mary M , 146
Peyton, 80, 82
Robert C., 64
Saunders, 145
Thomas, 19
Thomas J., 18
William, 68
William B., 24
William M., 18
Wright, 126
Cartwright
Lemuel, 111
William, 111
Caruthers
Andrew, 96
H C., 17
Carver
Thomas, 24
W. R., 125
Cary
Joseph, 152
William, 23
Casander
Margaret, 43
Case
John, 87
Casey
Barnett, 133
Dempsey, 110
Scina, 133
Cash
Bagan, 114
Jesse W., 129
Cashidy
Elizabeth, 151
Caskey
Elizabeth, 150
Cassady
Isaac, 153, 157
William, 160
Cassedy
James, 36
Cassidy
James, 34
Williams, 24
Casteel
William, 109
Caster
Malinda, 112
Catchum
Polly, 21
Cate
Ann, 21
G. B., 20
Joseph H., 117
Noah, 118
O. L , 115
Philip J., 21
Robert E., 118
William, 118
Cates
Daniel H., 38
Dixon, 24
Elizabeth, 24
Malaena, 84
Nancy, 24
Sarah, 24
Winney, 24
Catharine, 76, 102
Cathcart
Joseph, 121
Cavener
John, 65
William, 65
Cavner
Hugh, 48
Cawn
Elizabeth, 26
Cecil
Thomas, 119
Cecill
Joseph M., 119
Center
Lewis, 138
Chambers
Cain, 77
Charles, 11
Isaac, 11, 12, 13
Joseph, 32
William, 32, 105
William McCullen, 81
Chamners
Mary, 99
Prior, 99
Champe
A. K., 101
Amos K., 100
Chandler
Caroline, 12
Huldah, 103
James, 102, 136
John, 102
Maggie, 104
Thomas, 102, 136
William, 32, 88
Chaney
James W., 90
William, 84, 89
William [of Grainger Co], 85
Chapman
George, 126
James, 162
James Madison, 126
John, 71
Joshua H., 27
Leroy Pope, 126
Samuel M., 4
Thomas, 94
Wellington, 126
William, 71
Charles, 109
Jacob W., 78
John N., 72
Sallie A., 76
W. W., 73
William, 77
William A., 78

Charleton
Pointon, 150
Charley, 73
Charlotte
Violet, 58
Charlton
Ann Eliza, 162
Joseph E., 62
Victoria
Adalaid, 62
Chase
Milly, 162
Milly Frances, 162
Obed, 80
William Henry, 162
Chastain
John, 126
Chatt
Allen, 145
Chavis
Alexander, 100
Charity, 99
Chesney
Oliver, 145
Chester
Benjamin, 126
Elizabeth C., 161
Samuel G., 150
William P , 150, 153
William
Patterson, 148
Chidester
James, 53
Childers
Jackson, 88
Lotan, 97
William, 152
Childress
Ayres, 98
Creed Taylor, 100
James, 23
Marvell, 23
Mary, 100
Chiles
J. C., 5
Chilton
Isabella, 84
Joshua, 84
Chiser
Thornton, 37
Chismette
Thomas H., 73
Chisney
Moris, 150
Chittister
Alexander, 149
Chittyles
John, 149
Chockley
Joseph W., 62
Chopman
J. E., 6
Chorum
William, 31
Christian
Elizabeth Jane, 135
George, 136
John, 136
John M., 135
Lewis Z., 135
Nancy Ann, 135
Christie
John, 153
Christy
John, 153
Church
Robert, 150
Churchman
Rueben, 85
Chursant
Jonathan H., 55
Civils
William, 118
Clap
Henry, 22
Phoebe, 95
Clapp
Calvin, 145
Clark
Adaline, 128
Alexander, 128
Anderson, 128
Andrew J., 20
Daniel, 157
Elizabeth, 125
Hugh N., 99
Jacob, 159
John, 41, 125, 147, 150
Lewis, 135
Lucindy, 128
Mary
Tennessee, 125
Nancy Ann, 135
Sarah, 125
Thomas C., 130
Thomas J., 8
William, 36, 125
Williamson, 5
Clarke
John, 95
Clarke Co, MS, 117
Clarkson
Edward, 76
Claud
G. B., 30
Clawson
Josiah, 46, 49, 52
Claypole
Jeremiah, 38
Rebecca, 38
Tabitha, 38
Clayton
T. D , 120
Cleaveland
John A., 145
Clem
Michael, 151, 152
William T., 68
Clemm
Michael, 153
Clemmer
John F , 125
W. M., 125
Clemmons
George W., 82
Jackson, 83
S. E. (Mrs), 139
Cleninger
John W., 121
Clepper
T. W., 107
Cletcher
Stokes, 131
Cleveland
Ann, 121
Click
Henry Clay, 162
Jane, 117
Martin, 55
Clinch
Thomas J., 130
Cline
E H , 90
Fred, 78
Hanry, 90
Harvey, 92
Clinton, 28
Cloniger
Burton C., 144
George W., 144
John, 144
Cloninger
Daniel, 101
Cloyd
James, 149
Joseph G., 155
Cluck
P B , 122
Clum
Michael, 154
Cluts
Betsy, 48
David, 47
Mary, 47
Clutz
Sarah, 50
Coats
Charles, 126
John, 44
Joshua, 44
Cobb
Alexander, 70
Archibald, 104
P. A., 72, 75
Peter, 70
Cobble
John, 49
Joseph, 60
Cochran
George, 152
J. W., 16
James, 13
Cock
John, 26, 35
Leroy, 26
Susanna, 26
Cocke
John, 26, 32, 35, 38, 39
Pleasant S., 37
Stephen, 34
Thomas S., 37, 38
William, 35
William C., 35
William E., 36
William M., 41
Cockram
Anna, 120
Mary B., 120
Cockran
John L , 20
Cockreham
D. H., 74
Cofer
A. J., 138
Baty, 132
Coffe
Sarah Eveline, 88
Coffee
Eli L., 86
Sarah E., 86
Coffin
Charles [Rev], 48
Coffman
Betsy Ann, 150
Lucinda, 151
William, 160
Cofman
Conrod, 148
Jacob, 148
John, 149
Joseph, 146
Lucinda, 156
Mathias, 149
Robert, 156, 158
Sarah, 149
Sophia, 156, 158

William, 156, 158
Coggburn
Livonia, 63
Coggen
Owen, 160
Coggins
Edward, 69
Coiler
Alexander, 89
Coker
Esekie, 52
Lenard, 104
Nancy, 52
Coldwell
Elizabeth, 73
Cole
A. L., 81
Catherene, 81
Charles, 126
Isaac, 121
James Madison, 116
Joseph Alexander, 81
Patsy David, 81
Philip, 45
Sampson D., 23
Sampson David, 81
Sarah, 116
Wesley, 133, 134
Colehouse
John, 132
Coleman
Eliza, 58
Henry Montgomerty, 65
Mary Adelaide, 65
Sally, 61
Synthia Ann, 65
Colier
John, 137
Colison
John, 42
Collier
T. J., 20
Thomas, 48
Collins
Ambrous, 149
Ann, 108
Charles, 151
Daniel, 133
Delpha Jane, 124
Elisha, 26
Francis, 79
Garrett, 30
George, 41, 42
George Hendersen, 41
George W , 145
Henry, 150
Hetty, 27
J L., 31
Jesse, 124
John, 41
John M D., 31
L. William, 30
S. D., 76
William D , 118
Wilson, 30
Colston
James, 107
Columbus, 137
George, 20
Colville
R. W , 129
Colvin
John, 45
Mark A., 144
Colyer
Richard B., 89
William, 89
Combs
Samuel, 48
Comer
Archibald, 98
Condley
John V., 128
Condra
James A , 107
Conell
Christian, 118
Conley
Samuel, 151
Conner
Chloe, 86
Isaac, 99, 132
Thomas J., 132
William, 15
Conor
William, 16
Conway
Laura, 90
Mariah, 90
Conway, Sr
Henry, 47
Conzada, 61
Cook
Janathan, 60
Jonathan R., 56
Michael, 21
Reuben P., 25
Cook, Jr
John, 50
Cooke
Michel, 9
Robert F., 121
Cooley
Jessee, 118
Coon
John A., 122
Coonce
Harvy A. N., 144
Coons
Joseph, 82
Michael, 78, 79, 80
Coons, Jr
Michael, 79
Cooper
Archibald, 26
Azariah, 136
Barbary, 22
Burton, 10
Eli, 3
Isaac, 146
James, 147
Jane, 22
John, 130
John G., 5
John T., 70
Mary, 23
Nicholas, 146
Peter, 23
Sarah, 23
William, 2, 26, 147
William R., 5
Winnie, 146
Coose
William, 36
Coot
Howard S., 115
Cope
John W , 72
Minda, 16
Copeland
Jacob T., 89
James G., 87
James T., 124
John R., 124
Joseph, 86, 87
Coppinger
Elihu, 155
Corbet
Shadrack P , 91
Cordial
George, 112
Corland
Joshua, 147
Cormichel
Henderson, 76
William, 76
Cornutt
David C , 3
James, 3
William, 3
Corron
Michael, 27
Cotton
Enoch, 2
Couch
Elinezer, 76
Coulson
Thomas, 50
Coulston
Nathan, 7
Coulter
John, 13
Counts
Jessee, 35
Courtney
Annis, 73
Annis Rathbone, 73
James, 79
Jesse, 72, 73
Nancy W., 105
Courtny
Noah, 71
Courtry
Sally, 71
Cousins
George, 162
James C., 162
Covington
Elizabeth, 142
John, 141
Polly, 142
William, 142
Cowan
James, 109
John D., 65
Samuel, 10
William, 161
Coward
R. H., 5, 6
Thomas J , 5
William, 37
Cowen
Joseph H , 144
Cox
Allen, 97
Bartlett, 78
Brooks, 146
Gale, 33
George W., 68
James, 7, 89, 153
James P., 146
John B., 18
Narcissus, 146
Parm, 18
Rufus, 136, 137
Samuel, 18, 133
Samuel E., 143
Susan, 18
Thomas E., 113
William, 18, 69
Coyle
Craven, 96
Craddick
Drucilla, 46
John, 46
Rachel, 46
William, 46
Craft
Archillis, 146

Elias, 10
Olif, 146
Crag
Joab, 21
Craig
Jane J., 52
Thomas, 1
Craighead
Jane, 99
Mrs, 118, 119
Robert, 95
Thomas, 96, 97, 132
Craver
William, 75
Crawford
Barnes, 98
Ellinor, 76
Isaac, 67
John, 109, 111, 112
John H., 133
R A., 62
Robert A., 63
Samuel Joseph, 31
Thomas, 111
William D., 23
Crawford, Sr
John, 54
Creamer
George, 65
James, 65
Crenshaw
John W., 122
Cress
Daniel N., 92
David, 92
Eliza J., 93
N. L., 92
Uree, 92
William W., 93
Crews
Johnson, 21
Cricy, 146
Crider
Jacob, 25
Crippen
George, 95
Critz
Philip, 75
Crocket
Alexander, 97
Robert, 97
Crockett
Joseph H., 103
Mary, 99
Robert, 97
Cron
Caleb, 139
James, 139
Crosby
Abraham, 70
Crosier
C. G., 6
Cross
Absolom, 147
Ben, 147
Betsy, 52, 53
Elijah, 52, 122
Elizabeth, 52
George W., 84
Henry, 47
Joe B., 6
Mary, 4
William, 6
Crosswhite
A C., 92
Crouch
Alfred, 161
William H., 157
Crow
Henry, 117
Isaac, 117, 125
John, 45, 117
John H., 113
Patience, 125
Samuel, 138
William, 117, 131
Crowder
Nelson, 8
Croxdale
James, 44
Crozier
Arthur, 1
Carrick W , 101
Samuel N., 64
Crum
James G., 63
John, 60
Crumbliss
H., 138
Crumly
_____, 21
Charles D., 21
Jane, 21
Cruse
Rufus M., 128
Crush
Susan Ann, 100
Cryder
William, 15
Crye
John, 15
Culburson
James, 46
Cullen
John M., 96, 97
Culton
James, 113
Culvahouse
Edward, 136
Cumby
Minerva, 93
Cumming
Joseph, 15
William H., 15
Cummings
John, 12
Thomas, 8, 10
William, 15
Cummons
Mary, 155
Cunningham
Bennet K., 41
D. B , 120
George, 125, 142
J. W., 142
James R , 121
John, 109
Margarett, 108
Mary J., 104
Paul, 102
Pleasant T., 108
Samuel, 95
Samuel B., 156
Sarah, 142
Thomas, 26
William H , 110
Curenton
Robert, 84
Curry
David Simpson, 88
George, 37, 88
Margaret Adaline, 88
Thomas Alexand, 88
Curtis
E. R., 19
Hesakiah, 7
Cusack
John Black, 9
Cusak
John B., 9
Cutton
A., 114
Cutts
Coleman, 37
William, 91
Cyrus
Elsey, 34
Dabney
Paten R , 7
Dafferon
Edward C., 87
Dail
R. M., 5
William, 4
Dailey
Douthard, 11
John, 52
Williamson, 11
Daily
Daniel, 121
Douthet, 12
Houston, 11
John, 41, 83
William, 12, 13, 15, 40
Daley
John, 51
Dalton
Rubin, 44
William, 44
Dalton, Jr
Rubin, 33
Dameron
Abraham, 58
John, 152
Damron
Abraham, 61
William, 26
Dan
Samuel Lorenza, 91
Danahoo
George, 61
Danel
Thompson, 132
Danell
Ann, 116
Ezekial Melvin Obediah Jackson John Gusy Delamey, 116
Daniel, 73, 151
Edward, 85
Francis, 33
George, 145
George W., 145
Jane, 6
John, 33
Mary, 6
Mary Ann, 126
Nicholas, 145
Rabecca, 39
Ruth, 145
Rutha Jane, 145
Wesley, 145
William I., 126
Daniel, Jr
Edward, 34
Daniels
Jeannie, 6
Matilda, 6
Susan M. J., 6
Dankins
Abner, 84
Dann
Andrew, 107
Elizabeth, 107
John, 107
Matilda, 107
Sally, 107
Valentine, 107
Darcus, 157
Dardis
James, 95
Darling
George, 39
Darnin

Thomas C.,
129
Darter
John, 77
Darwin
Alexander, 129
Andrew, 129
James A., 126,
127
Polly, 129
Susan, 129
William P., 129
Daugherty
John Franklin,
138
Sarah Clay,
138
David
Assariah R.,
108
Azariah, 125
Rebecca, 78
Davidson
James, 3
Samuel, 2
Davis
Abraham, 28
Alexander, 100
Alfed, 18
Alfred, 5, 82
Allen, 123
Amanda, 71, 75
Andrew, 128
Archibald, 9
Baker, 83
Catherine, 104
Charley, 151
Eliza J., 104
Elizabeth, 104
Elizabeth
Matilday, 123
Ellen, 31
Ephraim, 56
George, 11,
126
George W., 123
Henry, 75
Hezekiah, 74
Hiram, 104
Hugh, 104
Isaac, 112
Isabel, 100
Jack, 83
James, 32, 145
James R., 112,
123
Janey, 35
John, 33, 77
John H., 123
Joseph, 143
Katy, 83
Lena, 155
Lewis, 33, 35
Manley, 102
Margaret, 83
Mariah, 83
Martha, 31
Mary, 104
Milly C , 104
Milton, 104
Ned, 83
Payton H., 71
Reuben, 128
Robert, 123
Robert B., 123
Russell, 104
Samuel, 17, 32
Susan, 104
Susanah, 128
T. A., 119
Thomas, 35,
55, 68, 83
Thomas P., 117
W. R., 119
Walter, 108
William, 5, 6,
90, 104, 128
William C , 124
Davison
Samuel, 156
Dawks
John, 95
Dawson
Mehala, 53
Rachel, 54
Thomas, 85
Day
Dorthula, 103
John, 126, 129
Sarah B., 103
Deaderick
J. T., 160
Deakins
James, 160
Madison, 107
Dean
Eliza, 72
Houston, 127
James, 94
James A., 111
John, 94
Thomas, 129
Thomas A., 111
William Calvin,
111
Dearin
John T , 129
Dearing
Sarah M., 129
Dearmon, Sr
John, 97
Dearstone
J. W , 68
Deathrege
George M., 116
Debkus, Jr
Jacob, 27
Debousk
Elias, 9
Debusk
Elisha, 58
Jonathan, 61
Mary Ann, 58
Dedman
Edith, 147
Deed
Eleanor, 152
Deeds
Hickman, 152
Vina, 152
Deever
John, 132
Delancy
Hiram, 95, 97
Delaney, Jr
John, 49
Delilah, 59
Delozier
Abe, 137
Dennet
Fleming C , 131
Denney
Francis, 158
Denning
R. M., 138
William, 35
Dennis, 134
Calvin, 97
Catherine, 56
Dilciana, 63
Eli, 33
Hezekiah, 50
John, 33
Joshua, 56
Josiah, 56
Lafayette, 63
Mary, 56
May, 33
Theodore, 63
Denny
Nancy, 95
Denson
Andrew J., 87
Margaret, 86
Susanah, 32
Thomas, 83, 86
Denton
Camden C., 87
Jacob, 82
James, 124
Denwoody
John, 55
Deputy
James, 68
James Franklin,
65
John, 65, 68
Derick
Andrew, 132
George, 132
Derrick
Enoch, 72
Marvel, 73
Nancy, 72
Derry
Aquilla, 160
Marion, 160
Devaney
B. J., 4
Devin___
Alfred, 154
Dew
Carter, 98
Dick
Henry, 81
Henry J., 86, 89
Jacob, 88
William, 81
Dickerson
Thomas I., 110
Dickey
James, 80
Samuel H., 123
Dicks
Henry, 68
Dickson
Charles, 113
Joshua, 125
William, 130
Dikes
Mary, 141
Dill
Eliza, 139
James William,
139
Dilley
A. J., 108
Andrew
Jackson, 108
Dillion
Christopher,
123
Hopey, 123
Nancy
Caroline, 123
Dinkins
Susan, 36
William, 36
Dinsmore
George, 66
Dinwiddie
J. M., 144
James, 50
John, 50
Dison
Sarah Jane, 68
Dixon
Edom, 110, 113
Eli, 113
John, 130
Onslow, 109
Dixon, Sr
Thomas, 1
Doak
John W. K., 62
Doan
John, 85
Mary, 109
Dobbins
Solomon, 26

Dobbs
Malinda, 26
Metilda, 34
Pheby, 26
Philip, 34
William, 111
Dobkins
Solomon, 28
Dobson
Joseph, 46
Mary, 46
Robert, 46, 49
Dobson, Jr
Joseph, 46
Dodd
James H., 112
John, 46
Mary, 59
Sarah Jane, 112
W. J., 68
Dodd, Sr
John, 51, 54
Dodson
James, 26
Margaret, 76
Oliver, 112
R., 76
Raleigh, 74
Vina, 76
Doherty
David Harrold, 82
James, 80
Dohority
Levina, 139
Levina Mary, 139
Donahoo
Robert, 55
Susan, 61
Donelson
Betsey, 130
Betsy, 130
Cresse, 130
Cressy, 130
Rhoda, 130
Donohoo
Enoch, 60
George, 58
James, 20
Letty, 55
Robert, 58
Donolson
Jesse, 131
Shepherd, 131
Donovan
Andrew, 96
Donoven
Andrew, 95
Doren
John, 137
Rufus, 136
Samuel, 136
Dorran
Sarah, 137
Dorren
James L., 135
Dorty
Elisha, 138
Doss
John L , 136
Dosser
Thomas E., 159
Willam, 154
William, 154
Doughty
Benjamin, 91
George W., 137
Douglas
Alexander, 79
Douglass
H. D., 124
Lawson D., 101
Younger, 32
Dove
Aaron, 162
Alpheus, 161
Dowell
John, 30
Down
John, 141
William H., 141
Downs
Joseph M. Filmore, 141
Doyl
Catherine, 94
Drain
David, 78
James, 45
John, 51, 156
Rebecca, 51
Thomas, 51
Drake
Francis, 130
Lewis J., 57
Sally, 130
William W., 59
Draper
Pryor Lea, 102
Robert, 75
Samuel, 101
Drauen
Wesley, 154
Draughtan
Louisa, 151
Drawn
Mary Jane, 157
Drayman
William Franklin, 62
Drinnon
William H., 89
Driskell
William Y., 133
Dryden
Joseph, 46
Dudle
Bartley, 57
Dudley
Watson, 52
Duff
Albert, 41
H. T., 40, 41
Hugh A , 37
James, 44
John, 40
Robert, 40, 41
Rufus, 40, 41, 42
Temple, 40
Duffield
George, 24
Dugan
Andrew Jackson, 109
Mack, 18
Duggan
Wilson, 142
Dugger
John, 134
Julius, 24
Duke
George M., 108
Dulaney
Jonah, 153
Dunahoe
William, 144
Dunahoo
George, 61, 63
James, 61
Dunahooe
George, 62
Dunavant
John, 38, 39
Duncan
Alice, 6
Benjamin F., 17
Calaway, 5
Enoch R., 122
George, 14
John, 1, 79
Robert D., 135
William, 120
Dungan
James L., 129
Dunham
William, 54
Dunkard
James K., 136
Dunkin
Isaac A., 89
Dunkum
William J , 136
Dunlap
Aaron T., 16
Hugh, 130
Samuel P., 18
William, 94
Dunn
Elizabeth, 127
N. B., 125
Dunnagan
Daniel, 47
Dunnehoe
Jack, 156
Dunnsmoore
Sarah, 28
Dunsmore
Mary, 29
Sally, 29
William D., 27
Dunwody
Adam, 55
John, 56
Dunwooddy
Adam, 55
Dunwoodie
John, 84
Dunwoody
Joseph R., 61
Duper
William, 122
Dyche
Benjamin J., 59
Christian, 53
Polly Ann, 59
Dycher
Isaac, 44
Jacob, 44
Dye
William, 147
Dyer
Amanda, 129
Charlton, 38
Frederick P., 129
George, 35
Jacob, 13, 14
James H., 40
John, 93
John C., 67
Joseph, 36, 37
Lea, 43
Margaret V., 129
R. F., 76
Dyer, Jr
Charlton, 41
Dyer, Sr
James, 32, 37
Dyke
Allen, 58
Hugh D., 58
Jacob, 48
Nicholas, 58
William D., 58
Dyke, Sr
Henry, 57
Dykes
James, 142
Mary, 142
Dyson
J. W., 20
Eagleton
John, 11, 14
Eakin
Alexander, 116
Andrew J., 115

Early
William, 155
Earnest
Jacob, 55, 56
Josiah W., 161
Thomas, 55
Easley
John, 38, 42, 43
Miller, 32
Warham, 36
Easterly
Abraham, 51
Francis M., 69
Jacob, 60
Philip, 48
Thomas C., 63
Eaton
Andrew, 34
Daniel, 39, 43
John, 131
Joseph P., 34
Patsy, 126
Pleasant, 34
Robert, 71
Samuel P., 72
William, 34
William K , 34
Eatons
James, 72
Eaves
Violet, 117
Ebben
Celia, 138
Eblen
John, 135
Eckel
Thomas R., 86
Eckel, Sr
Peter, 85
Eddleman
James, 56
William, 57
Edens
James, 24
Malissa, 77
Nathaniel T., 24
Edgar, 74
William J. J., 85, 91
Edgin
Eli Corrathers, 127
John C., 127
Matilda, 127
Edington
Allen, 38
Edmonds
David, 134
William, 91
Edmondson
A. C., 105
Peter, 105
William, 47
Edmonson
Samuel, 99
Wallace, 16
Edmundson
Solomon, 46
Edson
Amister, 75
Lawrence, 75
Edwards
Able, 154
Anderson, 108
E. E. Jane, 20
G. W., 20, 21
George, 45
James, 162
Jerry, 162
John B., 114
Mary, 162
Matilda, 20, 21
Matilda Ann, 21
Eggins
Edward, 8, 9
Eildridge, 155
Elder
Charles, 81
Daniel, 17
F M , 16
Marian, 16
Mary, 81
W. L., 17
William L , 17
Eldredge
Jesse, 132
Eldridge
John B., 117
Elen
Thomas, 105
Elenbaugh
Edward, 70
Eles
Elijah, 153
Eli
John, 97
Eliza, 99
Eliza Jane, 134, 135
Elizabeth
Elizabeth, 117
Elkins
Susannah K., 40
Ellege
Samuel, 142
Ellenberg
Henry, 63
John F., 69
Elliot
Harrison, 6
Elliott
George M., 86
Robert, 57
Ellis
Alise, 142
Daniel, 158
Elizabeth, 31
Ezekiel, 152
Jesse, 50, 54
Jonathan, 51
Samuel, 45
Thomas, 50
William, 79
William M., 135
Ellison
Ella Jane, 63
Joseph, 30
Joseph N., 91
Margaret, 91
Thomas, 30
Elliott
George, 83
Elmore
Thomas A., 90
Elroy
David M., 148
Elsey
Thomas, 148
Ely
Annis, 30
Emaline, 160
Emitt
Frederick, 14
Emmerson
Catharine, 154, 157, 158
Thomas, 153, 154
Emmett
Frederick, 16
George, 60
Emory
Mary, 120
Engert
Frederick, 122
England
Jacob, 63, 64, 66
Mariah Luisa, 27
Mary Ann Jana, 27
Thomas, 27
English
Allen, 59
Franklin, 68
Isam, 68
Jane, 147
John, 51
Entsler
John, 157
Noah, 160, 161
Epperson
Thomas N., 116
W. J., 116
Eppes
William, 30
Epps
Elizabeth Jane, 103
George W , 103
James, 95
William, 103
Erickson
Williamson, 114
Ervin
James, 49
James C., 66, 68
Sarah A., 68
Erwin
Calvin, 115
Elen, 143
Ellahugh
Martin, 106
John R., 115
Eskridge
Carpenter, 138
Estes
John B., 151, 152
John M., 150
Esther, 74
Esther, 121
Estip
Ibby, 47
Etter
Daniel, 47
Elizabeth, 47
Jefferson, 121
John, 47, 76
Mary, 47
Rebeckah, 47
Etters
Frederick W., 54
Evaline, 118
Evans
Barbara, 10
Elizabeth, 145
Evan, 125
George, 68
Hamilton, 43
Isaac, 145
James, 57, 60, 66, 70
Jesse R., 87
John, 148
Mahala, 58
Mary Jane, 90
Moses, 65
Newton A., 28
Richard, 65
Samuel, 154
Walter, 26
William, 60, 61, 146
Everett
Eppaphrodetus, 16
Orville, 123
Robert E., 17
Everhart
Mary Laura, 78
Evert
Philip, 47, 48, 50

Frank, 33, 74
William, 80, 81
Franklin
Lewis, 79
Riley, 97
Sarah, 84
Frant
Tillitha J., 2
Frasier
John, 114
Landon, 25
Frasley
Hiram, 128
John, 128
Nancy, 128
Frausen
Anias, 75
Frazier
Abner, 48
Andrew, 87
Beriah, 46
Fanny, 87
Jacob M. V. B, 158
James, 87
John, 73
Lorenzo, 111
Samuel, 126
William, 87
Frazior
John, 23
William, 23
Freele
Isaac, 1
Freels
Edward, 3
John T., 4
William S., 6
Freeman
Hiram, 154
Hugh, 27
Levi, 154
Lewis, 1
Sidney, 27
William, 27
French
Allen, 108
Henry, 49
Loffard, 83
Peter, 101
Fresham
A. S., 68
Freshour
George, 17
Jac, 17
Frishan
Smith C., 62
Smith Colombus, 62
Frost
George, 157
William Winfield, 72
Frow
J R., 18
T. J, 18
Frusley
Mary E, 128
Nancy, 128
Fry
George W., 91
Henry, 92
Isaac, 38
Sarah, 73, 76
W. C., 92
Fugate
Lee, 31
Fulington
David, 28
Fulkerson
Abraham, 41
Fulkes
Augustus B., 66
Deaderick A., 66
Nicholas N, 66
Fulks
Andrew J., 56
John, 56
William B., 56, 57
Fullington
Alexander, 28, 29
David, 29
Fultner
Asa, 18
Asa L., 17
Furguson
John C., 14
Furry
Sterling, 144
Futtner
John W., 13
G___t
John, 85
Gaddess
John, 162
Gain
Crampton H, 154
Gaines
Wilkerson, 151
Gains
Joseph, 153
Galbraith
G G., 6
Joseph P., 91
Galbreath
James W., 61
William, 131
Gallaher
Jefferson, 102
Gallen
Abraham, 117
Gallenwaters
Lucretia, 74
Polly, 74
Gamble
John N., 95
Samuel, 96
W. A., 119
Gambrill
R. W., 105
Gamman
Richard, 68
William, 68
Ganaway
Robinson, 103
Gann
Abraham, 79, 80
Eliz, 79
Lucinda, 115
Matilda, 83
Ranson, 83
Solomon, 79
Uriah, 92
Garber
Isaac, 162
Gardner
William, 47
Garett
William, 10
Garner
A. J., 3, 5
Allen, 15, 18
Griffin G., 97
Grifin G., 149
J. C. C. (Dr), 125
James, 82
John, 82, 86, 142
Sarah, 147
William, 15
Garnes
Adam, 153
Peggy, 48
Garns
Adam, 152
Josephine, 152
Garrard
Brittain, 12
Garrett
John, 145
Rueben, 145
William Anderson, 145
Garrish
William, 102, 103
Garrison
Jacob, 127
Garrott
Rubin, 144
Stephen, 144
Garst
William, 158
Garvin
John, 154
Gass
Charles, 59
Joseph G., 56
Mary, of James, 58
Samuel E., 89
W. T., 129
Gaston
John, 111
Gates
John, 149
Gatewood
Benjamin D., 124
Gatlin
Radford, 82
Gearin
Elizabeth Jane, 127
Rebecca Ann, 127
Geeslon
Alexander, 159
Gellespy
N. F., 19
Geno
David, 107
Gentry
Elizabeth, 67
John L., 101
Jude, 9
Lewis, 66, 67
Susanna, 10
Uriah, 10
George, 74, 94, 119, 122, 152, 160
Calvin, 110
Isaac, 110
Isaac Neuton, 110
Isaac W, 18
John C., 110
Mary Elizabeth, 110
Michael, 64
Susan, 110
William A., 110
Geroin
John, 154
Geron
Evalinda, 127
Gibbon
Nancy, 19
Gibbons
William, 94
Gibbs
James, 33
Obediah, 81
William W., 145
Gibson
James, 26
James K., 142
John, 119
Polly, 26
Robert, 8
Sally, 9

Spencer E
(Dr), 151
Thomas, 68
Giddeon
Randal
Franklin, 100
Gideon
Roger, 131
Gifford
Lawson, 154, 155
Giffort
Lawson, 153
Giger
George, 80
Gilbert, 7
Gill
Ben, 70
Gillaspie
Mark, 100
Gilles
___, 156
Gillespie
George, 150
George T., 52
Gillet
Andrew, 60
Margaret, 60
Gillett
James, 38
Noah, 84
Gilley
J. R., 108
James Riley, 108
Gillial
Andrew
Jackson, 109
Gilliam
Hardy, 107
Gillilan
William, 156
Gillis
Francis, 109
Gillmore
Samuel, 39
Gilmore
Elizabeth, 149
James, 9
John, 9
Gilton
Mauher, 153
Gingery
Mikel, 7
Gipson
Drury D., 29
Girtman
Daniel, 143
Givans
James, 79
Given
William, 159
Givens
Andrew J., 105
David, 78
Nancy Ann, 100
Gladden
Edward, 47, 48
Glossip
John Henry, 91
Glossup
Ruth, 79
Goan
David P., 91
Godbehire
John B., 127
Goddard
William, 17
Godfrey
Sam'l, 22
Samuel, 22
Godsey
Samuel, 22
Goff
James, 162
Goforth
Absolem, 149
Jemima, 46
John, 45, 46
Joseph, 46
Mary, 45, 46
Miles, 46
N. S. J., 161
Nancy, 149
Sarah Ann, 161
Goin
John, 37
Going
Anney, 34
Betsy, 35
Haulse Ellis, 78
John, 35
Rowland, 34
Goins
Minnie Allice, 31
Golden
William, 70
Goldman
Michael, 40
Good
Gimeral, 99
Gimerl, 133
Solomon, 56
Gooden
Lemuel, 57
Mary E., 66
Goodin
Matthew, 60
Goodman
Abraham, 135
Samuel, 53
Goodner
Caswell, 21
Goodpasture
Margaret, 148
Goodwin
Lawson, 25
Lawson Laury, 25
Gorden
James, 147
Gordon
George, 48, 49
Robert C., 47
Gorgey
Gabriel M , 76
Gosnell
J. E., 70
James E., 57
James Elbert, 57
Jesse, 60
Jessee, 61
Mary Emily, 60, 61
Gossett
John, 143
Gouldey
James N., 71
Gourly
William M , 25
Gowen, Jr
Nancy, 35
Gowens
Cynthia, 137
Obediah, 137
Obediah S., 137
Gower
Ely, 56
Gowers
Julia C., 156
Gowin
John, 34
Gowing
Henry, 34, 35
Grace
James K., 69
Jane Conway, 79
John, 79
Rebecca
Morrow, 79
Richard, 79
Grady
Carolina
Matilda, 99
Frances, 26
Franklin, 26
Gragg
James, 57
John, 57
John, of Polly, 57
Thomas, 57
Graham
Alice, 6
David R., 83, 84
George, 78
Jincy [Jane], 99
Joseph, 86
Mary Ann, 101
Rebecca, 124
Samuel, 40
Grant
James H., 23
John, 68
Richard, 57
Grantham
Willis, 38
Grave
Boston, 28
Graves
Akilen, 146
George C., 98
J. M., 137
John, 26
Joshua, 101
Lucy Jane, 28
Plesant, 144
Sarah, 28
Gray
Henry L., 4
James, 3
James F., 87
John, 49
Letha, 22
T A., 106
Grayham
John, 110
Grayson
Joseph, 112
Green
Addaline, 125
Alexander, 147
Allen, 7
Evan, 51
Jacob, 125
John, 75, 125
John O., 84
Levi, 159
Martin V B., 157
Martin
VanBuren, 159
Mary, 125
Mary Ann, 125
Richard, 108
Samuel, 154
Solomon, 93
Thomas, 20
William T , 159
William
Thompson, 157
Greenfield
Campbell, 11
John, 11, 12, 13
Greenlea
Eli, 41
Greenlee
Lewis, 124
Greenway
George, 107

James, 25
Rachel, 25
Greer
A. J , 91
Greer & Sparks, 158
Greever
C. T., 93
Gregory
A. C., 69
Benjamin, 115
Giles, 93
Isaac, 85
James, 114
John, 112
Tapley, 112
Gregory, Sr
George, 83
Grey
Matilda, 160
Greyson
J. W. M., 92
James W. M., 92
Griffey
Isoom, 9
Joseph, 9
Griffin
Andrew, 25
Catharine, 89
Elizabeth, 25
James, 25
Lucinda, 25
Mary, 25
Moses, 75
Sary, 25
Volney, 105
William, 9
Griffith
George, 158
James, 117
John William, 137
Mathew S., 7
Wilson, 30
Griffiths
W. S., 19
Griffits
Jane, 33
Griffitt
Henry, 127
Grigg
Joel, 110
Grigsby
N. B., 101
William, 11
Grimes
Allen, 161
Emanuel, 147
Grimsley
Caroline G., 159
James, 152
John, 149
Nathan, 160
William, 152
Grimsly
Lofton, 160
Grisham
George E., 161, 162
John, 115
Prior, 151
Thomas, 109, 115
Grissam
John, 147
Grist
Robert, 149
Grizzle
A. J C , 105
George H., 105
John, 99
Susannah, 99
Gross
Daniel P., 85
Groves
Eliza, 145
George, 99
Henry, 145
Sophia, 145
Grubb
Lucinda Jane, 29
Milly W., 29
Nancy, 29
Nichlis, 29
Thomas W., 29
Grubbs
Thomas, 51
Guein
_____, 35
Janny, 35
Samuel, 35
Guerin
Howard, 127
Jacob C , 127
Guffee
Alvin, 123
Guggenheimer
Henry, 64
Guin
James, 151
Guinn
James, 79, 150, 151
Nathan, 127
Thomas, 150
William, 83, 128
Gunn
William, 122
Gurtner
Rachel, 48
Guthrie
James, 47
Gwenn
John, 156
Gwinn
David, 24
Gyer
Jacob, 148
Gyre
Henry, 149
Jonas, 152
Hackaby
N A , 14
Hacker
Jacob A., 65
Julius, 131
Hackey
Joshua, 36
Hackler
Charles F., 113
Charles H., 113
Clarissa, 114
George, 114
George W., 115
Hustin, 114
Huston, 115
Morgan, 114, 115
William B., 113
Hagewood
Ruth, 130
Thomas, 130
Hail
George, 153
George W., 118
Hail, Sr
George, 148
Haily
Claiborne, 32
Hair
Isaac M., 12
Isaac N., 14
Julia, 156
Halaway
Jeremiah, 59
Halcomb
John, 120
Hale
Fletcher, 160
Joseph, 153
M. C. H., 5
Mark, 71, 161
Samuel, 108
Silus, 76
Stephen A., 83
Walter, 151
Winefred, 32
Hales
Thomas, 114
Haley
Martin, 134
Mary, 133
Hall
Daniel, 149, 151
David, 55
Edwin, 122
J. M., 18
John, 60
Joseph, 12
Mary, 19, 20
Milly, 5
Richard, 5
Thomas, 20
Halloway
Rachael, 78
Halls
George, 55
Ira, 52
John, 52
Halmark
Thomas, 94
Hamblen
James, 77
Margaret, 77
Orlena, 77
William S., 78
Hambree
George W., 136, 137
Hambrick
Emaline J., 113
Harrison, 113, 114
Malissa, 113
Melissa, 114
Hamelton
Nancy, 148
William, 145
Hamilton
Alexander, 137, 144
Andrew J., 137
Elijah, 27
Ezra A., 146
Frederick, 97
Hannah A , 91
James A., 27
John, 72
Lucinda, 91
Mary, 78
Mary Ann, 27
Sidney, 27
William, 144
Hamlet
James, 50
Hammer
John, 147
Hammock
James B., 109
John, 37
Joshua, 146
Messor, 109
Hammon
John C., 87
Hammond
Henry, 36
Hammons
Baxter, 32
Martha, 32
Sairah, 32
Hammontree
Daniel, 115
Jesse, 12
Jesse Franklin, 20

John N., 11
L. H., 106
Martha, 115
William, 12
Hampson
James, 147
Hampson,, 148
Hampton
A. P., 74
Dulaney, 160
John P., 120
Thomas, 160
Wade, 20
Hamrick
David, 25
Joel H., 25
Hanah
Ivory, 116
Hancock
Benton B., 141
Perry, 141
Hancoke
J. N., 88
Handcock
James, 14
Handley
Lardner, 96
Handly
Mary, 147
Haners
Avery, 116
Hanes
William, 80
Haney
William, 139
Hank
Henry, 140
L. C., 6
Hankins
Gilbert, 98
Hyram, 98
J. C., 64
Jefferson, 134
John C., 63
Ruth, 133
William, 34
Hanks
Franklin, 75
Hanley
Alexander, 93
Hannah, 73
Eliza, 159
George, 66
John H., 123
John W., 69
Hannars
Avary, 126
Harben
Arthur, 1
Jean, 1
Washington, 1
Harbin
Jacob, 41
Jane, 41
Harden
Joseph, 113
Hardin
Cornelius, 63
Cornelius B., 57
George, 54, 55
James, 142
Josiah R , 54
Robert, 101
Sampson, 55
Wiley, 120
Hare
Nancy, 156
Haris
Elijah, 99
Harlen
Benjamin, 74
Thomas, 74
Harless
John, 3
Harlin
Andy, 76
Harmon
Alexander J., 63
Elizabeth, 102
George W., 60
James, 102
James R., 68
Phillip, 159
William R., 58
Harold
James W , 63
Harper
Elizabeth Ann, 100
James, 104
Nathaniel M., 132
Harrel
James, 34
Harrell
Roadman, 42
Harriet, 119
Harriet Emilly, 87
Harrigan
Michael, 104
Harrington
Asberry, 56
Newton Carroll, 67
Pleasant, 76
Harris
A. N., 159
Benjamin C., 23
Columbus, 136
Elizabeth, 23
Elkanah, 65
Ezekial, 57
Franklin, 62
George L., 153
George W., 12, 101
Henry, 62, 63
Isaac, 98
J. C , 156
J. E., 160
J E. T , 159
James M., 100
Jane, 62
John, 59
John B., 10
John C., 152, 154
Jonathan G., 153
Lucinda, 153
Lydia, 21
Madison, 121
Mahala, 59
Mary, 20, 64
Nathanial, 41
Rose, 59
Sarah, 56, 156
Thomas C , 119
Willam O., 20
William, 152
William A., 152
William E., 59
William J , 93
William O., 20
William P., 21
Harris[on]
Abraham M., 56
Catharine, 56
Sarah Ann, 162
Harrison
Abraham M., 55
Andrew N., 67, 162
Catherine, 56
Elias, 27
Ezekial, 57
Henry, 63
Henry C., 157, 161
Isabella J., 162
Isaiah, 53
James, 157
Jerriah Isabella, 162
John, 126
Joseph, 47
Joshua, 86
Josiah, 54
Levi, 67, 162
Micheal, 148
Sarah E., 156
Solomon, 162
Harrold
James W., 56, 59
Hart
Alexander, 8
Andrew Jackson, 150
James E., 150
John, 76
Jonah, 151
Hart, Sr.
Joseph, 8
Hartley
Floyd, 72, 73
Hartman
Isaac, 157
Joseph, 62, 69
Hartsell
Isaac W., 158
Jacob, 151, 154, 156
Nancy, 156
Harvel
Joel, 124
Harvey
H. C., 104
James, 153
Jonathan, 131
Michael, 15, 17
Pror, 30
Harvy
Jonathan, 132
Harwood
Turner, 126
Haskell
Frederick S., 97
Jacob, 4
Hasler, 1
Eve, 1
Hasler, Sen
Michael, 1
Hastings
W. P., 19
Hatcher
J. W., 16
Leander A., 25
Thomas Robert, 159
Hatcket
James, 132
Hatfield
Ale, 138
Ally, 117
Eli, 139
Granville, 139
James, 139
James C., 117
John, 139
Martha, 139
Martha Patience, 139
Martin, 117
Oliver M., 139
William H., 139
Hatten
Orrington, 134
Hatton
Henry, 110
Mary, 59
Sara Ann, 59
Sarah Jane, 58

William, 133
Hattox
James, 17
Haun
Christopher, 52, 55
Jacob, 37, 70
John, 59
Haus
James, 160
Havely
Isaac B., 99
Hawkins
Henry, 31
York, 106
Haworth
Mary, 53
West, 53, 55
Haws
James, 156
Hayes
Janes K. P., 157
Joseph, 81
Hayle
Thomas, 108
Haymaker
John, 52
Haynes
Abraham, 48
Frankey, 48
Lazarus, 19
Haynie
Spencer, 97
Hays
Amanda, 86
Amos N., 85
Amos Napolion, 88
Daniel, 25
Delila, 82
Delilah, 83
Elijah, 67, 68
Frances Matilda, 81
Henry, 162
James, 49, 50, 86
James, son of Cyrus, 86
Jasper, 85
John, 85
John J., 85
John W., 85
Joseph C., 81
Levisca Emeline, 82
Rebecca, 158
Sarah, 86
Thomas, 65
Thomas E., 67
Hayse
Barnett, 44
Calvin, 30
James, of Cyrus, 85
Haywood
James, 4
Hayworth
Johnathan, 79
Hazlewood
Benjamin, 97
Joshua, 37
Rachel, 97
Head
George W., 92
Marilda J., 116
Mary, 92
Rachael, 92
William, 92
Headerick
Rolan, 152
Samuel, 152
Headrick
Elijah W., 62
John D , 13
William L., 136
Heart
Thomas, 17
Heartsuck
Peter, 50
Heath
David N., 43
Heaton
James, 62, 63
James V., 65
Thomas, 64
William, 62
Heburn
Henry, 94
John, 94
Heckson
Daniel, 33
John, 33
Hedereck
Alfred, 3
Hedgecock
W E., 105
Hedrick
Joseph, 147
Heilton
John L., 69
Heiskell
E D., 120
Hellum
William, 94
Helm
Henry, 82, 86
John J., 115
M. A., 116
W. C F , 86
Helms
John, 47, 48
Permelia, 152
William, 152, 156
Helmstetler
William H. H , 92
Helsley
Henderson, 104
Helton
Jesse, 150
John L., 69
Joseph, 150
Landon, 24
Melvina, 162
Patty, 24
Pheane, 151
Henderson
Delilah, 21
Elizabeth, 1
Fielding, 99
Harmon, 32
J. W., 6
James, 113
James A., 112
James H., 14
John, 32
Mary, 99
Noden, 80
R. P., 19
Robert, 9
Robert (Rev), 45
Rufus, 123
Samuel J., 121
Shadrick, 99
Thomas, 90, 106, 122
Hendrick
C. S , 72
Hendrix
Nathan, 23
Hendry
Edward, 64
William, 51, 52
Henegar
Charles, 68
Henigar
Jacob, 108
Henkle
Lemuel G., 154
Henley
John, 12
Henly
Joshua, 159
Henry, 33, 35, 114
Anderson, 13, 81
Clary, 65
Cyrus W , 129
Gabriel, 63, 65
Isaac A., 81
James, 15, 66
James (of William), 12
John F., 19
Lerah (fe), 115
Oscar, 65
Robert, 45
Samuel, 122
Sarah R., 115
W. R., 128
William, 79
Henshaw
David, 13
Henry, 34
Joshua, 37
Zemri, 14
Hensley
Margaret, 31
Henson
Archibald H., 161
Franklin, 160
James, 161
Mary Ann, 69
Rebecca W. E. C., 161
Richard P., 160
Richmond P., 160
W. R., 139
William P., 88
William T., 160
Herd
Elen, 72
Hernel
L. L., 29
Herrell
L. L., 29
Herrill
Mary, 109
Herrin
Granville, 19
Herron
William, 95
Hess
David, 25
William, 12
Hester
Ann, 63
Hetton
James Frederick, 63
Hewet
Nathaniel, 97
Hewett
Nathaniel, 97
Hewit
Nathaniel, 97, 131, 132
Hewlett
Edmund, 95
Hewry
William, 101
Hexon
Andrew, 51
Hibbs
Amos, 1
Malan, 6
Hice
Calvin A., 107
Polly, 107
Hick
John, 30

William, 41
Jabez, 84, 85
Jack, 37
James, 98
Ramsey, 98
Samuel, 45
Thomas, 125, 126
William, 33
Jackson
Andrew, 24, 153
Charles, 62
Claiborn, 6
Edmund, 61
Henry, 43
James, 24
Jefferson, 55
John, 3, 55
Luticia, 139
Mandy, 139
Margaret, 139
Nancy, 24, 139
Rhoda, 137
Simon, 3
Tennessee, 137
Thomas, 62
William, 24
William Henry, 139
Wilson, 37, 38
Jacob, 74
Jacobs
James W., 90
Jesse B., 22
James, 14, 19, 74
A., 126
A. R., 18
Edward, 159
Francis, 42
Jesse, 10
John, 10, 22
Mary, 157
Rollings, 22
Wesley, 42
Will W., 11
William, 22
William P , 141
James A., 41
Jameson
Benjamin C., 113
Jamison
William, 108
Jane, 155, 157
Janeway
Farrow, 27
Nancy, 27
January
Benjamin, 37
David, 39
Jarnagin
Aaron, 85
David, 85
Eliz., 85
Elizabeth, 85
Jane, 44
M___, 85
Martha, 44
Orlena, 44
Sarah, 85
T J., 44
Jeaneway
Daniel, 83
Jefferies
Andrew J., 59
Jemimar, 149
Jenkins
Henry, 27
Hugh, 23
James, 141
Jesse, 23
Jessee, 24
Larkin, 24
Parson, 77
R. F , 114
Jenning
James L., 155, 156
Jennings
Elijah, 4, 5
George B , 56
George W., 41
Royal, 37
Jennings, Jr
William, 53
Jeno
Calvin, 116
David, 116
Jenoe
Patsy, 116
Jeremiah, 158
Jerry, 121
Jester
Polly, 8
Jett
Polly, 99
Jewel
George, 48
Jewell
George, 72
Seburn, 48
Jinkins
Abraham, 142
Buster, 142
Charlotte, 126
Jo___
Rebecka, 8
Jobe
Abraham, 153
Joe, 94
John, 15, 35, 36, 37, 74, 88, 101, 112, 118, 148, 157
John Thomas, 87
Johns
Henry, 127
John, 127
Johnsen
Vincent, 41
Johnson
A. B., 105
A. D., 74
Abraham S., 65
Charles D., 114
Charles M., 106
Colombus, 126
David F., 143
Ellen E., 93
Ephraim, 37
F. M., 119, 137
Fanny, 29
George Marion, 28
Hannah, 82
Harrison W., 106
Henry, 74
Hetty, 20
James, 29
John, 55, 64, 68
John R., 101
Joseph, 60
Joshua, 158
Lewis, 121
Lyddia, 158
Lydia, 18, 82
Margaret, 46
Margaret Isabella, 101
Mary L , 18
Milton M , 114
Noble, 5
Patty, 29
Pleasant, 30
Polly, 126
Robert, 1, 82, 83
Sally, 119
Sparling, 159
Thomas, 82, 92
Thomas W., 111
William, 8, 60, 63, 82, 158
William B., 114
Wyly, 52
Johnson, Jr
Hiram, 26
Johnson, Sr
Hiram, 26
Johnston
C. M., 19
David, 153
E. R., 113
Elam, 153
Elem, 149
F. M., 137
Fanny, 28
Francis M., 137
George, 28
Hiram, 28
J. H., 120
James, 21, 28, 73, 134
James H., 99
John, 55, 154
John H., 137
Joseph R., 75
Mary Ann, 55
William, 50, 149
Joins
D. H., 121
Jones
Alfred H., 56
Andrew, 78
Benjamin, 155
C. R., 161
Charles, 10
Columbus, 127
Cuseanna, 53
Daniel, 28
David, 19, 71, 155
Dora, 123
E. E , 30
Edward, 127, 128, 130
Elijah, 26
Elisha, 26
Eliza J., 86
Emil M., 18
Francis, 8, 10
George, 71
George Houser, 98
George W., 85
Henry, 128, 147
Hezekiah, 14
Hugh, 36
Isbell, 78
Jacob K., 57
James, 12, 46, 53, 71, 155
Jeanette, 143
Jennie, 106
Jenny, 34
Joel A., 5
John, 9, 45, 78
John Alford, 38
John Alfred, 40
John H , 102
Johnston, 13
Joseph, 12
Joshua, 60
L. B., 140
Lafayette, 69
Margaret, 86
Mary, 19
Mary Ann, 53
Milas Jefferson, 19
Nancy, 10, 39, 86
Patsy, 53

Peter, 53
Phoebe, 29
Pleasant A., 86, 87
Polly, 126
Preston, 123
Reese, 109
Richard, 127
Robert, 71
Rufus, 66, 67
Sarah Jane, 67
Silva E., 67
Tabitha, 75
Thomas, 12, 30, 134
W. L., 19
William, 24, 37, 106, 140, 155
William D., 23
Jonesborough, 148
Jordan
Lewis W., 134
Moses, 79
Samuel H., 112
Jorden
Benjamin Franklin, 109
Joseph, 152, 153, 154
Jourdan
Mary, 80
Joy
Hannah, 104
William, 104
Julia, 73, 152
Julian
Isham, 110
M. L., 20
Justice
D. K., 69
Daniel, 69
Joseph, 1
Maria, 1
Mary, 141
Justus
J. A , 142
Mary Ann, 142
Kaneaster
Reuben, 123
Ruben, 124
Kannon
Bartlett, 94
Karns
Frederick, 100
Kay
James, 42
Kearns
Nicholas, 95
Keasling
Rueben, 58
Rufus, 57
Keeble
Richard, 16
Keedy
Sarah (Miss), 7
Keel
Henry, 27
Keen
G P., 106
Keeton
Benton, 111
Keith
John H , 128
Keller
Betsey, 67
John, 67
Phillip, 120
Samuel, 67
William N., 143
Kelley
Joshua P., 84
Margaret, 149
Payten, 124
Kelly
C , 104
David, 48, 52
Gilbreth, 7
Jackson, 153
James, 23
John, 133
Jonathan, 161
Mary, 151
Mary K., 150
Polly Kilsey, 149
Richard, 109
Ruth, 45
Sarah, 28
Thomas, 28, 113
William, 18
Kelsey
John, 157
William, 157
Kelsoe
Hugh, 9
Kendle
John, 50
Kenedy
Daniel, 147
James, 45
Moses, 45
Kenley
Mary D., 70
Nancy M., 70
Kennedy
George D., 53
James, 151
Jane, 61
John, 150
Robert, 150
Serena, 110
Thomas R , 156, 157
Walter, 96
William, 47
Kenney
J. P., 16
Kennon
Jeremiah, 12, 14
Patsey, 70
Kenord
Thomas, 150
Kensinger
William, 74
Keny
William, 66
Kerr
Calvin, 99
Elizabeth, 64
Henderson, 16
J. M., 16
John, 81, 98
Polly, 49
Thomas, 54
William, 94
Kerr, Jr
Robert, 45
Kerry
John P., 13
Kersey
Elijah, 77
Kesling
Christina, 57
Kestersan
Uriah, 61
Kesterson
John, 53
Martha, 23
Ketchum
B. F., 76
Ketteral
Terrersa, 83
Kexia
Polly, 48
Key
James, 43
John A , 15, 16
Joseph, 18
Maston A., 18
William, 16
William W., 15
Keyes
Conrod, 149
Keyhill
Alice R., 105
Kibble
William, 10
Kibble, Sr
William, 10
Kidd
Robert, 14
Kidwell
J. J., 90
John, 59
Kiles
Leannah, 79
Kilgore
Hiram, 46
Nancy, 45
Robert, 46
Killingsworth
Joseph, 71
Kimbrough
Duke W., 82
John, 86
John H., 124
Thomas, 82
W. P., 125
William S., 125
Kimbrough
Thomas, 86
Kincade
William, 144
Kincaid
Clingon McDonald, 137
John W., 44
Ritchey, 6
Kincannon
Thomas H., 117
Kincheloe
Enos, 160
Kinchelow
Samuel, 162
Kinder
Jacob, 42
King
George, 55, 147
Harriet E., 2
James, 61
John, 36
John H., 69
Joseph K., 79
Margaret, 147
Nathaniel W., 15
Penelope, 80
Riley, 142
Sally, 46
Sarah, 46
W. H., 106
William I., 73
Kingsley
Roswell E., 63
Kinkead
Philip C., 75
Kinnamon
A. K., 19
James, 18
Kinney
Harmon, 52
Kinser
Esther, 55
Jacob, 122
Sally, 48
Kinsinger
John, 72
Kirby
Alice G., 18
James, 33
Nancy, 33
W. F., 105
William, 33

Edward, 104
G. W., 120
Lea, 43
Mary C , 38, 39
Sam, 101
Samuel, 101
William, 14, 133
Lea, Sr
Ephraim, 16
Leach
Susan, 154
Leak
Richard, 103
Leaper
Matthew, 84
Leath
A. J., 4
G F. M., 5
Joseph, 4
Thelbert J.(Y?), .5
Willis, 1
Leboc
Henry, 13
Lebolt
John, 88
Leckie
John W., 100
Ledford
Delila, 126
Ledgerwood
A. P., 144
David, 101
Samuel, 144
Ledgewood
W. L., 146
Lee
Jansey, 25
Jonathan, 13
Rhoda, 93
Thomas, 20
Thomas F., 53
William, 11
William G., 71
William J , 93
Leech
David J., 98
Leigh
George, 94
Leinart
A L., 145
C. A., 4
Leith
Ebenezer, 79
Leman
Anderson, 109
Lemans
Washington A , 67
Leming
Robert, 53
Lemmon
John, 147
Lemmons
Robert, 62
Leng
James, 40
Lentz
Jacob, 48
W. R., 119
Leonard
F., 161
Joseph, 158
Leper
Mathew, 79
Lerned
George E., 122
Leroy
Ellen, 75
Joseph, 75
Lester
John, 46
Reuben, 46
Lethco
James, 87
Ritta, 87
Lett
Francis, 1
James D., 145
William, 1
Leuis
Thomas D , 7
Leuke
John, 140
Leukin
Rus, 150
Levi, 28
Lewellen
William, 105
Lewis, 43
Absalom, 92
B. S., 142
C W , 80
Coty, 132
Elizabeth, 98
Fanny, 84
Josephus, 103
Samuel, 150
William, 11
William V., 67
Z , 115
Licsenz
John, 9
Lide
John W., 34
Lien
Israel, 77
Lienart
John, 4
Ligget
Henry, 132
Henry, 131
William, 133
Liggett
Henry, 132
Light
Reuben, 76
Lightner
John, 56
Likenz
John, 9
Lilburn
Andrew, 152
Maria, 157
Polly Ann, 156
Lile
Ishmael, 23
Liles
Alexander, 132
Francis Marion, 133
Jasper, 133
Levi, 50
Robert, 132, 133
Lillard
Francis J , 121
Limerly
Jacob, 13
Linart
John, 6
Lince
Jacob, 50
Lincolen
Jessee, 51
Mordecai, 51
Lincoln
Isaac, 147
Israel, 76
Lincoln & Hieskell, 52
Lincum
William, 106
Lind
Moses, 98
Lindsay
Elizabeth, 53
John, 51
Mose, 98
Moses, 98, 99
William, 22
Lindsay, Jr
William, 22
Lindsey
John, 94
Moses, 96, 97
Robert, 97
William, 97
Line
Alfred M., 91
Joab, 88
Linear
Vanburin, 40, 41
Linebaugh
Jacob, 58
Lineberger
Nicholas, 148
Linert
Jacob, 5
Link
Ephram, 63
Linsey
John, 80
Lister
John, 53, 54
Literal
Robert, 64
Little
Christopher, 97
Elihu, 23
Elihu E., 23
Lively
Beverly, 84, 88
Livingston
Jesse, 42
Lizie, 91
Locke
John, 129
Joseph M., 119
Mary Ann, 119
Newton, 129
Thomas L. G., 119
Lockmiller
James, 118
Locust
Auston, 81
Loftis
Elizabeth, 3
Pleasant, 3
Polly, 3
Logan
James, 9
John C., 19
Loggins
Alexander, 158, 159
Lollar
John S., 131
Lonas
C. K. (wife), 70
James H., 70
London
James M., 20
Luther, 21
Long
Anny, 48
Eliza, 41
Isaac, 41
James, 147
Joel, 128
Joseph, 32
Nancy, 43
Samuel, 56
William, 95
William Jasper, 71
Longacre Jr
John, 79
Longbotom
Elihu L., 4
Longbottom
Lyhue, 3
Longmires
John, 153
Longworth
Sally, 92
Looney

John, 76
William, 59, 60
Looper
Joel, 139
Lord
Claudius B., 106
Lotspeech
William, 85
Lotspeich
William, 84
Loues
Jane, 30
John, 30
Susan L., 30
Loughly
J. Y., 124
Loury
William, 13
Love
Anderson, 61
Eliza, 25
Jack, 17
James T., 84
John, 46, 49
John S., 61
Joseph, 95
Joseph N., 133
Livina, 61
Robert, 10
Samuel, 25
Samuel H., 99
Thomas B., 109
William S., 12
Loveday
James, 3
Lovel
Drucilla, 144
Samuel, 144
Lovell
Drucilla, 145
Matilda, 145
Lovely
Charles, 3
John P., 3
Lovitt
Charles, 66
Charles A., 66
Low
Abner, 37
David, 30
Henderson M., 57
Isaac, 111
James, 106
James R., 57
John, 30
John R., 69
Robertson, 57
Ruthy, 57
Lowe
Adison C., 111
Barten, 41
C. R., 6
Lowery
James, 109
Lowry
Elizabeth, 128
Henry, 16
James, 79
James M., 61
Mariah, 62
Mrs, 128
Loyd
Anderson, 88, 89
John, 8
Robert, 38
William, 88
Lucas
Samuel, 33
Lucky
Rufus, 59
Seth W., 153
Lucy, 43, 160
Ludmilk
A J., 68
Lunn
Charles, 8
Luster
George, 77
Lutrell
Caswell, 133
Lyle
Elbert, 91
J. Nat (Dr), 91
Nancy, 79
Samuel, 152, 153, 154
Samuel A., 156
William M., 11
Lyles
Delilah, 48
Holly, 49
Levi, 49
Nancy, 49
Polly, 49
Lynch
George W., 75
Jesse, 45
John, 30
Lynn
Asberry, 137
Lyon
Daniel, 99, 100
Jeremiah, 133
Lyons
Clarissa, 103
Daniel, 99
John, 98
Matilda, 104
Lyons, Jr
John, 103
M____t
John, 86
Mabe
George, 72
Mabry
William, 112
Mabs
Frank, 77
Maccashlin
Robert, 147
Maclin
William, 10
Maddox
Levi H., 75
Maderis
Robert, 4
Madisen
Eldridge, 77
Madison, 90
Madison:, 90
Magee
Anderson, 65
Andrew, 65
Robert, 65
William, 65
Magill
James, 50
Mahallow
John, 48
Mahan
Robert L., 132
Mahog
Willet, 63
Mahoney
Everett, 152
William, 20
Mainas
Susan, 126
Maines
Jackson, 25
Majors
Smith, 95
Malaby
Jane, 95
Malaney
Harvey, 68
Sevier, 69
Malcon
John, 10
Malicoat
William C , 37
Mallett
Jane Amandon, 73
John, 73
Levi, 73
Malvina, 73
Mary Jane, 73
Mallicoat
Rachel, 41
Rhoda, 39
William C., 42
Malone
Louisa, 120
Samuel, 70
William, 115
Maloney
John, 55, 61, 62
Robert, 47, 48, 53
Maloney, Sr
John, 51
Malony
Robert, 52, 53
Maner
Meshah, 90
Manes
Godfrey, 92
Mange
William Hambleton, 25
William Hamilton, 25
Manis, 77
Duke, 89
Fanny C., 140
James, 75
John, 75
May (?Mary), 74
Minerva, 72
Manley
Luena, 87
Mann
George, 73
Thomas, 32
Mansfield
Elizabeth, 134
John, 81
John W , 139
Maryann, 134
Nicholas, 130
Norman, 140
Thomas, 79, 86
Manual
George, 65
Manuel
Alpha, 63
Maples
Jackson, 84
Marion, 146
Nancy, 146
Rebecca, 146
Redman, 142
Marcum
Arthur, 22
Eli W., 111
Gabral, 29
Nancy Louisa, 111
Peter, 26
Polly S., 111
Marefield
Samuel, 93
William, 93
Margaret, 19, 43, 74, 103, 104, 157
Margrave
Drury, 130
John, 130
Margrove
Samuel, 132
Marks
Jacob, 156

Patsy, 156
Markwood
Lewis A., 154
Marney
Robert, 132
Mars
James J., 22
Marsh
Abell, 152
James, 55
Marsh, Jr
Henry, 151
Marshall
Benjamin, 86
J. C., 104
Sally, 26
William, 17
Martha, 74
Martha Jane, 87
Martin
Caroline, 135
David, 32
Delila, 135
Elizabeth, 111
George Washington, 135
Hannah, 157
Isaac, 32
James, 135
James R., 136
Jesse, 117
John Wesley, 38
Joseph, 156
Joseph B., 138
Leroy, 115
R B., 70
Robert, 89
Saloma, 71
Samuel J. B , 108
Timothy, 136
William, 44, 111
Willie O., 117
Martin, Jr
Lewis, 84
Mary, 87, 138
Mary Ann, 75
Masan
Robert, 61
Thomas J., 135
Mason
A. G., 155
Frank, 92
James, 102
John A., 62, 64
Robert, 61, 62, 64, 109
Sarah Jone, 109
Massa
John, 47
William, 47
Massey
Anna Jane, 8
Calaway, 5
Caloway, 5
Elias, 5
James, 8
John, 5
Josiah, 5
Polly, 51
Sherrod, 102
Massy
Callaway, 4
Joseph, 6
Mastin
George W., 25
Mathes
E. L., 158
Mathis
Ancel, 134
Calvin, 65
John, 158
Rebecca J , 158
William E., 162
Matilda, 73
Matthews
James, 54
John, 53, 56, 59
Matilda, 99
Robert L , 99
Matthus
Ambrose, 101
Mattocks
Joseph W., 67
Maumpine
Benjamin T. H., 12
Maupin
E L., 15
Maupine
Elbert Lafayette, 12
Harriet Maranda Jane, 12
Morgan G., 12
Thomas Dewitt Finton, 12
Mauris
John, 45, 50
Maxwell
Ferdinand, 162
Jacob, 162
Joseph C , 105
Martha, 114
Samuel G , 158
W. N., 105
May
Isaac, 162
Jessee, 156
John, 152, 156
Marlin, 156
Samuel, 160
William, 158
May, Sr
John, 108
Mayes
Calvin, 116
Henry, 33
Mayfield
Abraham, 117
Elizabeth, 134, 160
Isaiah, 134
Martha, 160
Martha Jane, 134
Noah, 68
Maynard
Mary Lucrecia, 19
Mayo
George W., 113
James, 112
Mays
John, 33
Jonathan, 28
Mayse
Anderson, 33
Sherad, 33
William, 43
McAdams
Robert, 151
Thomas M., 151
McAdoo
William G , 3
McAfee
Archibald, 59
McAffry
James M., 104
Patsy, 100
Thomas, 100
McAffy
Terrence, 95
McAlister
Elijah Monroe, 125
John, 65
McAllister
George, 162
John, 148
McAmish
Mary, 50
McAmos
James, 44
McAmy
John, 94, 95
McAnally
C. W , 40
Charles, 35, 38
McAndrew
William, 20
McBath
James, 98
McBee
John, 39, 144
McBride
Amos, 49
Eliza Ann, 89
James D., 54
John, 59
Marcus, 89
Martin, 56
Samuel E. H., 89
William, 97
McBroom
James, 26
McC_____
Robert, 10
McCade
John, 150
McCaffry
Terence, 97
McCall
Robert, 45
Sarah Jane, 108
McCallie
David E., 12
Samuel, 120
William T , 112
McCammon
O. P., 18
McCampbell
John (Minister), 96
McCamy
John, 130
McCanse
James, 126
McCarroll
James T., 138
Sarah L., 138
McCarter
A. W., 142
John, 141
Mary, 141
McCarty
Buina V., 77
McCathren
James, 160
McCauley
Eliza, 74
McCawlie
James, 13
John, 13
William, 13
McCeahen
John, 149
McClain
Alzira, 104
Andrew, 13
Carrick, 104
Francis M., 103
James, 104
John, 12
McClanahan
Samuel H., 101
McClane
Robert A., 86
McClary
William, 158

McClellan
Barbara, 130
David, 130
William, 102, 103
McClister
John, 81, 83
McCloud
James M., 100
McCluer
Jane, 17
John R., 17
McClure
John, 16
John R., 16
Thomas, 153
William, 4
McCollum
Alexander, 12
McConkey
Elizabeth, 120
Joseph, 120
Rachel, 120
McConley
James L., 64
McConnell
Franklin, 57
Isaac M., 16
James, 95
Thomas, 95
McCord
H. J., 120
William B., 62
McCorkle
John, 153
Samuel B., 60
Sasmuel B., 61
McCormack
Samuel, 131
McCoy
Dennis H., 53
Elisa, 52
Isaac, 99
J. C., 16
William, 22
William H., 66
McCracken
John, 152
McCrarey
Ann, 83
Thomas W., 83
McCrary
William, 27
McCraw
Napoleon B., 24
McCrossky
John, 44
McCroy
John M., 116
McCubbins
John, 26
McCuistian
James, 86
McCullen
John, 96
McCulley
J. W., 17
J W. M., 17
Joseph, 112
McCullough
John, 11, 12
W A , 18
McCully
John, 10, 11, 12
William, 18
Wm. Abraham, 18
McCulpin
Absalon T., 64
George M., 62
Hanna Jane, 63
Keziah, 62
Thomas Alexander, 62
McCurdy
Robert, 10
McCurry
James R., 41
John, 51
McDaniel
Crawford, 127
George M , 133
Rhoda, 127
Rody, 127
William, 51
McDonald
John, 128
Martha J., 121
Orlena Jane, 108
William, 8, 121
McDonell
Luticia, 127
William, 127
McDonnald
Charles W , 109
McDonnell
John, 109
McDonold
Charles W., 111
McDougald
Malcome, 131
McDowell
Julina, 27
Livonia, 27
McEldry
Edmund, 96
McElhaney
Allen, 32
Arch, 36
N. H , 43
McElrath
H. M. D., 113
McElwee
William E., 137
McFadden
David S., 14
McFaddin
Joseph F., 72
McFarland
Andrew, 64
Clara, 64
John, 81
Oliver, 72
William, 64, 148
McFee
Thomas, 11, 12
McGass
Samuel G., 84
McGee
James, 79, 81, 83
Robert, 51
McGhee
James, 20, 98
McGhee, Jr
James, 95
McGill
William, 123
McGinnis
Abraham, 150, 152
John, 149, 150
McGlaughlin
Lawrence, 73
McGlohlin
Sary, 147
McGlothlin
Charles, 14
William, 140
McGloughlin
James L , 73
Mcguff
Ed, 147
McGuffin
John, 63
McGuire
Cornelius, 78
Silas, 90
Silas A., 90
Silas M., 91
Thomas A , 90
McIlherin
John, 16
McKahen
George, 47
McKamey
William, 131
McKamy
Barton, 4
Elizabeth C., 4
Martha J., 4
McKee
Alexander, 9
Elizabeth J , 6
McKeehan
George W., 23
Western, 29
Willam H., 120
William J., 23
McKeehen
Patrick, 55
McKemy
Barney, 57
Minerva, 58
Rebecca, 57, 58
McKenry
Samuel, 14
McKenzie
E. M., 161
Margaret P., 121
McKerny
Robert, 48
McKie
Allexander, 147, 148
McKinley
Samuel, 99
William, 31
McKinney
Charles I., 72
McKInney
George W., 91
McKinny
Daniel, 39
McKinsey
Alexander, 116
McKinzie
Alexander, 112
McKorkle
John, 159
McLain
Andrew, 11
Daniel H., 69
Francis, 102
Joseph Grant, 69
McLaine
Warden, 71
McLamore
William, 98
McLane
Gordon, 71
McLaughlin
James, 45
McLellan
William D., 61
McLelland
William D., 62
McLemore
John, 123
McMahan
James P., 140
John, 28, 86, 142
Mrs, 104
Sanders, 140
Wilson, 140
McMahon
James, 104
Joseph, 147
Sevier, 123

David, 38
William, 42
Mineck
Samuel, 127
Minerva
Jane, 159
Mingle
Rebecca, 14
Minich
William M., 127
Minis
John, 121
Mink
John, 24
Minnic
Isaac, 126
Minnick
Peter, 127
Samuel, 126
William, 127
Minter
Mathias, 81
Minton
Calvin, 135
Miranda, 60
Mis___
John, 8
Miser
Joseph, 16
Michael, 18
Miskell
Charles, 96
Robert, 96
Mismer
George, 50
Mitchel
Elijah, 41
George, 91
James Calvin, 38
James R., 40
William, 37
Mitchell, 96
Frederick E., 73
James, 15, 85
Mary Ann, 65
Robert, 36, 72
Ruth, 32
Sally, 149
Samuel D., 159
Thomas, 149
Thos., 149
MItchell
Nathaniel, 78
Mitzger
Frederick, 100
Mize
Robert, 28
Mizer
Hartwell, 117
Michael, 117
Moad
Loadermilk, 21
Moffett
William W., 87
Mohog
Willet, 60
Moline
Cressein, 125
Molly, 35
Mona, 155
Monday
Abner, 102
Monger
G. G., 4
Monroe
Houston, 69
James, 109
Mark, 145
Pryor L., 144
W. G., 145
Monset
John, 85
Montgomery
James S., 9
John, 94
John W., 135
Rufus K., 22
Moody
John, 34, 154
William, 85
William M., 37
Moon
Daniel, 76
Moses, 155
William, 113
Moon, Jr
William, 115
Moor
William, 26
Moore
Andrew J , 136
Caswell, 145
David, 52
George, 96
George R., 87
George W., 135
Henry, 89
Jackson, 108
James, 15, 39, 117
John, 117
Joshua, 99
June, 160
Lucinda, 156
Maria Elizabeth, 136
Mary, 50
Patsey Self, 34
Polly, 98
Rachel, 34
Rhoda, 39
Rice, 32
Robert, 161
Rufus, 92, 93
S. L , 6
Samuel, 6
Sophia, 161
Squire, 145
Stephen, 34
Thomas, 117
Thomas Mordecai, 34
William, 36, 161
Moore, Sr
Moses, 45
Moorehouse
G., 104
Gilbert, 103
Moppin
Thomas Dewit C., 14
More
Rice, 36
Morehouse
Gilbert, 102
Morelack
Franklin, 68
Jerry A., 68
Morelock
Henry S., 69
Thomas, 69
Moreur
Reuben, 79
Morey
Ira, 156
Morgan
Allen D., 43
Frankling, 22
Isaac, 55
J M., 44
Richard, 78
Robert, 48
Rufus, 37
Thomas, 101
Washington, 129
William, 80
Morier
Reuben, 79
Morrall
John R , 143
Morris, 74
Addison C., 52
Gideon, 147
James H , 104
James M., 132
Jesse E., 132
John, 59, 71, 161
Sillie, 68
William, 80
William W., 111
Morrisett
R. M , 73
Richard M , 78
Morrison
Barten, 63
George, 64
Isaac B., 63
James, 58
John, 64
William H., 118, 119
Morriss
George, 121
John, 121
Morrisson
Nathaniel, 108
Morrow
Adam, 68
Charrels, 101
Ebenezer, 65, 68
John, 57
Morse
Marion, 80
Morton
Isaac W., 14
Meredith Y , 25
Quin, 1
Mosegy
John, 81
Moseley
Isaac, 17
Mosely
Dimman, 161
Enoch, 157
William, 147
Moser
Abreham, 2
James, 152
Mosley
Jesse, 47
Moss
E. T., 115
George, 159
J K., 31
Jack, 158
Mary, 29
Sary Jane, 158
Moulder
Henry, 34
Mouler
Henty, 150
Mount
Isiah, 81
Mountcastle
George, 76
Joseph, 76
Moyers
Alfred I., 82
David, 78
Frederick, 35
Jacob, 80, 81, 83
John, 79
Thomas S., 7
William, 82, 83
Mozier
Elizabeth Jones, 45
Muceller, 28
Muddy Creek, 84
Muller
Lu, 90
Mullins

Absalem, 93
David, 31
George W., 144
Susan M., 31
William R., 136
Mumford, 155
Mundy
Abner, 102, 103
William, 26
Wilson, 26
Munsey
Harriet, 129
James Albert, 129
Mollie Jane, 129
Munsul
Martha, 75
Murdock
Wright, 76
Murley
Wenny, 79
Murphey
E. S., 65
Pleasant, 31
Thomas, 47, 57
Thomas J., 65
Murphy
James M., 142
Joana, 104
John, 141
Joseph M., 101
Joy, 104
Murray
Huston, 140
Isaac, 161
Jemima, 87
Thomas D., 96
Murrel
John, 69
Murrell
Onslow G., 111
Murrey
Ann, 148
Murrin, Sr
Robert, 11
Murry
George, 27
Jessee, 30
John, 145
Permley, 27, 28
Pleasant, 27, 28, 87
Polly Ann, 27
Samuel, 87
Sebray, 28
Thomas, 2
Thomas A., 88
Musgrove
Elijah, 132
Musselwhite
Joseph F., 124
Myers
Eleanor, 15
Elender, 14
Elenor, 15
Eli, 13
George W., 40
Jane, 125, 140
John E , 66
Lucinda, 51
Mary J., 14
Matilda, 14
Robert, 13
Sally, 52
Myers, Jr
Philip, 13
William, 48
Myers, Sr
Philip, 13
Myrick
Jacob T , 53
Myrik
John, 81
Naff
Jacob, 154, 156
Naff & Coffman, 160, 161
Nail
Andrew, 132
Nair
Tennessee T , 25
Nance
Archibald, 98
Betsy, 2
Isham, 1
James M , 11
Peter, 98, 99
Pryor, 102
Nancy, 33
Narkleroad
William N , 143
Narramore
Thomas, 140
Vesta, 140
William F., 140
Nash
Thomas, 42
William, 29
Nassy
Henry, 132
Nathan, 87
Nathaniel, 143
Neal
A. B., 109
Grimes, 26
John, 87
Nease
Joseph, 62
Neathery
Robert, 95
Samuel, 95
Thomas, 96
Ned, 79, 138
Needle
Elizabeth, 122
Neff
David, 84, 89
Neil
Jepetha, 31
Nelly, 33
Nelson
Agnes, 151
Charles, 103
David, 152
David Grant, 105
George W., 55
Margaret, 151
Martin L., 87
O. P., 160
Orvelle P., 155
Netherland
John, 75
Netherly
Robert, 97
Nethery
Thomas, 95, 96
Newberry
Elias, 68
John, 117
Joseph, 67, 68
Lucinda, 54
Newbery
Mary, 146
Newby
John, 7
William, 7
Newcom
John, 71
Nancy, 71
Newcomb
Elizabeth, 122
Moses E , 122
Newcum
John, 71
Newell
Samuel, 44
Newkin
Dianna, 33
Newman
Ann, 146
Bird, 108, 109, 114
Ewen
Jefferson, 83
Granville, 86
James C., 90
John, 114, 147
John A., 90
Jonathan, 49
Madison, 84
Polly, 23
Rebeca, 115
Rebecca Jane, 90
Samuel, 83
Samuel N., 90
William, 23
Newman, [Jr],
Aron, 81
Newton
I. B , 21
Nicely
Jacob J., 89
Nichols
Alfred, 140, 141
Dock, 161
James, 90, 92
Richard A., 140
Richard N., 140
William, 57, 61
Nicholson
George, 80
James M., 90
Night
Lewis, 113
Nipper
Sarah M., 17
W. H., 105
Nite
Doc, 70
James F., 70
Rachel L., 70
Nix
Daniel Jones, 125
Francis Barto, 125
Nixon
John, 106
Thomas, 107
Noah
Richard, 59
Noe
Daniel, 31
Jacob, 32
John J., 40
Rufus, 31
Noe, Sr
David, 44
Noel
Jesse, 2
John, 1
Martha, 2
Martha J., 2
Nooncaper
Andrew J., 91
Rebecca Ann, 91
Norman
Anthony, 5, 6
James, 6
Mathew, 118
Samuel, 5
William, 5
Norris
Alfred, 3, 36
Isaac, 145, 162
Nelson, 96
Parelell L. D., 146
Patsy, 96
William, 144, 152
North
Eliza, 40

Margaret, 135
Maria, 135
Rhodes, 135
Powell, Jr
Rhodes, 135
Powle
Henry, 82
Prasise
Leanadan A., 4
Prather
Jeremiah, 60
Jonathan, 62
Pratt
Charles, 68
James, 99
John W., 104
Presley
John, 52, 98
John Wesley, 139
Levi, 52
Matilda, 52
Rebecca, 52
Presnell
Charlotte L , 159
Prestley
Charles, 10
Preston
James, 132
Price
E. H., 139, 140
Henry, 108
Hiram, 60
Hiram T., 57
James, 157
Jefferson D , 119
Lee, 118
Marcus F., 23
Sarah, 118
William, 18
Pride
Allen, 131
Prince
Celia Malinda, 124
David, 5
William A., 125
Pritchett
John, 127
Private
Hiram, 26
Proffit
Auston, 30
Proffitt
Amanda, 76
Lucy, 76
Provence
Isaac, 90
John, 90
Samuel D., 90
William, 89
Province
Isaac, 90
William M., 90
Prudence
Visa, 88
Pruet
James, 67
Martha, 67
Pryor
A J., 88
Andrew J., 87
Skipyou, 132
Pucapile
David, 32
Pugh
L. V., 16
Pullen
E , 70
Leroy, 33
Purciful
Martha, 45
Peter, 44, 45
Thomas, 44, 45
Purkepile
Katharine, 42
Purkeypile
John, 37
Purselley
James, 135
Putman
Benjamin, 116
Putteet
John, 138
Pyott
Samuel, 134
Qualls
Neicy Ann, 100
Quals
Aaron, 99
Quarle
William, 81
Quarles
Betsy, 82, 83
James, 81
Joseph, 82, 83
Polly A., 82
Polly Ann, 83
William, 82, 83
Quilliams
George, 142
Leander, 142
Quin
James, 105
Quinn
Edward, 55
R__ley
Hugh, 109
Rader
Calvin M., 143
Jesse, 54
John, 47
William, 56
William, of Jno., 57
Rafter
Charles, 140
Ragan
George W , 15
Mrs, 157
Ragdale
Benjamin, 109
Ragsdale
Benjamin, 108, 109, 110
John, 107, 131
Lewis F , 101
William, 131
Ragsdell
Robert Hardin, 64
Rail
Mary Ann, 137
William, 137
Rainwater
Andrew, 16
Jackson, 16
Martha, 16
Miles W., 88
Thomas, 16
Raler
Jasper, 31
Rambo
E. M , 69
Elbert M., 63
Ramsay
J E., 122
Ramsey
John, 120
Samuel, 96
Randolf
James, 148
Randolph
Robert, 110
Raney
Josirah, 7
Martha, 7
Nancy, 7
Range
Jacob, 24
Johnothan, 24
Ranken
John, 79
Ranken, Jr
Thomas, 79
Rankin
Anthony, 58, 62
John, 55, 56
Samuel, 91
Samuel B., 19
Thomas, 11, 80
Thomas C., 55
Rankins
William L., 93
Rann
Nancy, 88
Rawles
John A , 112
Rawlings
D R., 106
Ray
Benjamin, 44
George W., 105
James T., 21
John, 44
Joseph, 44
Luritha, 27
Susannah, 44
Rayburn
Newton M., 115
Rayl, Jr
William, 32
Rayl, Sr
William, 32
Rayle
George W., 136
Mary A., 136
Raynor
John, 12
Reace
Clark, 128
Read
John T., 20
Mary Jane, 20
Noah, 20
Reader
Andrew, 55
B. W., 4
Reader, Jr
John, 51
Reagan
Alexander, 13
John T., 16
Rear
James B., 40
Reave
Sophia, 70
Reaves
George, 58
James G., 60
Robert, 56
Rebecca, 140, 154, 155, 156
Rector
George, 58
Sarah Jane, 111
Redenhours
George, 62
James, 62
Redman
Andrew, 25
Redmon
Andrew, 25
James, 30
Reed
Charles N , 142
David, 62
Phelps, 31
William, 155
William Franklin, 138
Rees
David, 56
George, 56
Reese
George A., 88
James, 56

Joseph B., 85
Reeve
Samuel R., 67
Reeves
James G., 63
John, 55
Robert, 55
Register
Francis, 48
Reid
John L., 51
Reid, Jr
John L., 51
Ren
Margaret, 61
Reneau
Marcus, 141
Renner
John, 68
John H. (or B), 68
Noah, 62
Renshaw
James H., 103
John, 34
Rentfroe
James, 115
Reons
Henry, 83
Reynolds
Ann M., 38
Joseph, 59
Margaret, 66
Mary Jane, 67
Ruth Malinda, 69
Sarah, 45
William, 101, 134
William H., 69
Rhea
Eli, 4
Jane, 103
Robert, 54
Robert B., 143
Rhinehart
Caswell, 118
James, 118
Nancy, 53
Polly, 53
Rhineheart
Jesse, 117
Rhoda, 80, 82
Ricardi
John B., 104
Rice
Augustus, 81
J. W., 75
Milly, 124
Nianetta, 80
Richard, 33
Richards
Betsy, 77
Edward, 86
Elijah L., 109
Hannah, 115
Isaac, 140
John, 67
John V., 109
Thomas, 22
William, 78
William H., 115
Richardson
Drew, 9
Eli, 72
George, 26
Gideon, 9
James, 45
John S., 67
Richeson
Cass, 121
Harrison, 121
Joseph, 9
Moriah, 122
Peter, 121
Richey
Andrew, 45
Robert, 14
Richson
Drury, 9
Rickats
John, 80
Ricker
William S , 67
Rickets
Reuben, 99
Ricketts
Benjamin, 99
Ridenhour
David, 1
Ridenour
David, 146
Ridlin
Elisha, 107
Rigg
W. B., 128
Riggle
George W., 126
Riggs
Edward C , 91
John, 83
Lewis, 83
Right
Anderson, 42
Betsy, 151
Jane, 40
Millikan, 42
Nancy, 89
William, 151
Rigney
William, 96
Riley
John D., 74
Patton, 74
William, 64
Rimell
Jacob, 51
Rinds
Rotison, 115
Rinehart
Nancy, 54
Rinker
George, 48
Ripley
Alfred E., 13
David S., 67
Risden
Isaac, 139
Risedon
Fletcher, 96
Risler
John, 154
Ritchey
J. H., 14
Rite
Charles H., 63
Isaac, 124
Ritter
Levi, 2
Roach
A. S., 44
Absalem, 43
Absalom, 41
Jasper, 44
Jasper N., 44
John, 44, 91
William, 36
Roach, Jr
Absalom, 41
Roach, Sr
Absalon, 38
Roan
Archibald, 45
Roane
William, 95
Roark
James B., 75
Robbins
Henry, 76
Samuel, 2
Roberson
Cyntha, 112
Henderson, 112
Rufus B , 7
Robert
Joseph, 30
Roberts
Allen, 23
Amee, 46
Ann, 148
Harriet, 141
Isaac, 157
James, 54, 148
John, 46
Levi I., 142
Mary, 23
Michael, 109
Roda, 148
Samuel, 95, 141, 142
Sarah, 148
Thomas Bradford, 82
William, 25, 46, 141, 157
Roberts, Jr
William, 141
Robertson
Benjamin, 116
Elijah, 147
James, 114
Jesse, 11
John, 114, 144, 147
Samuel, 70
Thomas, 34
Robinson
Charles, 68
Isaac, 120
James, 49, 127, 130
John, 49, 115, 126
Joseph, 135, 137
William, 58
William B., 62
Willoby, 97
Robison
Delaney Churchill, 111
Easter, 19
James, 19
James C., 110
John, 58, 152
William Hutson, 110
Rochold
Tolbert, 124
Rockhole
Tolbert, 124
Roddy
Alexander, 12
Calvin, 18
Jesse, 127
Moses, 94
Philip, 95
Roddye
James (Col), 32
Rodgers
D. F , 6
James, 45, 100
John, 101
Joseph, 59
Matelar, 74
Thomas, 101
Roena, 88
Rogers
A. L., 76
A. R. T., 114
Benjamin, 8
David, 120
David S., 71
Harbert S., 75
John, 105
P. L., 103
Thomas, 115

William, 115
Rogers, Jr
David, 28
Roggers
Roda, 124
Rollins
George, 124
Louisa, 124
Nathan, 124
Romines
Asa, 145
Jerry, 145
Rorer
William, 11
Rose
Alexander, 54, 58
Elizabeth, 155
Ery Jane, 155
Frank, 13
James, 50
James F., 13
Jeremiah, 151, 152
John W., 62
Levi, 50
Marian, 101
Mary, 62
Mary Ann, 61
Robert, 50
William, 100
Rosodey
Roderick, 152
Ross
Ellen, 161
James, 2, 51
John A., 65
Robert, 2
William, 69
Ross, Jr
William, 49
Roston
James G. B., 101
Roten
Effy, 92
Roulstone
George, 93, 94
Routh
John, 84
Stephen, 41
Rowe
William, 39
Rowlan
Joab, 140, 141
Rowles
John A., 112
Rowlet
Charles, 16
Ruble
George D., 58
Harriet, 58
John C., 58
Joseph, 58
Marcus, 69
Perry W , 70
W., 153
William A., 58
William J , 67
Rucker
Cordelia, 44
Cornelia, 44
Emily, 44
John, 3
Matilda, 44
Permelia, 44
Permelia A., 44
Rudd
William, 114
Ruen
Isaac, 24
Ruffian
James, 4
Rule
Henry, 12
Rumbaugh
James H., 63
Runnels
Ann Malessa, 38
Runnion
George, 12
Malinda C., 19
Reuben, 124
Runnions
Elizah C., 19
Runnolds
Nancy, 38
Runyan
John K., 142
Runyon
Loanie West, 10
Rush
Cathrine, 7
Hugh Mc., 7
Isaac, 126
James M , 41
Joseph, 112
Joseph T , 7
Mary Jane, 41
Meredith, 36
Samuel, 42
William, 42, 108
William D., 41
Russel
James Riley, 123
Mary Hood, 123
Sarah Ann Elizabeth, 123, 124
Thomas, 19
Russell
Alexander, 145
Andrew, 28
Bembre, 55
Bluford, 59
Carey, 55
Cary M., 158
David M., 55
Emberson, 55
George, 64, 71
H. B., 20
James, 57, 60
Jim, 71
John Morris, 73
Major, 123
Malen, 65
Mary, 28
Matthew, 71
Milly, 99
Thomas, 37, 52, 55, 60, 64
Willam A. V B., 124
William Anderson VanBuren, 123
Willis H , 28
Zaney, 156
Russle
John, 9
Ruston
Calvin, 92
Ruth, 111
Rutherford
Campbell, 22
Ryan
Elizabeth, 79
Elliston, 81
James, 81
Joseph, 53
William, 79
Wyly, 81
Ryland
John, 153
Rymer
J. W., 124
William, 124
Saffell
L. B., 18
Salling
James, 144
Sally, 73
Salmon
John B., 135
Salter
James, 151
Sam, 71, 74, 160
Samples
Charlotte, 139
Elizabeth, 139
Sampson
Mrs, 160
William, 84
Sams
Jacob C., 157
Samuel, 74, 121
Sanders
Abraham, 127
James, 20
William T., 123
Sandford
S. L., 18
Sands
Celia, 50
Doctor, 50
Henry, 150
John, 52, 150
Rachel, 50
Sanly
Nicholas, 136
Sanson
Amos, 71, 72
Elizabeth, 71
Sappington
John, 131
Joseph, 130
Nancy, 130
Sarah, 74, 91
Sarah Jane, 59
Sarahphiner
Nancy, 158
Sartin
Lewis, 32
William, 85
Sasseen
Edward R., 81
Satterfield
Eliza, 92
Emly, 145
Su, 92
Satts
Daniel N., 64
Saulsbury
James M., 69
Saunders
John, 96
Savage
Jesse, 139
Sawney
Elizabeth, 62
Frances, 62
George W., 62
Smith, 62
Scaggs
Lewis, 6
Scales
Mary Ann, 138
Scalf
Amanda, 156
Elizabeth, 156
Scarborough
Mary J., 5
Mary Jane, 4
Scarbrough
E. C., 135
William, 6
Scarlet
Stephen, 86
Scarlett
Abraham, 84
John, 84, 86
Lewis, 84
Ruth, 84

Snyder
Robert, 75
Solmon
Washington, 134
Solomon
Jesse, 134
Jessee, 38
John, 43
W. P., 119
Sopers
Mary A., 74
Soward
Henry W., 137
Spahr
A M., 143
Sparkman
George, 40
Henry, 42
Spears
E. M., 77
James, 73, 162
John, 156, 157
Joseph, 162
Joseph T., 18
Margaret, 162
Mary, 98
Nathan, 162
Rebecca, 18
Samuel, 162
Sarah E., 74
Sarah Elizabeth, 73
Spence
James, 129
Spencer
George M., 60, 67
John, 135
William A., 11
Spillers
William, 27
Spoon
Abraham, 35
John, 35
Nancy, 88
Spriggs
Elizabeth, 37
James, 37
July Ann, 37
Mary, 37
Nancy, 37
Sprinkle
Charles M., 68
Charles W, 67
Manning, 67
Sprowl
John, 80
Spurgen
James, 142
Spurgeon
George, 55
James M., 59
Squibb
George F., 160
John K., 57
St John
G W, 161
Stacey
R. H., 73
Stacy
Jefferson Monroe, 127
Staephan
Chappel Car, 26
Stafford
John, 141
Margaret, 87
Stakely
John, 119
Stamper
Jesse, 23
Standfield
Samuel, 51
Standley
F. H. Bratcher, 22
Reuben, 22
Rhoda, 22
Stanfield
James, 111
Stanton
Samuel Montgomery, 159
Starnes
George, 47
J. J., 77
Jackson J., 75
Jacob, 150
James H., 37, 42, 43
John, 72, 73
John E., 74, 77
Pleasant H., 75
Staton
James, 157
Statsworth
Amos, 39
Elizabeth, 39
John, 39
Martha, 39
Nancy, 39
Samuel, 39
Thomas, 39
William, 39
Steed
Campbell, 21
James, 111
Steel
Mary, 48
Samuel, 48
Steele
Burton, 143
John D., 5
Stegall
Nero, 119
Richard, 134
Richard A., 136
Stephen, 150
Stephens
Allen, 22
B. M., 68
George, 83, 131
John H, 162
Joseph, 12, 80
Lorenzo, 140
Noah, 140
Samuel, 151
Solomon, 140
Stephens, Jr
Andrew, 54
Stephenson
Andrew R., 123
Elijah, 124
Thomas, 162
William, 147
Stepherson
William, 20
Steptoe
Alexander, 49
Sterling, 43
Sterm
John F., 69
Steuksbury
Jacob, 2
Stewart
Adeline, 119
James, 126
Jane, 103
Samuel, 119
William, 3
Stiff
Edward, 81
Stiles
Aurelius, 122
Still
Charles, 146
Stillmant
Thomas Hants, 148
Stillmant, Sr
John Hants, 148
Stirling
Hariet A., 16
Stockton
James, 10
Stoffle
Mary Ann, 54
Stokes
Cletcher, 131
E. J., 5
Edward S., 117
Elias, 4, 5
William A., 4
Stone
Alexander, 34
Andrew P., 93
Ellen E, 93
John, 93
John S., 128
Washington, 55, 60
William Preston, 89
Stonesifer
John A., 60
Stout
Aron, 148
Daniel, 148
David, 25, 148
David L, 13
George, 148
John L., 92
John W., 8
Magdalin, 148
Moses, 148
William S., 13
Stover
Joseph, 80
Stow
Robert, 133
Strain
Allen, 9
John, 10, 147
Stranahan
Charles C., 7
Stratham
Elizabeth, 91
Straton
Absalom, 148
Stratton
R. H., 106
Striplen
John, 83
Strong
James Monroe, 109
Stuart
Adeline, 115
Caladonia, 74
George, 54, 155
George W., 7
James L., 7
John A, 15
John C., 74
Joseph, 15
Lucinda, 54
Martha, 153
Milly, 7
Murray, 126
Phoebe (Mrs), 159
Sarah Ann, 103
Thomas, 155
William, 74
Stubblefield
George, 26
Martin, 32
Robert, 38
Stubbs
Claborne W., 109
Stuffel
Polly Ann, 54

G. W., 5
Isaac, 34
J. C., 18
Jesse, 127
Jesse M., 150, 151
Jessee M , 154
John, 12, 126
John W., 120, 128
Loyle B., 101
Malinda J., 136
Malinda Jane, 135
Moses C. R., 129
Polly, 50
Polly Ann, 135
Samuel, 140
Stephen, 106, 107
Vandenburgh, 81
William, 9, 81, 112
Zachariah, 97
Zerelda M., 135
Thomson
Isaac, 34
Thornburgh
Ai, 81
J. M., 90
John, 90
Montgomery, 84, 86
Richard, 83, 86
Thornton
Levi, 80, 82
Thorp
Calvin, 117
Thrasher
Benjamin, 96
Rebecca, 94
Thurman
Isah, 9
John, 7
Samuel, 9
Thurmon
Isley, 15
John, 15
Tidwell
Betsy, 51
Elizabeth, 49
William C., 115
Tildy, 74
Tillery
Coffield, 118
Jacob, 118
Letty Ann, 118
Polly, 118
Samuel H , 118
Sarah, 118
Tilley
Elizabeth, 93
John C., 93
Tilly
Albert N , 93
Tilson
James S., 106
Jesse, 9
William, 25
Timmons
Matthew, 101, 128
William, 13
Timons
Matthew, 98, 99
Tindell
Joshua, 100
Tinker
William, 98
Tinly
John, 99
Tinney
Eliza Jane, 113
Tipton
A. D., 77
Abraham, 23, 25
Brian, 1
Elbert W., 69
J W. H., 18
James J , 24
John, 147
Jonathan, 1
Joseph, 138
Mary, 138
Minerva, 1
Robert C., 69
Samuel, 147
Sarah, 1
Tittsworth
Charlotte, 92
Todd
Gillaspie, 85
John, 84, 85
Loe, 1
Martha, 85
Tolbert
James S., 37
Toliafero
Charles, 132
Toliver
Abraham, 36
Hartley, 105
John, 36
Tomlinson
Thomas, 74
Tompkins
William, 161
William E., 56
Tool
Michael, 45
Toole
William, 13
Torbert
John, 111
Townsley
Isaac, 29
James, 16
William, 39
Tramwell
James, 138
Nancy Jane, 138
Patsy, 138
Traynor
John D., 20
Tredway
Eliza, 79
Isaac, 79
Trent
James Madison, 103
James Patterson, 103
John Ryburn, 103
Margaret Lucinda, 103
Milly Caroline, 103
Trevillion
Joab, 85
John, 85
John C., 85
Joseph, 85
Pleasant N., 85
Rhoda R., 85
Trimble
James, 45, 130
Jane, 45
Sarah, 45
Trobaugh
William, 55
Trobough
George, 57
Trogden
Abner, 34
John William, 89
Solomon, 41
Troop
James, 53
Trott
Gillispie, 83, 85
James, 38
Trotter
Jasper, 122
Trout
George, 95
Trusler
Joseph, 24
Trusley
John, 128
Mary E., 128
Tilmon, 128
Tuck
Mary L., 16
William, 16, 17
Tucker
J. R , 21
Jackson, 132
John, 30, 88
Lucretia, 69
N. B , 158
Reese, 152
Richard, 21
Samuel, 9
Tucker, William R. of Athens, 107
William, 78
William R., 108
Tuder
J. W., 142
Tullock
Zachariah, 161
Tunnell, 5
John, 4
Samuel, 3
Turbott
James, 147
Turk
Archibald, 10
H. L. M., 119
James, 9, 10
Mandy H., 119
William B., 15
Turley
Thomas W., 38, 40
Turnby
George, 80
John C., 80
Turner
Elijah Elsmore, 19
Jacob, 3
John, 8
John Fothergill, 93
Nathaniel, 134
Sterling T., 136
Thomas, 41
Vincen, 20
Vincent, 19
Turnley
Adeline, 86
Elizabeth M., 86
Esther, 87
George, 80, 86
Isaac, 87
James A., 108
John C., 88, 91
Joseph F., 86
Turnly
George, 82
Tutle
Absalom, 130
Tyler
Irah, 151
Tyra
Dianah, 91
Elizabeth, 91
Parmeanus, 91
William R., 78

www.ingramcontent.com/pod-product-compliance
Lightning Source LLC
Chambersburg PA
CBHW062025270326
41929CB00014B/2325

* 9 7 8 0 8 0 6 3 4 9 6 6 4 *